BROAD OCEANS

OCEANS

AND

NARROW SEAS

John Townend

The Larks Press

Published by
The Larks Press
Ordnance Farmhouse
Guist Bottom
Dereham, Norfolk NR20 5PF
01328 829207

June 2000

Printed by the Lanceni Press
Garrood Drive, Fakenham

British Library Cataloguing-in-Publication Data
A catalogue record for this book is available
from the British Library

ISBN 0948400 91 9

ACKNOWLEDGEMENTS

It would have been impossible to write an autobiographical account like this one without the continued support of a host of friends. My thanks to them for their help in reading and commenting on my draft efforts, in particular to Mike Prodger, who made time despite his work load as an assistant editor on the *Daily Telegraph*.

David Thomas FRAS, a professional writer, encouraged me from day one and has been kind enough to advise me as things progressed. He introduced me to Alan Francis of the Naval History Branch of the Ministry of Defence, which supplied vital factual information, and it was the help and guidance of the staff at the Public Records Office that enabled me to verify a variety of events. To them all I am deeply indebted. I also wish to convey my gratitude to my old 'Sparker', Charles Milner and my Captain, Ronnie Seddon, for supplying information and correcting my chapters about MTB 718. I have attempted to be factual and unbiased in my story but must apologise if, despite my best efforts, I have failed.

Latterly I am indebted to Giles Scott-Giles for his technical help and to Mrs Susan Yaxley for her editing skills and confidence to publish these memoirs.

John Townend

CONTENTS

WAR - '....YOU ARE JOINING THE NAVY'

I was helping my father build a bonfire in the garden. He glanced at his watch and beckoned towards the house. I can see us now, as if in a video replay. My father switched on the radio and relit his pipe. Big Ben struck the hour and our Prime Minister completed his short speech with the words, '...we are now at war with Germany.' My heart was thumping. For some time my father had predicted that this would happen, and now it had.

The following summer my young cousin and I watched the first air raids over Harwich. It was exciting fun to us and I could not wait for my seventeenth birthday to volunteer. My older friends at school were now returning in uniform and I felt cheated.

My school, Lancing College, had been evacuated to four country houses in Shropshire. My house was settled in Moor Park, just outside Ludlow, a lovely old house with long-established grounds, having a most peaceful air.

Germany had spread its bombing raids from London and the major south coast ports to other cities. One night, during my last term, I woke suddenly; the drone of a lone aircraft had woken me. Lying very still, I could hear the other boys' blissful breathing. Then a lightning-like flash lit the room, followed by an enormous explosion, which shook the house and rattled the open windows. The bomb, or land mine, had not done any damage to us or to the house, so I told the boys to go back to sleep. Lying there in the approaching dawn light, I remember thinking how odd fate was. Had the pilot of the plane dropped his load a few yards further on, he would have ended the lives of all the boys in the house. He would never have known, and they (who had been evacuated from the south coast for their safety) would never have known - and this book would never have been written.

My second recollection of my final term is of our cricket match with Shrewsbury School, one of the best school sides in the country that year. We had looked forward to this battle, but in the event they thrashed us. I seem to remember that we were bowled out for around 68 - of which I made over 30.

The third and most important event I recall was the arrival of an interview panel from the RAF. They interviewed some of the older boys who had volunteered. As a result of my interview they recommended me as 'potential fighter pilot' material. I was thrilled. With the Battle of Britain still so clear in our minds, such a recommendation was far too important to be passed on to my family in the weekly letter home; this news I would keep till the holidays. So it was at our first breakfast that I was telling my father about it when my mother interjected,

'I had enough worries with your father flying during the last war. *You* are joining the Navy.'

It is chance remarks like this that fashion people's lives.

'Are you an officer or a man?'
The author dressed to join HMS Night Hawk

CHAPTER ONE – *NIGHT HAWK*

My mother had moved us in 1941 to a gardener's cottage on a Cornwall estate whose owner was crippled. Because there was no room for all our family in the bungalow, the owner allowed me to set up house in some rooms over the lighting engine and stables, across the yard from the big house. In return I was responsible for maintaining and running his engine, which supplied the big house with electricity via great banks of batteries. We, of course, used candles and paraffin lamps. He also lent me two guns, a beautiful little double-barrelled 20 bore and an old .410 with the longest barrel I have ever seen. With these, and the run of the estate, I kept his and our larder filled; meat rationing was not a problem in such a plentiful countryside!

The young farmer, whose father had recently bought him the local farm, employed me and I soon learned about hedging and ditching from a wonderful old Cornishman who was an expert on the countryside and all that moved in it. The only tractor on the estate was a Fordson. By relieving the farmer during his meal breaks, I also learned about the various tasks from him. He paid me sixpence an hour, which was the going rate, and by working all the hours available I felt rich!

A friend, some years older than me, owned a small pram dinghy, which he kept in Percuil creek. I borrowed this each week to take our family Nannie to Falmouth to do the shopping. The row of around three miles saved having to drive ten times this distance, and with petrol rationed this was vital. On one of these visits I met a young RNVR officer in the dockyard. During the course of conversation he let slip that they were expecting a new harbour launch to be delivered. Immediately I asked about the possibility of obtaining a position as a crew member, pointing out that it would be helpful to gain such experience prior to joining the Navy. He agreed to consider my request and asked me to contact him in a couple of weeks' time when the new launch should have arrived.

On my return home I told my parents and my farmer employer what I had arranged. In due course I again met the RNVR officer, but he told me the launch had been sunk by the enemy on its way down to Falmouth. I was bitterly disappointed, and must have shown it, because the officer led me into an adjoining office, told me to wait and disappeared. Five minutes later he beckoned me to follow him. I found myself face to face with a four-stripe bemedalled Royal Navy Captain - as I was to learn later, Captain Minesweepers Falmouth!

'I understand you need to obtain sea experience prior to joining the Royal Navy,' he said. It was spoken as a statement rather than a question.

'Yes please, sir,' I replied, wondering what ideas he might have. To my utter astonishment he then continued,

'Fine. You'd better go home and inform your parents, collect some clothes and report back here at 1830.' Turning to the RNVR officer he said, 'Perhaps you'd arrange for a boat to collect this young man and take him out to HMS *Night Hawk*

Fix him up with a kitbag and hammock. She'll be lying at the coaling jetty.'

The interview was obviously over. I thanked the Captain very much and left with the officer.

As soon as I could I collected Nannie and rowed home - my parents were as amazed as I was at my good fortune. I threw a spare pair of pants, some socks and my shaving tackle into a case and returned to Falmouth. At the appointed hour the officer met me. I was given a kitbag, and a hammock, which was tied up like a long sausage. The boat, engine running, was waiting, and off we went to find HMS *Night Hawk*. Sure enough she was lying alongside and the boatman threw my kitbag and hammock on to her deck as I clambered rather awkwardly over the side. I felt very conspicuous, dressed in a blue polo-necked sweater, my school blue suit and long sea-boots. I remembered reading in a book about an 'Officer of the Watch' in harbour and set off to find such a man. Eventually, having reached the bridge, I found an officer leaning over the compass apparently deep in thought.

'Excuse me, sir,' I said in a rather nervous voice, 'I've been told to report to your ship.' He eyed me suspiciously.

'Are you an officer or a man?' he asked. Thinking as fast as I could, I replied honestly that I was not an officer. With that he led me back down the various ladders to an open hatch forward. 'Sparks!' he shouted down the hole, and a tousled head appeared. 'Take this chap below and settle him in - we can sort out his details in the morning.' He turned and disappeared, I collected my gear and Sparks helped me below with it.

He was, I suppose, only a couple of years older than me but had that confident air which old hands exude. He sat me down and produced a mug of steaming, very sweet tea, which tasted strange because it was made with tinned milk. 'Are you a survivor?' he asked. When I told him how I came to be aboard he was intrigued. Space below was so cramped that we moved into his wireless cabin where he introduced me to a Belgian fisherman who had recently joined them; my schoolboy French helped us to converse and he seemed delighted to have someone to talk to.

Once the men going ashore had left, we moved back into the mess-deck. It had been the fish-hold until the ship had been requisitioned by the Admiralty in 1940. She had then been converted to minesweeping and the fish-hold became the mess-deck. However, there was barely enough space for them all to sling their hammocks - which reminded Sparks, 'Is your hammock made up?' he enquired. I looked at him blankly, and he unravelled the rope surrounding the 'sausage'. 'Bloody typical!' he complained. 'Those shore-based wallahs don't even know how to set up a hammock!' Paying careful attention to everything he did, I watched as he showed me how to set up my hammock. It was my first lesson aboard *Night Hawk* and like all the rest, which were to follow over the ensuing weeks, invaluable.

That night, my first in a hammock, I took hours to get to sleep, but then slept the sleep of the dead. I awoke with a start to find people falling out of their hammocks, grabbing their clothes and disappearing up the ladder to God knows where.

I followed as fast as I could. The cold fresh air on deck cut into my lungs and I found myself in a very basic washroom. The basins were made of stainless steel, there was a cold tap to each and to obtain hot water one pushed a button, which squirted live steam into the cold water. This gave the place a peculiar sweet smell and having washed I returned below to the mess-deck. Then the stale stench of our night's quarters hit me!

There was no time to talk, just swallow a breakfast and a mug of tea, which someone produced, and return on deck for stations for leaving harbour. Not having any idea what to do or where to go, I followed a small group of men on to the forecastle, helped pull in the head-rope and fore-spring, held a large tyre fender over the side while the Captain manoeuvred his ship, helped the others 'square up' the forecastle and 'fell in', standing at ease. HMS *Night Hawk* steamed slowly out of harbour. I stepped backwards as the long swell made me over-balance and the man in charge of the forecastle party barked, 'Stand still!' My first day at sea had begun.

As soon as we had left harbour we went to 'cruising stations'. I was told to report to the Captain's cabin, which I found underneath the bridge. Here, I was collected by the officer I had met the night before. He turned out to be the First Lieutenant and took me in to the Captain. Having introduced me, he left to return to the bridge. The Captain was intrigued to learn how I came to be aboard but could not have been nicer or more helpful. Having satisfied himself about me, he handed me over to his Coxswain who took down whatever details he needed to enable him to claim for my victuals, confirmed I was not old enough to draw my 'tot' and gave me details about my watch. The whole of this took perhaps a quarter of an hour and I was back in the mess-deck telling Sparks what had happened.

When you know you know nothing, and are as keen as I was to learn, it is surprising how quickly you pick things up. This small vessel, only 307 tons, was launched in 1915. She was coal-burning still, and since the First World War had been fishing until requisitioned in 1940. Now she sailed each day to keep the swept channel clear of ground mines, one day to the west of Falmouth, the next to the east. She had an old saluting-gun mounted on her foredeck to defend herself against aircraft, and a couple of 'maxims' on the bridge! I really felt the part as I became one of the gun's crew or stood my turn as lookout. It took a time to become accustomed to steering a compass course, but very soon I was able to carry out all the new tasks and, very important to me, I had not become seasick despite a long session in the engine-room with the engineer Chief PO while she had rolled her way back up the channel. The hot sweet smell of the steam, mingling with the smell of 'soogee', had nearly caught me out, but concentrating hard on his detailed description of how everything worked had saved the day!

Some weeks later I received news from home that my papers had arrived with orders to report to HMS *Raleigh* for initial training. I informed my Captain who gave me a piece of signal-pad stating I had permission to leave the dockyard - this was my only authority to leave HMS *Night Hawk*! Came the day, I wished Sparks and my other friends farewell, returned my gear to the naval base and returned home. So much had happened in such a short space of time, I talked non-stop for hours.

Many years later, when fishing my own inshore vessel off the south west of Ireland, I bumped into old *Night Hawk*, she had survived the war, been de-requisitioned in 1946 and then, fitted with a diesel engine, was continuing to earn her keep, fishing once more. As my first naval experience she will always hold a special place in my heart.

CHAPTER TWO - *RALEIGH, DRAKE & SHROPSHIRE*

As a result of my time aboard HMS *Night Hawk*, I decided to report at the Training Base dressed in my same blue polo-necked sweater and school blue suit, plus polished black shoes, far less conspicuous than the smart suits and shirts with collars and ties worn by the other new entrants. Such anonymity helped to avoid being instantly categorised by one's 'cell mates'!

Directed by the Leading Seaman at the gatehouse, I made my way to a collection of Nissen huts. As I entered, a leathery-faced, elderly, Chief Petty Officer was calling out names. 'Sir,' I shouted as my name was called. Swinging round to face me, his eyes looked me up and down.

'Take this lot outside and fall them in, in four ranks facing the roadway,' he said. 'You are Class Leader.' I swallowed and made my way outside, followed by a most undistinguished group of nearly thirty men. They were from all walks of life, ranging from university and industry to labourers and schoolboys like myself. By the time the Chief emerged, I had managed to cajole them into some sort of order. Few of them had ever 'fallen in' in their lives before and, as I was about to find out, some did not know their right from their left!

The Chief looked them over with a disdainful and disapproving look. Someone muttered an aside to his mate and sniggered. 'Silence in the ranks!' barked the Chief. His voice was so powerful that it commanded instant attention. He then told me to march this squad to our allotted Nissen hut (Mess Number 74), halt them outside and await his arrival. After a couple of attempts I managed to manoeuvre this raggle-taggle gang into some sort of order, march them to the hut and halt them. I realised at once just how valuable my previous training as Company Sergeant Major in the OTC at school was going to prove.

Standing outside in the roadway, the Chief then told us what our new programme would consist of: in twelve weeks we would have been turned from useless, ignorant civvies into smart and knowledgeable embryo sailors. He was the Senior Chief Petty Officer in the establishment and he expected his classes to pass out with the top marks! Turning to me he said, 'Carry on Leader. Dismiss this rabble and get them settled in. I'll see you all tomorrow as scheduled.' His bandy legs carried him off and we entered the hut, which was to be our home for the next three months.

I placed my case on the first top bunk (the room was full of metal-framed double bunks with a pillow and mattress on each). A fresh-faced, obviously ex-public-schoolboy placed his case on the bottom bunk. We introduced ourselves, shook hands and sat on the edge of his bunk smoking cigarettes.

Looking back, I am amazed at just how quickly the Navy managed to knock us into shape. By the following Monday morning our thirty civvies had been categorised and given medicals, had signed various forms and marched for miles up and down the roadways between the huts . Our first taste of the parade ground was an unforgettable experience. Several thousand sailors and some WRNS were all being shouted at by people with enormous voices. Somehow the right orders were obeyed by the right groups and the whole thing went off as planned. We learned that the Senior Chief running the Gunnery School was called Chief Petty Officer Fenton. At our first meeting with him he informed us that, after God, he was the most important man at *Raleigh* and 'Don't forget it!' he bellowed. Certainly he was the most feared!

The punishment meted out by this man, should one be sent to him for some misdemeanour, would probably start with an invitation to carry a 100lb shell balanced on your forearms, hands facing upwards, for a gentle run round the perimeter of the parade ground, while either he or a subordinate watched from the centre. The encouragements received during these extended circuits were of a shouted and very nautical sort. One dare not drop the shell as one was running since it would have taken your foot off, but eventually one's legs and arms just could not keep going. It was as one approached that stage that the torturer would close in. We watched him break even the toughest and most stubborn of men, and only the very stupid risked taking him on!

Chief Petty Officer Rooke was a strict disciplinarian with a heart of gold. He was a survivor from HMS *Courageous*, sunk at the very beginning of the war, and had been at Raleigh ever since. The Navy had been using 2/4 rank drill when we arrived but now had to learn the new 3-rank drill. Fortunately for me I had been in the OTC when these new drills were introduced so was able to help.

As the weeks passed we gradually grew in confidence. One of the gang, an old sweat who had been in the Irish Army, found out that a lady cook of enormous proportions ruled the canteen. She was lonely and, as he had undoubtedly 'kissed the Blarney Stone', he became her admiring consort. If we could produce a small, secret working party to help the ladies who set things up for their mass feeding operation, we would be suitably rewarded with secret supplies of bread, butter and tins of jam or marmalade! A simple scheme was produced whereby I was able to march my mess, along with all the other marching squads, up to the canteen without anyone noticing our couple of missing men. As we were all constantly famished, such additional supplies were a wonderful boost to our morale; the ration of one slice of bread per man per meal was little use to hungry chaps!

My friend, Graham Sumner, lived in Cheshire and so chose to spend his weekend leaves with me in Cornwall. He was a tall red-headed young man. Our mutual interest in the countryside was shared while wandering around with guns at my home. All our spare time we spent dreaming up trips to be made after the war, exploring the UK on horseback.

Towards the end of our time, the establishment held an inter-division boxing competition. A young Scotsman from the boxing booths of Glasgow won his weight. Not long after this I was furious to learn that the same man, having picked a fight with his Class Leader in his hut, had then knocked him out. The end result of this was for the man to be put back a class, which was exactly what he wanted - it was the second time he had done it!

My fury was because I had learned he was being assigned to our hut. I collected my cap and set off to see Chief Rooke. We had got a first-rate class with no troublemakers and were all set to pass out with top marks; the introduction of this man would spoil everything. 'Rooky' listened patiently. He explained that 'orders were orders' and that he had never had a failure since he had joined Raleigh. He most certainly was not intending to have a failure in the future. The interview was over and feeling rather depressed I returned to my hut. I sat on the edge of Graham's bunk and lit a cigarette.

'What did Rooky have to say?' Graham asked. I told him what had been said and in his usual level-headed way he led the conversation back to our mess. 'Do you think it might be prudent to have him sleep under you here?' he said, pointing to his own bunk. I really had not got round to thinking about things at all, but immediately decided his suggestion made a lot of sense.

'Good idea,' I replied, and in no time Graham had moved all his gear to the far end where there was a spare space. The Scot Smith arrived full of bounce and was quite put out when told that his locker was open and his bunk was under mine. He was all set to argue when I turned to Graham and announced we were off ashore.

'See you later on,' we waved as we left. On our return he had started a card school for money, something we had banned for obvious reasons. When 'pipe down' was sounded Smith was still capering around. Thinking our wily old Chief just might pop in to see everything was in order, I told Smith to 'get turned in'. His immediate response was to challenge me to make him!

Grabbing my pillow I jumped off my top bunk on to the highly-polished floor. He swung his pillow viciously at my head and I ducked just in time. The momentum of his blow took his stockinged feet from under him while my bare feet held me held me firmly in position. There was an almighty 'whack' as my forehead struck his temple; he fell like a poleaxed ox!

The whole incident took barely twenty seconds and had been witnessed by the entire mess. I slapped his face to bring him round and as he opened his eyes I said with great authority, 'Now will you get turned in.' Before he could say anything, I grabbed my pillow and climbed back to the safety of my top bunk. After such god-given breaks you do not push your luck! It may seem extraordinary, but it is nevertheless true that from that time on we never had any trouble from Smithy. He became a whole-hearted member of our very happy class and passed out with us, with excellent marks too.

Before we left we held a collection in the mess to buy our old Chief a present. The back page of my seamanship manual still has a pencil list of some of the names and their contributions. It may surprise some to learn that not only did we feel grateful to this old man who had knocked us into shape but were delighted to give up at least a day's pay to show our gratitude. He had tears running down his cheeks as we made our small presentation and we ran away in embarrassment as we too started to feel our emotions erupting.

We all left for a couple of weeks' well-earned leave. The majority of us would never again meet, but we did not even think about that then. We had joined HMS *Raleigh* like new boys at school; we left some thirteen weeks later like experienced hands. From memory, *Raleigh* had a population of around 4,000; each week, as classes passed out, their places were filled by new intake. We had gradually gained knowledge and confidence.

HMS *Drake* was quite different; it was a transit camp of around 10,000 constantly moving people, and almost all of them had been to sea! Once again we became 'new boys', and every day was spent doing odd jobs and waiting, ears pricked, for the loudspeaker announcement that would spell out our future.

'The following ratings report to the Reg Office at once!' The crackling voice of the Tannoy system called out an interminable list of ordinary and able seamen. We dropped our shovels and ran to the office. This was the third time in the past few days we had 'reported'.

'Get fell in over there,' barked a petty officer, 'and answer your names as I call them out. Ordinary Seaman Townend, Yates...' Along with the others named we sprung to attention - this was it!

My joy at being drafted to a ship at last was dimmed when I found that my friend and I were to be parted. We were both going to cruisers, but they were different ships. At the time we accepted it and swore to keep in touch; after all we had plans for 'after the war'. It did not occur to me that I would never to see him again - he was lost in submarines as a young sub-lieutenant.

HMS *Shropshire* was a London Class cruiser of 9830 tons. She had been launched in 1928 and when we joined her at Chatham she was just completing a refit. She was lying alongside and I remember thinking how vast she was as I lugged my kitbag and hammock up the steep gangway. Once aboard, we were hustled down ladders, along passageways, through watertight bulkhead doors to the Regulating office, a tiny office on the starboard side bursting with people and papers! A weary old Chief Petty Officer was calling out names. 'Where the 'ell is Smith?' A brief silence, then he started again. 'Townend!'

'Here, sir,' I answered in a strained shout. He handed me various papers, which detailed my new functions in my new ship, obtained my signature in several places (God knows what I was signing - I was far too scared to ask!) and dispatched me. As I left to try and find my way back to where we had left our kit I could hear him calling,

'Smith, you bastard....'

16 Mess was on the port side of the mess-deck (odd numbers to starboard, even numbers to port). There were around twenty men to each mess. The mess consisted of a scrubbed, wooden table, bolted to the deck, and scrubbed, wooden benches, which were movable, either side of the table. This was to be our new home. Each man had a metal locker into which he placed his kit; any kit found lying around went into the 'scran bag' and one had to buy it back with 'pusser's soap'; such odd

rules had been started in Nelson's time and who were we to comment? It was the Navy's way to keep 'Jack' tidy. And it worked! Your own messmates made sure you were clean! Your hammock was stowed, properly lashed, in the adjacent hammock netting, a 'stable' for hammocks!

It is difficult to explain in words just how totally lost we felt in amongst all those 'old hands'. It was like being dropped into a maze. The loudspeakers made incoherent noises following a shrill piping to alert all to listen. We spent our early days desperately asking our mess mates, 'What was that pipe?' Eventually their patience would run out 'Why don't you wash your f........ ears?' It was a miracle that we managed to turn up at the right place at the right time. But within a very few weeks we could find our way about blindfold and had learned the jargon of the loudspeakers, though at the time it seemed to take an eternity.

Since these ships had been laid down, new guns, W/T and Radar equipment had been installed, all of which meant extra crew to be housed. This made for very cramped conditions; in fact it was very difficult to find a place to sling a hammock. Being new boys, we were rather like young blackbirds trying to find a nesting site for the first time. No sooner would one start to sling, than an old hand would appear from nowhere. He would either tell you to 'push off' in suitably naval language, or ask if you knew that Dinger Bell slung there!

After a couple of weeks we sailed. This, I thought, is the life. We were joined by some destroyers and made our way swiftly northwards up the east coast in filthy weather, wet, cold and windy. My cruising station at that time was as a lookout on the ADP (air defence position) high above the bridge. We swung back and forth, seated on swivel seats, searching the horizon constantly for any sign of enemy aircraft. Woe betide any man who failed to pick up anything that moved before the officer in charge. Radar in those days was not developed as it is today and often it was the lookouts who spotted trouble before the new-fangled radar.

We arrived at Scapa Flow and marvelled at the great fleet mustered there. Our Captain's job now was to knock his ship into shape as quickly as possible. We carried out a crash working-up programme: every part of this ship was 'exercised'; every man learned, from actually doing the job, what had to be done both by day and at night. The weather, as always in those latitudes, was hostile to say the least; almost constant rain and gales, along with the biting cold, made for misery and I soon found out that it was better (warmer) to volunteer to work in the frozen holds of the meat-storage ships than to work as a deck party!

I can only recall one run ashore. As the drifter rolled its way shorewards with its cargo of NAAFI-bound sailors, I bumped into a friend from school. He was older than me and was sporting the uniform of a Midshipman RNVR. We had both played games for our school, but now there was just time to share a few casual words before he went off to the Officers' Club and I made my way to the NAAFI. Ordinary Seamen were even lower than RNVR midshipmen, Mr Christian!

At last we were sailed to Greenock. Rumours abounded that we were bound for

Russian convoys, so we all wrote home asking for sweaters and warm clothing. To add to the congestion, we now embarked soldiers and, shortly afterwards, sailed to join up with some destroyers, an aircraft carrier and a host of large liners, whose decks could also be seen to be full of soldiers. We sailed west into the long Atlantic swell, our destination a mystery.

After a few days our course was altered towards the south. Then, one Sunday after church, on the Marines' mess-deck, our captain announced that we were bound for warmer climes! He was not able to tell us more than that at the moment but after Scapa and the Russian convoy rumours we were all delighted, especially the large South African contingent aboard.

The aircraft carrier and some of the destroyers had peeled off to go to Gibraltar. We alone now 'mothered' the convoy from the centre, while the remaining destroyers guarded the flanks. It is odd how memory fails to recall events that would have been milestones for me then. The log of HMS *Shropshire*, Monday 13th April 1942, notes that she crossed the equator in longitude 15 degrees 35 minutes west at 1700. The first crossing of the equator is a special day in the lives of all young explorers, but, until I read this recently, I had forgotten all about it. I can remember my first sight of the African coast, palm trees swaying and a smell all its own wafting out to greet us. Freetown was an incredible first experience. I can remember painting ship wearing a regulation topee; today it seems all a bit bizarre, but then we were nearer to Nelson's navy than we were to the Royal Navy of today.

Half the convoy sailed on to Cape Town. We now took ourselves to Durban, the idea being that we would then sail back to collect the first half and take it to Madagascar and assist in the invasion of that island. At the time, of course, we had no idea where we were going or what we were going to do! All we knew was that having arrived in Durban, early one morning, we were not allowed to go ashore. Fresh food and water were loaded, as was fuel. That evening we slipped away and sailed south at top speed. The captain told the ship's company over the loudspeaker system that we were off to collect the other half of the convoy to invade Madagascar - tremendous excitement. Soon we would be firing our guns for real, destroying the enemy. At last we knew where we were bound. What we did not know was that, at that very moment, we were running head on into one of those storms for which the Cape has been famous for centuries.

By first light the next morning, the ship had been forced to reduce speed, and soon the enormous swell, some 50 feet high, had physically lifted the forward twin 8-inch turret, snapped its strengthened-steel locking-bolt like a rotten carrot and swung it round to face aft! Gradually all the armament positions were closed down except one pom-pom. Virtually all hands were closed up in the spaces below decks. Armed with buckets we slid our way back and forth bailing out cold, oily water from the shell-handling rooms. On every mess-deck, specially made wire handling ropes were joined to each metal upright, providing handholds 'tween decks. Even these could be seen to be stretching and loosening as the ship 'moved' to the enormous forces pounding her. We were all scared!

It was the first time in my life I had ever seen anything like this. I had read about storms at sea and tried to imagine them. Nowhere had I ever read anything that even remotely described what we were seeing for ourselves. The noise was unbelievable. I suppose, in retrospect, it was the shock at suddenly being made to realise just how fragile even a 10,000-ton armoured cruiser is, in relation to what the elements can offer.

I believe it took us about four times as long as it should have done to make this passage. I can recall, after the initial fear, the great pride I felt that our ship could cope with such a battering and, for the final few days, delighted in the ferocity of the storm. Standing on the 4-inch gun deck, where the overlap plates were situated, (two overlapping metal plates lay over each other, unfixed by rivets, to allow movement) we could watch the movement of the ship's hull as she drove her way up a mighty 50-foot wall of water, teetered for a moment on the crest, then, propellers thrashing, surged down the other side. The noise on deck was quite deafening. As the mountainous seas swept past, their wind-blown crests hissing, we cringed behind the guns for shelter.

In the trough between the swells, her momentum would drive her bows deep into the approaching sea. Great sheets of storm-blown spray would be hurled way over the superstructure and tons of solid water would cascade aft along her length. The sheer weight of this water would cause her to shudder like a palsied man as her own buoyancy lifted her bows clear and her propellers drove her ever upwards. I only wish I had had a camera in those days.

Even the 40,000-ton liner New Amsterdam, took all day to overtake us; we were steaming at ten knots, which just gave us steerage way, and were making good about four, she probably five! Thus it was that we missed the invasion and all its excitement.

However, on the positive side, it put us in dock for three weeks and gave us the opportunity to see Cape Town. As we entered Simonstown Bay, Table Mountain stood proudly covered with her 'table cloth', just as the photographs had shown. There were three 'springboks' in my mess and their advice to us was to book in to the Navy, Army & Air Force accommodation as soon as we got to Cape Town. This we did; for a charge of only sixpence a night we became entitled to membership of the best Services Club I have ever been in.

The beds were in dormitory fashion, spotlessly clean with the linen changed each day baths and hot water unlimited. All the most eligible girls and ladies of Cape Town did volunteer work for this home for servicemen. The meals were excellent and fresh fruit (presented by well-wishers) was freely available on each table! Even our meagre pay enabled us to live like lords.

We had found out that there was a riding stable at Kloof Neck (near the top of the mountain), so next morning, after a quick look round the shops, we boarded a bus. Already on the bus were a group of young ladies wearing riding habits. Shyly we asked one of them if they knew where the riding stables were at Kloof Neck and, to our delight, they said that they were going there themselves. By the time we arrived we had split up into four pairs and the owner of the stables, sensing this, managed to organise things in such a way that we were all mounted at the same time and departed together. It was not until some months later we learned that he was a retired Chief Petty Officer!

This first breath of freedom was magic after so long aboard. The opportunity to live like normal young folk for a short time, to be able to talk to pretty girls of our own age and to laugh again', was marvellous. Half way up the winding road, Alan's horse did something I have never seen before or since. He had drawn a rather stubborn animal and had great difficulty in persuading it to accompany the rest of us. Quite suddenly, without any warning, it just sat down in the middle of the road! Alan's face was puce with embarrassment as grinning motorists crept slowly past. He stood up, kicked his feet clear of the stirrups, and begged his mount to get up! No response. By this time we had all gathered round and one of the girls dismounted. I am ashamed to say that we were laughing so much that we sailors were quite incapable of helping him. Poor Alan, but from then on his 'Girl Friday' and he were inseparable!

My own girl friend was called Dinty Spence. She was a slim blonde and kindness itself. It was she who took us to her home and who wrote home to let my folk know that she had met me. Until they received her letter my parents had no idea where in the world I was. During the war it was she and her parents who very kindly sent my family Christmas parcels of dried fruit long after I had left South Africa.

Our week's leave flew past; dejected (but rejuvenated) we returned to our wooden benches and the rough and tumble of life on board. Soon we were sailed, this time alone, and when the Captain spoke over the loudspeakers it was to inform us that we would be involved in 'South Atlantic Patrol'; this would involve long stretches at sea, searching for the odd enemy ship trying to use the South Atlantic to escape back to Europe or to supply their submarines, or trying to intercept enemy raiders. These latter would include some of Germany's most powerful capital ships. In retrospect we were lucky not to have been so involved!

My cruising station had been changed to 'masthead lookout'. I was very proud of this change when I realised that with four watches, there were only four men aboard picked out for these duties. In good weather, alone in the vast wastes of the southern ocean, I really enjoyed my time in the crow's nest. One bright, sunny afternoon, a massive albatross kept its effortless station ten feet away, wings outstretched and beady eyes glancing to left and right. Without any apparent effort, it would suddenly swoop to almost touch the oily waves, swing over them at zero height and curl back and up to keep me company again without a single flap of its wings. On such days the sea was a marvellous blue and, with a cloudless sky, there was no visible horizon; the two blues just merged. Inevitably, in such a vast wilderness, sightings of other vessels were few indeed, but I was able to watch nature for hours at a time. Huge whales, their spray-breaths giving them away, would trundle past; dolphins would keep us company, playing in our bow wave for hours.

We also had our storms. I remember one such when I had fought my way into the small metal cylinder, which surrounded the swing-chair masthead position, at first light. It had taken all my strength to do so and the noise of the wind in this exposed position, along with the constant spray splattering against the mast behind me like shrapnel, made it very difficult to hear the voice of the officer of the watch on the bridge through the sound-power telephone which was our only means of contact.

'Masthead lookout closed up,' I bellowed down the phone. There was a long pause, then my telephone 'call-up' sounded. I picked up the phone and dodged below the level of the shielding to try and hear the message. A voice was querying something. I bellowed my message again - another long pause. Because of the constant spray I could see virtually nothing with my eyes, and binoculars were impossible. The phone whined again.

'What the hell are you doing up there?' A strange voice demanded an answer. Before I could say anything it continued, 'Report to the bridge at once!' The line went dead as I automatically responded, 'Aye aye, sir!'

Getting up to the masthead had been difficult, but going down was very frightening. One had to get out of the small surrounding metal cylinder and, hanging on for dear life, reach round the cross-trees to find the welded ladder footholds which ran up the rear of the mast. This mast sloped backwards and with the force of the wind trying to blow me out like a flag, it took all my strength to make my way slowly down each rung of the ladder. At last, as the ADP superstructure took the full force of the gale, I was able to increase the speed of my descent. Flushed, soaked and out of breath, I reported to the bridge. The Officer of the Watch alerted the Captain, who was seated in his chair. He turned slowly and looked at me. I felt as I used to do when confronted by my headmaster.

'What in heaven's name were you doing up there?' He pointed skyward. I replied that my orders were to close up at first light and these orders had not been countermanded. 'Have you no brains?' the Captain said and turned back to his contemplation of the weather ahead. I saluted and hurriedly left the bridge. When I arrived back on the flag deck the Petty Officer, in charge of our watch, gave me a real roasting. It transpired later that it was he who was held responsible for not telling me not to close up!

These long patrols had few moments of action; I can only remember a couple. One night we were all called to stations. Mine was on the port searchlight. The ship was turning at high speed as we closed up and the shuddering and wind noise made it hard to hear the sound-powered phones.

'Burn light behind closed shutters,' the voice ordered. As communication number I passed the order to the searchlight crew. A switch clicked and one could hear the unmistakable fuzz as the arc lit up. A few moments later the voice was

AB John S.Townend,
D/JX 303588, 1942

giving more instructions. 'Bearing red 100 stand by.' The searchlight layer eased the light to the new bearing - we waited. Our ship had now eased her speed. 'Open shutters,' came the order. Immediately a vivid pencil of white light sped across the sea and showed a ship travelling on a course parallel to our own. She was rolling slowly, and black smoke was issuing from her old funnel. A signalman on our bridge was flashing a message by light. During the long pause that followed we wondered when she would fire at us; all our guns were fixed on her old hull. Or was she acting as a decoy for a submarine, which even now was getting into position to torpedo us? Our searchlight still shone out pin-pointing our position. Eventually, the ship started to flash her response to us. After what seemed an age the voice on the phone ordered us to, 'Close shutters and switch off port searchlight'. We did so and almost at once the ship healed over as she turned away and increased speed. Action stations were closed down and cruising stations were reinstated. We lucky ones returned to our hammocks.

On another occasion I was employed just above the propellers right aft, sorting out some gear with a couple of friends. It was late morning. Working in the adjoining space, separated by a watertight door, were another group of sailors. Suddenly the action station buzzers sounded. We made our way to the watertight door, but as fast as we undid the clips on our side some idiot on the other side did them up again! This meant we had to wait until they were all clear of the compartment before we could get out! By the time I arrived on the upper deck as ammo-supply number to the starboard pom-pom, the Petty Officer in charge was 'hopping'! I started the electric winch and began hoisting boxes of the heavy ammunition on deck - those eight-barrelled pom-poms ate ammunition! Once again we steamed at speed, spray flying, ensign straining, only, eventually, to close down and revert to cruising stations. In retrospect we were lucky not to have bumped into any of the enemy capital ships; at the time I felt most disappointed.

The next time we returned to Simonstown some of us were told to parade in our number one suits. We were to attend a selection board being held in our Captain's cabin. As a result, ten of us found ourselves on our way by train to Port Elizabeth. Very excited, we all knew that we were entering another phase of our development. We were now 'potential officers'. Stage one had been completed; if we could make it, stage two lay ahead.

CHAPTER THREE - *GOOD HOPE.*

At the same time as Field Marshall Rommel was approaching Cairo, a Royal Navy Captain flew into Alexandria from London, with orders to open a new naval training establishment. This was to intercept potential officers and, like HMS *King Alfred* at home, turn them into officers. Setting up such a school in Africa would save having to bring sailors back to the UK and then send them out again. Fortunately for us, this Captain decided that 'Alex' was not a very suitable site for such an enterprise (it looked as if the Germans could well be occupying it before too long!) and he set off to seek a place in South Africa. He ended up by taking over a brand new hotel seventeen miles outside Port Elizabeth on the coast. When we arrived we were amazed. The very smart staff of Indian waiters, in full regalia, treated us as VIPs and waited on us just like first-class peacetime visitors. The contrast to the mess-decks we had all just left was incredible. After a wonderful civilised breakfast that first morning we were fell in and our new Captain addressed us.

He explained how he and we had arrived in this heavenly spot, apologised for there not being any suitable naval equipment to train us (suitable groans from us all), but went on to explain that our first task was to make friends with the local residents. Army trucks would take us to PE each Wednesday afternoon for 'sport', and on Fridays, for those entitled, for weekend sport and leave. Immediately we were to form a rugby team and he had arranged the first fixture against the local Public School first fifteen for the next Saturday afternoon. What a start! Fifteen of us ended up playing against those very fit schoolboys. Naturally, after at least a year of naval life, we were out of practice but it was very noticeable how much we had been hardened over that time and, despite being out-run, we won - not least because of the quality of our South African colleagues.

It has become fashionable since the war for people in this country to become anti-South African, rather than anti-apartheid. We appear to have forgotten how many South Africans fought and died alongside our men. At the same time they suffered from internal terrorists, called OBs, of Dutch-Boer origin, who were anti-British and pro-Nazi Germany. The same people were pro-apartheid after the war, but the vast majority of ordinary South Africans, the children of those brave people who fought with our men, were not in agreement.

Gradually, as the weeks passed, we settled into our new routine. A parade ground was constructed, as were new buildings to house the inevitable six-inch BL guns. We spent much of our time playing rugby, golf on the hotel course and swimming in the largest open-air pool in the country, which was filled by each high tide from the sea. We studied the same subjects, to the same depth, as our King Alfred colleagues at home but had many more distractions. One of mine was a lovely young lady whose parents had kindly invited me into their home for a couple of weekends. They had a lovely home and she was as pretty as a picture. Looking back, she must have felt I was terribly 'slow'. I was still at the stage when I put every girl I became fond of on a

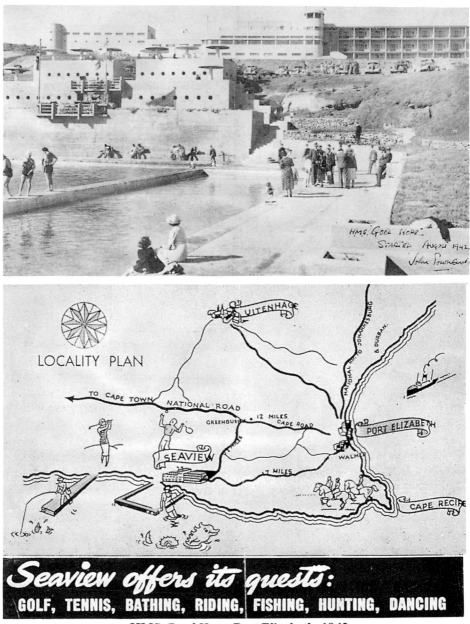

LOCALITY PLAN

TO CAPE TOWN NATIONAL ROAD

UITENHAGE

NATIONAL ROAD TO JOHANNESBURG & DURBAN

GREENBUSH • 12 MILES CAPE ROAD

PORT ELIZABETH

SEAVIEW

WALM

7 MILES

CAPE RECI

HM.S. GOOD HOPE.
STARTED AUGUST 1942.
John Townend

Seaview offers its guests:
GOLF, TENNIS, BATHING, RIDING, FISHING, HUNTING, DANCING

HMS *Good Hope*, Port Elizabeth, 1942

pedestal, became totally loyal, but would not dare even to kiss her in case she rejected my advances. What wasted opportunities!

A few weeks before the exams I began to realise that I was in danger of failing, due to lack of really hard work. My understanding of spherical trigonometry and the theory of astro-navigation was nil! I had no problem with anything of a practical nature, but on the academic front I was a clot!

More by good luck than my hard work, I was one of the fifty-odd sailors of that first class to pass out. If you were over 21 you became a sub-lieutenant; under 21 you became a midshipman. Along with my friend Frank Yates, I became a midshipman. In the UK we would have gone to any naval tailor, had our uniforms made and they would automatically have had the correct regulation coloured patches on the lapels to indicate we were 'mids' RNVR; RN had white ones. In Port Elizabeth this proved a problem. No one knew the right colours! Frank and I must be the only midshipmen to have had to go to a ladies' outfitter to select the right shade of silk to have our patches made up!

After a final party, suitably attired in our new finery and feeling very self-conscious, we said our final farewells. Relief at having succeeded was watered down by the genuine sadness at having to say goodbye to so many very close friends. Some of us had been together ever since we had joined. How distant those days now seemed!

When we were interviewed at the end of our course, the Captain asked us to what sort of vessel we would like to be appointed. For the second time during my short naval career I asked to go to Coastal Forces. He smiled and congratulated me on my choice; I was delighted. Their Lordships at Admiralty, however, thought quite differently. Midshipmen (especially RNVR ones) needed to be properly educated in naval ways and a capital ship-of-the-line was the right place to knock sense into young men with 'lower deck experience and radical ideas'!

Thus it was that Frank Yates and I found ourselves on the train to Durban. We were to report, not to a small Coastal Forces craft, but to the only battleship available! I was horrified. I had seen the way the midshipmen were treated in HMS *Shropshire*; they were worse off than we were as A/Bs! A battleship would be much worse.

Because the OBs had blown up a railway line, we were routed via the mountains to the north and west, visiting Ladysmith en route, an extended but fascinating journey.

CHAPTER FOUR - DURBAN TO MOMBASA

It was very hot. The bright sun beat down from a cloudless sky as our native taxi-driver delivered us alongside HMS *Warspite*; she lay there 'sweating'. The heat as we made our way up the after gangway on to the quarterdeck was oppressive. We saluted as we crossed the brow; a Midshipman RN asked our names and introduced us to the Officer of the Watch. Looking us up and down in a rather disapproving way, he sent a side boy to find the Sub of the gunroom. He ordered a sailor to collect our gear from the jetty and suggested we wait by the huge 15-inch turret out of the way. A young RN Sub-Lieutenant suddenly appeared and we shook hands. He led us below to the gunroom. This was a large, long 'room' on the starboard side of the ship. Its scuttles were open and the wind shutes collected whatever breeze there was. Overhead old-fashioned deck-head fans waved their languid arms slowly around. I looked at Frank and knew he was thinking the same as me. No way!

We were introduced to the 'snotties' nurse', a brisk Lieut-Commander RN who would be our mentor and tormentor! Later on we were wheeled along and introduced to the Commander, a senior and imposing figure who gave the impression of having heard about RNVR midshipmen but had never been totally convinced they existed!

At lunchtime we met the rest of the gunroom. It was worse than one's first day at boarding school. The RN mids seemed so young. We had not realised how quickly our time on the mess-deck had aged us. As soon as we could, we obtained permission to go ashore. We found a clean, out-of-the-way café and ordered the cheapest omelette on the menu. We had to find a way out of our present predicament. Some sailors who had had too much to drink were eyeing us with distaste. Eventually, one of them got up and came over to our table.

'Why are you looking at ush?' he slurred. 'Bloody little stuck up snotties....'

I shall never know what made me think of it but I suddenly had a brainwave. Hooking my feet over the cross member of my chair (hidden by the tablecloth) and resting one hand for support on the table, I stood up. The added six inches enabled me to tower over the man. In my best lower-deck language I looked down at him, pointed to my RNVR patches and said, 'Six months ago I too was on the mess-deck. Why don't you f... off and leave us in peace!' He did! The only trouble was we had to re-order. We dared not leave before they did or they would have seen just what height I really was!

As we made our way back through the dockyard we noticed two Hunt class destroyers. Discreet enquiries revealed the fact that they were due to escort HMS *Warspite* to Mombasa. Frank and I tossed a coin - we would each board one destroyer and see if we could 'bum a ride'.

I strode up the gangway to board HMS *Blackmore*. The duty Quartermaster welcomed me aboard as a human being and informed me that the Officer of the Day was the Navigator - he took me down to the tiny wardroom and introduced me. The Navigator, an RNVR Lieutenant, asked me if I would like a drink and offered an open packet of Senior Service cigarettes.

'Please sit down,' he said. 'What can I do for you?' This was so different to the 'big ship' approach that I was overwhelmed and told him so. He grinned.

'Somehow,' I told him, 'I need to escape from that gunroom. Would it be possible for his Captain to request a midshipman as an additional watch-keeping officer (dogsbody) for the passage to Mombasa?' He had listened in silence as I poured out my heart.

After topping up my beer for me he rose. 'You stay here,' he said. Ten minutes later I was in the Captain's cabin. He too was an RNVR Lieutenant. I was in luck! He laughed in good-humoured fashion as I confirmed what his Navigator had told him.

'Return to your friendly battleship and say nothing to anyone about this meeting,' he said. 'Leave things to me and trust me. I can make no promises but certainly we will request your help for our escorting duties!' I was absolutely thrilled. I had never thanked anyone more sincerely.

When I reached the jetty Frank was already waiting. His beaming face told me all I needed to know. He too had been successful! With light hearts the two conspirators waltzed up *Warspite's* gangway, threw carefree salutes as they crossed the quarter-deck and made for the gunroom bar.

The following morning we were told to prepare ourselves to meet the Captain. The Sub of the gunroom delivered the message with a leer. 'The old man doesn't like mids,' he said.

Half an hour before our appointment we were sent for by the snotties' nurse. 'Just wanted to see that you were properly dressed,' he said, and dismissed us.

We arrived outside the Commander's cabin ten minutes before we were due to report to the Captain, knocked on his door and were told to wait. At exactly five minutes before the time the Commander had us outside the Captain's cabin door. We were nervous and wondered what this Captain (who did not like mids) would look like. The Captain's cabin in those old battleships was immense. It was furnished like a beautiful drawing room with lovely desk, sofa and chairs. Pretty chintzy curtains covering the portholes and a neatly-arranged vase of flowers completed the picture. Behind the desk sat a handsome, bemedalled man. His face, tanned above a spotless white collar, smiled kindly as he shook both of us by the hand. We stood in awe, our caps held tightly under our left arms, and waited.

He was saying that he had been interested to note we had both been together ever since training. He had served in a cruiser as a young officer and now that we were starting out on our careers he was sure we would do very well, assuming, of course, we kept our noses clean. A glance at the Commander showed me that he was nodding assent. Quite suddenly he stopped in his review of our past and looked at us hard.

'Today I've received a signal from the Captains of the two destroyers due to escort us to Mombasa requesting that you be lent to them for the passage for watch-keeping duties.' I dared not even glance at Frank and, feeling my face getting red, stared straight in front of me. Trying to show no emotion, we stood silently waiting for his next comment. To our great relief he continued, 'I have replied to their requests that I think it would be wonderful experience for you both. 'We grinned as our eyes met. He was speaking again. 'Can't think,' he was saying to the Commander 'how they knew we had just received these two young gentlemen aboard can you?' The Commander shuffled his feet uneasily and replied that he had no idea. Our first and last interview with the Captain was over. He shook us by the hand again and, with a wicked look in his now twinkling eyes, mumbled something about 'using one's initiative'. We were about to break free!

The occupants of the gunroom, when they heard about our new appointments, were absolutely furious. For two just-qualified RNVR mids to be given the chance to join the two destroyers - it was infamous! Frank and I kept our own counsel, but early next morning we left.

The trip up to Mombasa was terrific. I was treated as a grown-up apprentice and, as a result, learned very quickly. We zigzagged our way, keeping station on our charge as she lumbered through the ocean. Flying fish preceded us and dolphins played in our bow wave. The blue, blue Indian ocean stretched as far as the eye could see and no one would have known there was any danger but for the incessant 'ping' from the asdic compartment. Certainly, nothing could have been further from my mind than war. I was at sea in a destroyer, I was learning from the Navigator and the other officers, I could not have been happier in a cruise liner. It was magic!

On our arrival at Mombasa we had a nasty shock. My Captain sent for me. 'Terribly sorry,' he said. 'Just had a signal to send you ashore.' I was flabbergasted. On the jetty I met Frank with his gear. He had had the same message from his Captain. The powers that be had decided that, if there were berths available in destroyers for training, it was RN mids who should be filling them not RNVR ones! We joined the shore base and awaited further orders. At least we had escaped from the battleship and our short time aboard the destroyers had made us hungry for small ships.

The following day we were told to report to the Censor's office. Here a young officer with glasses informed us that we would report daily and assist in the task of reading all the letters from the mail office prior to them being sent onwards. It was a most unpleasant task; having to read other people's mail made one feel faintly 'unclean', and since one was also obliged to cut out (with a pair of scissors) any reference to places, one could finish up with a letter in tatters! I knew because I had received such a missive and had wondered not only what the offending section had mentioned but, rather more to the point, what the other missing piece over the page had said! The monotony was sometimes relieved by finding letters in French. Our schoolboy French was hardly up to the task but we dutifully did as told!

The officers' mess was a collection of 'Basher huts' joined by concrete pathways and surrounded by native trees and gardens. A resident family of baboons regularly raided our rooms, which were open at the top to such visitors. Anything left lying around would disappear. Other resident visitors tended to appear after nightfall and consisted of all the creepy crawly creatures that live in the jungle in that part of the world. We pretended not to be fearful of these, but each night we would race to get under our mosquito nets. Last man had to switch the light out, and that meant crossing the room in the dark. One night Frank trod on a large black centipede and his shriek woke the whole block!

There was a mad doctor, I remember, who collected scorpions. These creatures would congregate outside the washroom, attracted by the bright outside lighting. We kept well clear of such things and our only deliberate contact with the insect world was to get a praying mantis drunk at the bar. These harmless insects were drawn by the light and we would place a small drop of liqueur on their extended fore legs; they would then clean this off with their mouths, like kittens washing their faces. Quite soon they would start to wobble about, just like drunken sailors the world over. We thought this was hilarious and I suppose, in retrospect, it was a reasonably harmless pastime. Certainly I never met any mantis that suffered from an addiction to alcohol due to such antics!

Ashore one afternoon, we found a garage willing to hire us a car. It turned out to be a Ford, built in 1925. The Indian salesman promised us it was in 'top class condition, Sahib'. With great pride we paid him the deposit and drove back to the officers' mess.

It was just before dinner when we arrived. The mess was full, with several officers sitting on the open verandah. As we drove up I suddenly realised that the brakes were having no effect. I tried to change down into a lower gear. The resultant noise, as well as the extended double de-clutch acceleration, was horrendous. All that happened was that the car flew into neutral and the speed increased as we sped past the verandah, heading for the flowerbeds. I hauled the steering wheel to the right as far as it would go and we swept round in a grand circle, which we had to continue to do to lose headway, circling the tall mango trees and central flowerbed. Eventually, the constant pressure on the hand-brake brought our steed to a halt. Two very embarrassed midshipmen stepped down. The comments from our audience were mainly of the unprintable variety and we hurried away to our room. We would forgo dinner and make an early start next morning.

We had learned about a super beach some miles to the north and, armed with instructions as to how to get there, we set off just after first light. Although the car started first try, she stalled shortly afterwards and, despite all our efforts, would not re-start. After about half an hour we were wondering what to do when a chain gang appeared with their warder. We explained our predicament. In no time at all the chain gang was pushing us at a great lick. Sure enough she fired and by keeping her revs up for the rest of the day we never had the same problem.

The first part of the journey took us on a metalled road through the built-up area of the town; then the houses became more spread out till we ran into solid jungle on a very rough single track. We had to assume we were going in the right direction since we would have had one heck of a job to turn round anyway! After an hour or more we arrived at a glade with native huts and fires. When we enquired about the beach they just pointed ahead, and sure enough, as we rounded another bend in the track, the jungle thinned to reveal a most beautiful curved white sandy beach. The blue Indian Ocean was calm and just a whisper of surf ran up the sand. We were enchanted and started to drive very slowly on to the beach.

We had just left the shade of the surrounding tress when the trouble started. Our front left wheel suddenly slewed inwards and the car came to a stop. The sand surrounding us was beautiful, fine, white coral sand but it was not ideal for supporting a jack that now needed to raise the front wheel-axle to enable us to see where the problem lay. The garage had not supplied any sort of tool kit. We were stuck.

We decided to have some sandwiches and consider the options. It was pretty obvious we had somehow to obtain some tools and make good a repair to enable us to return. We spun a coin and Frank walked off to a bungalow that could be seen on the very far side of the beach. An hour later he returned with a screwdriver, a hammer, some heavy wire and a pair of pliers. Now to work! It took us all day - we never even stopped to enjoy a bathe under that tranquil sky, but by late that afternoon we had 'botched' the wheel back into almost a fore-and-aft position. We did not dare to risk driving any further on to the beach and backed the car very slowly on to the harder soil under the trees. We returned the tools to the bungalow. With fingers firmly crossed we entered the jungle and with considerable care retraced our tracks. It seemed to take forever to reach the metalled road, which we did just as the last light began to fade. We parked the car and went to the bar.

'Good day?' questioned the friendly Lieutenant who had explained how to get to the beach. We nodded, not daring to tell him the truth.

'Super spot,' said Frank. 'Many thanks for your most helpful directions - we owe you a pint!'

The following day we returned our famous Ford to the Indian. He could not understand when we told him about the failing brakes or the fact that she refused to start 'She is first class lady, Sahib, never lets me down in many years.' When we showed him the wire holding the left wheel in position he was full of admiration. I have often wondered whether anyone ever took our wire off - probably it stayed with that old car for the rest of her days!

We had now been ashore for over a month and were becoming bored. At last news came through that we were both to join an old cruiser called HMS *Dauntless*. It seemed the powers that be had compromised. A light cruiser gunroom was infinitely better than a battleship gunroom, and we were still together!

We looked forward to the arrival of our new home with interest. Although there were those who explained that she was an old First World War ship and hot as blazes, it did not matter to us. She was our way out of our current existence and we sought news of her arrival each day.

CHAPTER FIVE - *DAUNTLESS*

This lady had been born in 1917, a full six years before Frank or I had arrived on this planet! We eyed her warily as the motor cutter landed us alongside with a bump. It was 1400 on the 10th November 1942.

A bronzed Australian RNVR Lieutenant, the Officer of the Watch, welcomed us aboard. This was encouraging! A pleasant RN Midshipman organised for our gear to be taken below and accompanied us to the gunroom. Here he introduced us to the other occupants who were relaxed and friendly. We could be happy here, a quite different feeling from that encountered in the battleship gunroom. The other mids were soon telling us all about the various officers with whom we would come into contact - they had just completed the 'first chapter' when our new snotties' nurse arrived. He turned out to be a young RN Lieutenant who treated us as adult beings. We were informed about our duties and warned to be ready to meet the Commander at 1630. After this we would be taken to meet the Captain.

'Between now and then,' he said, 'I've arranged for you to be shown round the ship. I suggest you get to know your way around as soon as possible. We are due to sail tomorrow at 0500.'

The Commander was an elderly man with the reputation for ill temper, especially first thing in the morning. Our first meeting was short and to the point. He was of the old school and believed midshipmen should hardly ever be seen, and for preference should never be heard, and those sentiments referred to RN mids! RNVR midshipmen were almost beyond his comprehension! He looked at us with his watery blue eyes and sighed heavily.

'You are Townend?' He eyed me up and down.

'Yes, sir,' I replied, wondering what was in store.

'I see from your duties that you are to be my 'doggy' - do you know what those duties involve, boy?' I was taken aback, and stuttered that I had been making enquiries. Before I could finish, he rounded on our snotties' nurse. 'For Christ's sake, how long have you had these idiots under your wing?' Without waiting for any response he went on. 'You,' pointing a dagger-like finger at me, 'will report to me here at precisely 1745. Is that clear?'

'Yes, sir,' I replied and the three of us beat a hasty retreat. Once out of earshot, the young Lieutenant turned to us and grinned.

'Well,' he said. 'You have now met our gallant Commander.' He paused to allow some sailors to pass us in the gangway. 'He'll be less amenable when you meet him tomorrow morning.' He grinned again and led us aft to meet the Captain.

Our Captain was the most delightful man. He asked us about our careers to date and, since we had been together from the start, only one of us needed to reply; Frank acted as spokesman. He then gave us what information he could about the ship and its proposed programme. We were due to sail very early next morning, but would be spending Christmas in Simonstown.

'Which one of you will be responsible for the motor cutter?' A nudge from the young Lieutenant prompted me.

'I will, sir,' I said.

'Have you had any experience in driving these boats?' He looked me straight in the eyes.

'I'm afraid not, sir, but I will be starting to learn later on this evening for the liberty men.'

'Good,' he said, 'because you will be driving me around the tankers in the Gulf and I do not like being either kept waiting or dunked in the sea!' He smiled broadly and wished us well. The interview was over and we went back to the gunroom.

At 1740 I knocked on the Commander's door.

'Wait!' a voice shouted. At 1745 the Commander appeared, walked straight past me as if I were not there, and was fast disappearing down the passageway. I replaced my cap on my head and set off in hot pursuit, almost at the double. I arrived on the quarterdeck just in time to hear him chastising the Officer of the Watch. To my unpractised eye the place looked immaculate; to the Commander's experienced eye the place looked 'a bloody mess!' And he was in the process of telling the unfortunate officer exactly what he felt when a signalman arrived, saluted smartly, and handed him a signal. The incident was closed.

The side party ran around the quarterdeck seeing to the various things the Commander had mentioned as being incorrect. He walked briskly forward, followed at a smart canter by me. This was what being a 'doggy' meant! I began to understand where the rather odd term had come from. It described this job exactly and very explicitly! One followed the Commander as closely as possible; his every wish needed to be dealt with at once. Not only did he expect you to have excellent hearing but also, on occasions, to be able to read his mind. He would wave a hand in a general direction. 'For God's sake go and sort out those fools,' he would say as he disappeared up a ladder. I would glance in the general direction of his waving hand and run off. On my way there I would try and think about what my glance had shown me. I would arrive, out of breath, and salute the officer in charge of whatever working party was in question.

'Commander's compliments,' I would blurt out. 'Could you please hurry along.' The usual response was unprintable. I would turn and be gone before I was abused further. Doggy then set about trying to find his 'owner'. He never told me what his planned movements were. It was a matter of telepathy trying to guess where he had gone. Eventually, when I had caught up with him, he would look at me and ask in a disapproving voice where the hell I had been; he had work to do and could not wait around all day for lazy good-for-nothing RNVR snotties! I soon learned to grin like a puppy which had been rebuked and salute in recognition. It worked wonders!

That evening, for the first time, I found myself in the motor cutter. This was terrific, my own small boat! She had a large leading seaman, my Coxswain, at the tiller. A bearded pirate, whose grizzled head appeared from nowhere, turned out to be my stoker-engineer and two sailors, one forward and one aft, manned their boat hooks in a most seamanlike manner. I was indeed a very proud young man.

I shall never forget that first liberty boat run. As we approached the jetty to land our load of liberty men we were overtaken by the faster, more modern, liberty boats from other ships in the harbour. The closer we got to the landing jetty, the more congested the approach became as every ship's boat jostled to land its cargo of impatient men. Naturally I had never seen anything like this before and was wondering how to cope when my Coxswain whispered in my ear,

'OK if I take over, sir?'

'Yes indeed,' I replied, totally at a loss as to how to proceed.

Although the other boats were more up-to-date and faster, we had a secret weapon, which they did not have: we were fitted with 'kitchen rudder gear'. This simple, but very effective, invention enabled us to place our bows between the jetty and another boat and by using the secret weapon we could muscle in. Inevitably such queue-jumping behaviour enraged the opposition while delighting our own liberty men. The end result was that our men got ashore ahead of the opposition while the two boats' crews and their officers bandied words and shook fists! I realised for the first time why it was vital to have such powerful, piratical fellows in my boat's crew! For my part, having served my time on the lower deck, I was able to silence the more gentlemanly RN midshipmen with such a flow of abuse that even my own crew were shocked!

For the first time, later that same night, I also learned the difficulties and dangers inherent in separating out your own liberty men from all the others in the mass of men, all impatient to return to their hammocks and sleep off their surfeit of local brew! Once again I realised the value of my 'pirates'. Leaving me in the boat, my Coxswain leapt ashore. In a stentorian bellow he shouted 'Dauntless!' A movement in the seething mass spilled out a small group of sailors who proceeded to board us.

'Sit down you bastards!' The stoker's bearded head appeared. I just stood there bemused and silent. Eventually, after a swift head-count, my Coxswain told me we could now return to the ship. In the inky darkness I had the utmost difficulty in finding our ship. Fortunately my Coxswain had a much better idea of the geography of the place and in due time we landed our valuable cargo without incident. As I turned in that first night I realised just how much I had to learn.

It seemed I had only just dropped off when I was shaken to get up. Already I could hear movement on deck and, hurriedly shaving and throwing on my uniform, I just had time to swallow a cup of tea before my wrist-watch told me to report to the Commander.

'Special sea duty men close up.' The preceding pipe had warned us of this order. I knocked on the Commander's door. 'I'm coming blast you!' was the immediate response. I stood aside and, my Commander pushed past and set off for the bridge. I followed in hot pursuit.

The ship had been moored to two buoys; the warps attached to the buoy astern

25

had already been recovered (these were the noises I had heard when I woke). There were a lot of people on the bridge but there was an air of quiet competence. Below, men feverishly hauled on warps, winches rattled, signalmen were hoisting flags and orders could be heard. I stood very still behind the Commander, attentive to every detail. Suddenly, a movement indicated that the Captain had arrived. He returned the Commander's salute and wished everyone a good morning. The Navigator and he then had a short discussion about their plans for leaving the harbour and he gave the necessary orders to set things in motion.

At a signal from the bridge the final wire rope connecting us to the buoy was slipped from the forecastle with a splash. I glanced at my wrist-watch - it was exactly 0500 as the signalman on the forecastle hauled down the Union Jack. Orders had stated that we would sail at 0500 and we had. I was seeing at first hand what the Navy meant by being punctual.

As we passed other ships, according to the seniority of their captains, we either 'piped' them or they would 'pipe' us. The crew, fallen in and immaculate, facing outboard, would be called to attention each time and we would salute from the bridge. It felt like a peacetime review, not a warship sailing to face the enemy, but such traditions help to preserve the morale and good discipline of the fleet.

As the engines increased their throb we felt the old lady get into her stride. We were off to Durban. I was quickly brought back to earth by the Commander shouting for me.

'Sir.' I jumped to face him.

'Get down and tell that quarter-deck officer he is the son of a useless bitch. Unless he gets those warps sorted in double quick time, I'll personally have his balls for my breakfast! Get going!'

I sped off down the various ladders as fast as my young legs would carry me, ran down the deck, avoiding the small knots of sweating sailors busily making ready for sea, and saluted the officer in question. He was in no mood to talk to midshipmen bringing comments from the Commander or anyone else; he was sorting out a 'cat's cradle' of wire ropes all determined to go their own way.

'Get to hell out of my way, Snottie,' he said in an undertone 'before I kick your arse!' I glanced up at the bridge nervously.

'Commander's compliments, sir,' was all I could say before his boot arrived. My rugby training ensured that I had turned and was on my way back to the bridge. I had just swept round a corner when I came face to face with my Captain. I flattened against the steel bulkhead. The Captain paused and turned to face me. He had a twinkle in his blue eyes.

'Did you deliver the Commander's message, Snottie?'

'Oh yes, sir,' I stammered.

'What did you say?' he queried.

'Commander's compliments...' I began, but he was already chortling his way towards his breakfast - perhaps he too, in his day, had been a Commander's doggy! In retrospect the job taught me a whole host of things, but in my Commander's case it was very necessary to learn them pretty quickly!

It is surprising how quickly the long-established naval routines absorb newcomers and enable them to become integral members of the team. Within a couple of days of being at sea we were absorbed and going about our various allotted tasks as if we had been at it for years rather than days.

The only extra duty we had as midshipmen was one of schooling. *Dauntless* carried a schoolmaster, a kindly man whose unenviable task it was to teach us the theory of navigation. The two RN mids were both clever and knowledgeable about such subjects; I was 'thick'. I had no trouble in actually taking sights but trying to understand the mathematics was totally beyond me! Fortunately our time at school was small in comparison with all our other duties and, as the other duties were all of a very practical nature, I concentrated my energies on them.

We made a brief stop in Aden and then sailed back down to Simonstown. Shortly after our return a notice calling for cricketers appeared on the gunroom board. I had represented the ship against the RAF in the Gulf so I entered my name. To my delight, the following afternoon, I was sent for. It seemed that I was to attend the 'nets' at the Test ground (Newlands) in Cape Town. Naturally, I was thrilled to bits.

A couple of us attended as ordered. We found a small group of other Naval personnel already bowling when we arrived and a large older man, in immaculate white flannels, was organising things. Rather nervously we joined them. The older man came over and shook hands.

'Nice of you to turn up,' he smiled. 'Tell me something about your background.' I looked at the young Lieutenant and awaited his reply. When he finished I followed with my scant details.

'Fine,' said the man, who turned out to be the Pro at Newlands. He was an old England cricketer whose name escapes me. 'Please pad-up,' he said to the Lieutenant, and throwing me a ball said 'Let's see what you can do with that!'

The afternoon flew past. It was tremendous to be playing under the eye of such a man. He coached us and, after a period of fielding practice, sent us back to our ships with instructions to return the following afternoon for a further session.

On the Friday, I was sent for by the snotties' nurse, and to my astonishment he congratulated me! Apparently I had been selected to represent the Navy at Newlands the following day. I could not believe it and returned to the gunroom in a daze. Frank asked me what the snotties' nurse had found to complain about. I just looked at him and grinned.

'You'll never believe this,' I said. 'You know those 'nets' I've been attending all week. Apparently they have been using them to select a team to represent the Navy against a South Africa side tomorrow on the Test Ground - and I'm one of the eleven selected!'

'You jammy bastard!' His words arrived at the same time as a cushion flew past my ducking head.

Saturday dawned bright with large white clouds sprinkling the blue sky. The rail journey to Cape Town had never taken so long, but I was one of the first to arrive and was already on the field practising when the captain called us together. He had won the toss and put them in to bat. After the first few overs I had the feeling that their batting looked considerably sharper than our bowling! However, there was no prouder youngster than me that afternoon as I sprinted around the field. If only my father could have been there to see his son actually playing on a Test ground.

As their score mounted, so did the black thunder-clouds. Quite suddenly, as happens there, a flash of lightning heralded a torrential downpour. We ran for shelter to the pavilion. It soon became obvious that there would be no further play - such a sad end to what had looked like being a day to remember for ever.

The South African players now entertained us in royal fashion. Unfortunately for me, I had not yet learned that it was prudent on such occasions to refuse politely any drinks offered! I can faintly remember finding my way back to the station at Cape Town, but do not remember the ride back to Simonstown. The walk back to the ship was unsteady and my eventual collapse in the gunroom was heralded by shrieks of mirth from those still aboard.

'Our conquering hero has returned, but vanquished, poor chap, by the demon alcohol!' Hoots of laughter filtered into my befuddled brain as I lay, uncaring, and slept.

Early in the new year we were sailed north to Bombay in India. I had always wanted to visit the Indian continent. My godfather had joined the Indian Army at the end of the First World War, having been commissioned from the ranks and earned an MC in the Gunners during the war. His stories, on his infrequent leaves, had merely increased my curiosity. Now we were to see the Taj Mahal for ourselves.

At our first opportunity Frank and I went ashore. We made for the Taj Mahal Hotel, as I believed that my godfather, now a Brigadier General, was billeted there with his wife. The smell of India had wafted out to us as we had approached Bombay, but the oppressive heat and the concentration of smells as we landed one can never forget. The mass of people pressed against us and we soon realised that either a taxi or rickshaw was going to be necessary. Eventually we managed to hail a ruffian who assured us he would have us at the hotel in no time. As we got into this contraption, I felt almost ashamed - the slim and bony man pulling us looked hardly strong enough. His mouth was smeared blood-red with betel juice and his shallow lungs seemed due to burst as he set off. I felt we should really have reversed the position had we only known where to go!

On arrival we paid him off and gave him a small tip for his pains His gratitude was an embarrassment. Even our own meagre five shillings a day would have fed his family royally for a while. We entered the massive portals feeling very small fry. A crowd of well-dressed people and senior officers were casually moving about. We made our way, avoiding the 'brass hats', to the reception desk. Summoning up all my courage, I asked for the room number of General Hawkins. The rather superior personage behind the desk looked at me.

'Who,' he enquired coolly, but very politely, 'are you?' I explained falteringly that I was his godson and had been told in a letter from home (I produced a rather moth-eaten piece of paper) that my uncle was billeted in their hotel and I would like to visit him. The personage studied my letter and rang a bell under the counter. An even more stately official appeared. He asked me some more questions and having read the letter handed it back to me. With an imperious wave he summoned an Indian servant, immaculate in his colourful uniform.

'Take these two gentlemen up to room number 102,' he ordered. We followed, our shoes sinking into the deep carpeting. A scented lift took us up to a spacious landing where our escort knocked on the numbered door. I had never met my uncle's wife, but it was she who answered the door. Naturally she showed some surprise at the sight of two bronzed young men in rather off-white well-worn naval tropical uniform. She smiled sweetly and invited us inside. Shyly we entered and sat on the edge of our chairs. She immediately eased the tension by pouring us long, cool and very welcome drinks. She was friendliness itself, but despite her best efforts all we could muster was rather stilted conversation for around half an hour. As my eyes roamed around the room, they settled on a photograph standing on the grand piano in a silver frame. I got up and walked to the piano.

'Are these your children?' I asked. My aunt smiled an affirmative. I was thinking hard. So far as I knew, my uncle had two children. Here was a photograph of three bonny youngsters - what should I do? I turned and looked at my aunt. 'I suppose there couldn't be two General Hawkins in India at the moment, could there?'

She immediately replied 'Oh yes, my dear! The other one is at the moment in Delhi!' I looked at Frank and we started to laugh. The lady joined in - we had got the wrong General Hawkins. To her eternal credit, having established that we had no family ties at all, she stood us a marvellous dinner and could not have done more for me even if she had been my real aunt. To my eternal discredit I do not remember ever writing to thank her for her kindness. If she ever reads these lines I trust she will forgive my lack of manners.

The Navy had kept ships in the Gulf for many years. Before the war, they had patrolled these waters, acting as policemen. They intercepted white slavers, drug-traders and arms-dealers. They took a medical interest in the isolated coastal communities and helped the local rulers to keep the peace. With the advent of the war they had added the mustering of oil convoys to these tasks. Such varied duties now fell on us.

However, because of the intense heat, their lordships only kept the 'duty' ship on station for around three months at a time. In an old cruiser like ours, there was no proper ventilation below decks and when I visited the lower electrical control rooms on my midship rounds (even in the middle of the night with the temperature on deck at 0 degrees) the temperature in these spaces would be over 130 degrees! The duty electrician would be wearing only a towel around his waist, and one hand would be hanging in a bucket of tepid water to try to cool himself down as he patiently sat out his watch. By the time I returned to the bridge to report, 'Midships rounds all correct, sir,' to the Officer of the Watch, I would be soaked in sweat. On the bridge, the watch would be wearing greatcoats against the near-freezing night air!

It was not surprising that men cracked up, working in such conditions. Hence the three-month turn-around of duty ships. Even so, it was not uncommon for stokers and others working 'tween decks to have to be sent ashore suffering from heat stroke.

We carried two doctors, a Lieutenant Commander and a young Lieutenant. The young Lieutenant was an expert gynaecologist, which naturally caused him considerable ribbing from both the men and his colleagues.

The first oil convoy was already collecting when we arrived. The weather had turned nasty and a very short choppy sea was running as I lay alongside our after gangway waiting for my Captain. By now I had had enough practice to handle the boat myself; my Coxswain controlled the crew. I decided it would be safer to 'lay off' and informed the officer of the watch accordingly. Some minutes later I could see the Captain standing at the head of the gangway and we eased alongside. The ladder was rising and falling twenty feet or more as the short swells swept past and the ship's roll did not help. The Captain made his way slowly down the ladder and at the right moment jumped into the strong arms of my Coxswain.

'Let go!' I screamed and the sailor forward released his boat-hook's hold on the standing rope. The stoker eased the engine to full power and I thrust the tiller hard over to port, simultaneously opening the 'buckets', which controlled our ahead-astern movement. We lolloped our uncomfortable way towards a large tanker. The Captain, sheltering as best he could from the flying spray, raised his head to have a look at the first of his 'calls'.

'Take a dummy run, Snottie,' he ordered. I slowed down and did as he bid. The tanker's ladder was rising and falling like our own. It was going to need very good judgment and timing from our Captain to be able to jump at the right moment on to their platform. Slowly we wallowed our way round in a spray-swept circle and I started my approach. The Captain, holding his briefcase and swaying in tune to the swell, was standing in front of me. The bow man stretched out and grabbed the standing rope. I allowed the boat to ride closer to the tanker's gangway platform; it rushed upwards missing our side by inches, stopped for a second at the top of its travel and came rushing down again, threatening to crush our small boat. I manoeuvred to keep our boat just clear of this charging 'lift', ably assisted by my practised boat's crew. The Captain looked unconcerned and was waiting for the right moment to jump. With perfect timing he arrived on the platform just as it tore back upwards again and shouted for us to lay off. This we did.

As we all congregated aft and lit surreptitious cigarettes, out of the weather and out of sight, I asked the Coxswain for his comments. He reckoned I had got the idea but suggested that it should have been carried out with rather more style.

'Bit too cautious,' he said. I was still thinking about this remark as we returned to collect our Captain an hour later. My first attempt to get alongside was a disaster, much too fast and my poor bow man almost lost both his boat hook and himself overboard. I swore quietly to myself and circled for a second try. This time an awk-ward sea the critical moment, pushed our bow away from the tanker and the bow man's boat-hook collected only fresh air and sea water! Our Captain stood stoically at the head of the ladder looking down at us. I felt very small indeed as I turned round again for a third attempt. This time things worked out and we managed to retrieve our Captain without any further damage. Having carried out these same manoeuvres alongside several other tankers, the Captain told me to return to our ship for lunch. We were delighted and although I was soaked to the skin, as were my crew, a surge of pride warmed me when the Captain, on leaving the boat turned to me and said:

'Well done, Snottie. You haven't dunked me yet have you?' and, turning to the crew, said 'Thank you, men. Please carry on.' I saluted and grinned at my crew as we made our way to the 'boom' and made our bucking boat fast, clambered up the hanging swinging ladder and made our individual ways down to our respective messes to change into dry clothes and to satisfy very hungry tummies!

I loved the freedom of driving my little motor cutter around and would request permission to set out on any pretext. I am not sure that my gallant boat's crew were quite as keen as I was but they were always good-humoured and never let me down. During all the times I had to land our Captain aboard rolling tankers, I never saw him show anything but full confidence in our ability to do the job. Such an attitude was vital to give me the confidence needed and must have taken great courage on his part.

The nearest I ever got to dunking him was one occasion when I mistimed a wave; he was about to jump and just stopped in time, but his cap went spinning away in the wind! We swung round in double-quick time and managed to recover this rather soggy item. The Captain was not impressed, but even under those somewhat difficult conditions he merely looked me squarely in the eye.

'I suppose,' he mused out loud, 'if snotties have to use their Captains to learn ship-handling, their Captains should be grateful if it is only their caps that get soaked!' I apologised again and grinned ruefully at my Coxswain. Our Captain was a real gentleman and never made mention of this unhappy incident afterwards. So far as I know, neither the Commander nor the snotties' nurse was informed.

As the weather improved, so did my ability to handle my small boat. Soon we had called on all the assembled tankers. They had received all their orders and the day came when they sailed away. It was time for us to revert to the old pre-war patrols.

CHAPTER SIX - SMALLPOX EPIDEMIC.

A quick glance at the map will show where Khasab Bay is. This small village nestles below huge, sheer cliffs, rising straight from their base to around 3,000 feet. At the top of them lie the vast deserts of Central Arabia. At the base lie small land-locked bays, holding tiny, isolated islets of soil, which has been tilled by a local population in almost the same way since the Bible was written.

We had steamed slowly into the Bay, the Navigator and Officer of the Watch checking various bearings with the bridge gyro-compass as we approached our planned anchorage. The forecastle party was standing ready, the blacksmith with his sledge hammer raised above his head.

'Two cables...one and a half cables...' the Navigator was speaking in his quiet voice and the Captain had his hand held high carrying a small flag. 'Stand by,' the voice continued. 'Now!' The Captain's flag was immediately dropped. At the same time the blacksmith's hammer hit the slip holding the starboard anchor cable in check and, with a muffled rattle, the linked chain shot down the foredeck like a frenzied snake. A signalman, standing right in the 'eyes', was raising and lowering his arms to show the bridge, by flag signals, how much cable had run out. The forecastle officer told the capstan operator to apply the brake and waited for the bridge to give further instructions. Slowly the ship came to rest as her engines were put astern. Almost as soon as she was moving astern, the engines were stopped and she rode to her cable.

'Thank you, Pilot' said the Captain to the Navigator. 'Carry on Commander.' Then, turning to the chief yeoman, he added 'Yeo, please collect the interpreter and bring him to my day-cabin.'

We had embarked a most extraordinary Arab, the interpreter. He looked for all the world like something out of Lawrence of Arabia. His flowing robes were held in place by double-breasted bandoliers, a short Lee-Enfield graced his shoulder and at his hip hung a service revolver. Several hand-grenades were supported by the traditional belt round his waist, as was his beautiful curved knife, worn as a Scot would wear his sporran. I never saw him without these arms at least. His bright eyes stared from beneath his head-dress without a flicker. He was a truly impressive character.

As soon as we had anchored, the motor cutter was 'piped away'. I was told by the Officer of the Watch to proceed ashore and collect the local Wali; I was to bring him back for a meeting with the Captain.

As I approached the beach we could see a small knot of Arabs on the shore. As we got closer we could see that they were all armed to the teeth. They reminded me exactly of the pictures of Arab pirates I had seen as a child, and I was glad to feel the six foot plus of my Coxswain alongside me. The Wali was accompanied by his bodyguard and there was no way we were going to be allowed to return without each and every one of them! I had to accept the inevitable and returned to the ship loaded to the gunwales. The Officer of the Watch had seen all this through his telescope and once the Wali had been given a suitable welcome (piped aboard and a

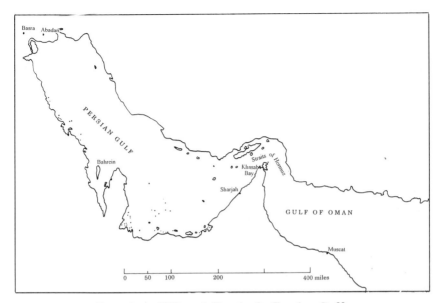

Location of Khasab Bay in the Persian Gulf

Royal Marine Guard to inspect) he let me know that he did not consider the 'hangers on' as necessary to the proceedings. They had all followed the Wali on to the quarter-deck and were even then in the process of negotiating deals with his 'side party' and any other sailors they could way-lay! I explained that I had had no option and went below to get a drink.

After a couple of hours we were called away to return the Wali and his gang of ruffians ashore. Later that day we landed a medical party with the young doctor in charge. It appeared that the village was suffering from a smallpox epidemic and the natives were dying like flies. While we ferried the various necessary people and their stores ashore the doctor took stock. Soon he reported to the Captain that he was running out of lymph, the vaccine needed to safeguard the remaining population. Signals were sent to the RAF at Basra and they arranged to fly new supplies to Sharjah, a pre-war Imperial Airways airstrip. In the meantime we up-anchored and sailed for Sharjah.

On our arrival I was ordered to take the Sub of the gunroom ashore. Together, feeling very conspicuous with our Service .45 revolvers strapped to our waists, we left the boat on the beach and made our way through the narrow streets of the little town. We hardly saw anyone during this time, but eventually met a man as we approached the outskirts. He spoke no English and we spoke no Arabic, but we drew pictures of aeroplanes, made flying noises and gyrated around like lunatics and eventually his toothless face lit up and he smiled. Pointing with a withered arm in the general direction of some sand dunes, he led us forward. The day was very hot and dry. The sun beat down from a cloudless sky and the sand under our shoes was hot enough to burn unprotected flesh. We trudged along, sweating profusely, until eventually, through the heat haze, we could see the hangars, but it seemed an age before we actually made our entrance to their officers' mess.

Our reception was marvellous; large cool beers were thrust into our hands and we had to be careful not to outstay our welcome. It was very tempting to accept 'one for the road' but we needed to get back and had already taken much longer than had been estimated. I wondered how my boat's crew were coping. Armed with our precious cargo of life-saving lymph we made our weary way back to the beach. I need not have worried. As usual, when one leaves Jack Tar to please himself for a couple of hours he will find a pleasant and relaxing way to pass the time. They had had a wander into town (forbidden before we landed!) and, as a result, by the time we returned, were surrounded by an admiring group of children and some not-so-young ladies. They had been given a plentiful supply of fruit and dates, and their cigarettes had been bartered for odd items. We launched our boat and made our way back to the ship.

That evening, as we sailed south again, I remember thinking how strange the world was. Here we were in a cruiser in the middle of a world war, running back and forth, at considerable expense to our country, just to save a few hundred Arabs in a tiny village miles from anywhere. Would they or their children ever know how they came to be saved and by whom? But as I dropped into a deep sleep I felt that to have been able to help such poor people fitted into my idea of 'how the British should behave'.

Anchored once more in Khasab Bay, I landed the new supplies for the doctor. He returned with me to the ship and had a long meeting with our Captain and the senior doctor. It now transpired that we were going to have to sail and leave the medical party for a while. When I next took the doctor ashore we also landed more food supplies and I wished them luck.

It was time to muster another convoy. This time the sea was smooth as a mill-pond, the oily surface broken only now and then by a shark's fin as it lazed along seeking its prey, or by an enormous splash as a huge manta ray would hurl itself ten feet into the air. It would land flat on the surface to dislodge the parasites, which had attached themselves to its great body, and the resulting noise sounded like a revolver shot.

We were now ordered to travel up to Basra, the first ship, I believe, to have been so invited since before the war. We were to host an official reception for all sorts of worthies and this was to be followed by a reception ashore, hosted by the Khoramshar Yacht Club. I can remember standing on the bridge watching and listening as the Navigator and the local Arab pilot negotiated the various bends and sandbanks on our journey up the famous Shatt el Arab river. I could feel the excitement rising as I realised that we were sailing up the confluence of those historic rivers Tigris and Euphrates.

As our powerful engines drove us up against the strong tide, we could marvel at the skill of the local dhows as they dodged back and forth to take advantage of each puff of wind and eddy of current to make their way up this mighty waterway, just as their forefathers had done for centuries.

The only thing I remember about the Yacht Club Reception was meeting a real live millionaire. In 1942 there were not too many about! Looking back, we were too unsophisticated and naive to appreciate such a party. Pints of beer with the boys after a rugby match was still our scene, not gently waltzing a lovely lady into an alcove!

I was delighted when we at last anchored back in Khasab Bay and I could return to running my motor cutter ashore. I was fascinated by the medical party's experiences and was very excited when the doctor said I could accompany him to visit the Wali in his palace. This was an experience I shall never forget.

As we made our way across the hot sand, the sun shone so brightly that even its reflection from the sand hurt one's eyes. The palace was a large, imposing fort-type of building. The entrance stood out like a black hole in the brilliant light. As we entered this 'hole' our eyes, unaccustomed to the relative darkness, were temporarily blinded. The interpreter, who was leading, had just stretched out his hand to knock on the huge iron-clad door when a noise from behind made us all jump out of our skins. The hairs on the nape of my neck stood up and my heart missed a beat. I reached for my revolver. As I turned I could see about a dozen fully-armed men pointing their guns straight at us; they had been sitting quietly watching our approach from seats dug into the walls some five feet above eye level. Totally hidden from anyone entering, they had waited until we were fully occupied and blinded by our new environment - this was the Wali's Guard in action and very impressive it had been. They would have had all our throats cut before we had time to fire a single shot!

The great door swung slowly open and we entered the hall of this incredible palace. Since the object of this visit was for the doctor to talk to the Wali, I could only really glance around, but I remember seeing an old pre-war accumulator-driven radio sitting in pride of place. I wondered vaguely if the man who had sold that to the Wali had returned once the accumulator had given up the ghost - it would be prudent, I thought, to keep well clear if one wished to remain in one piece.

Of course, in those days, as had been the case for centuries, virtually the only way of obtaining either news or new products of any sort was to buy them from the trading dhows which visited each year. These wonderful vessels would sail with the monsoon winds from East Africa to India and then from India up the Persian Gulf before returning back again to their East African home ports. These same small ships we would intercept at sea and have to search for contraband, arms or slave women. Occasionally one would come upon them in mid-ocean, without wind to blow them or water to keep them alive. On those occasions we would steam round them (in case they were being used by enemy submarines as a decoy) and would drop them wooden casks full of water. Often the number of bodies on board these small craft had to be seen to be believed - great sailors and brave people.

35

The doctor's conversation with the Wali was eventually brought to a conclusion when the doctor threatened the Wali with the Sultan of Muscat. Apparently the doctor had learned that though he thought he had vaccinated all the people he had not in fact vaccinated any of the Wali's wives! For fairly obvious reasons this was a subject that needed very diplomatic handling and the mind boggles when trying to imagine how our young hero, through the interpreter, managed to get his delicate message home without having his throat cut! His final threat worked, however, and arrangements were made to have a curfew set up that night. At that time the whole harem, escorted by his eunuchs, were walked the short distance to the palace. One by one the ladies were thrust forward by a eunuch from the left of the great hall, the doctor and his attendant carried out their vaccination tasks and another eunuch grabbed the lady, dealt with her and thrust her towards the right-hand door, out of the great hall. The doctor told me afterwards that some of the ladies were so shy that they would not even bare their arms but tore a small hole in their sleeves. All were very heavily veiled, but his guess at their ages showed a range of many, many years!

The medical party had had to organise the burning of all the contaminated houses and bodies. While we had been away they had lived in a second palace close to the sea and each morning were in the habit of taking an early morning dip. One morning, shortly after we had sailed, they were surprised to see a pile of old Arab clothes lying on the beach close to their quarters. After they had had their swim, one of the party, more curious than the rest, was even more surprised when he lifted one of the garments to find a body inside it! He called the doctor. A man of middle age was found; he was alive but had had the whole of his stomach burned like an overdone fillet steak. Someone had evidently dropped a red-hot plate of metal, about a foot square, on his tummy while he had been stretched out on his back.

The unfortunate individual had been carried to the beach, probably in the hope that our medical party would find him. The doctor was furious and went straight to complain to the Wali who explained through the interpreter that this man had been caught red-handed robbing the palace strong room. There had been other men involved and so this one had been 'encouraged' to inform the authorities who the other folk were! It was all really quite simple. In that country, at that time, no one thought there was anything strange, let alone wrong, in the actions taken. The doctor returned to his quarters in the palace and set about nursing this chap back to health. The shock alone would certainly have killed most Europeans, but by the time I was being told the story, the man concerned was walking around with only a slight stoop, all smiles and very willing to give one a quick flash to show his horrific scars!

A further twist to this extraordinary tale came later. The Wali had mentioned to the doctor that he had a headache and he gave him an aspirin. Some days later, out of courtesy when they met, the doctor asked after his headache and was disappointed to learn that the tablet had had no effect. Puzzled, he asked the Wali to remove his headgear and let him examine his head. After some hesitation the Wali did so. To his astonishment the doctor saw a very large and unclean wound. He asked the Wali when this had happened and how. It soon became clear that one of the rascals had hit him over the head with a crowbar the night they had been caught robbing his vaults. He had been walking around with a badly fractured skull for a fortnight - no wonder he had complained about having a headache! The recuperative powers of these people were incredible as was their ability to put up with the most awful disabilities as if they were nothing at all.

Navy save a 'sick' town

IN response to an appeal from the local sheik, who was a representative of the Sultan of Muscat and Oman, a medical party from the cruiser H.M.S. Dauntless recently put ashore at a town in south-eastern Arabia and stamped out an epidemic of smallpox.

The party, led by two R.N.V.R. surgeons, vaccinated 3,095 people—1,000 on the day they landed.

When the Arabs saw the swollen arms of those who had been vaccinated, crowds of envious relatives came demanding to have their arms made to swell, too.

"Only Allah"

The surgeon-lieutenant removed one of a child's eyes to save the sight of the other. Soon afterwards ten blind men asked to have their sight restored. The doctor assured them : "Only Allah can cure the blind," and they departed satisfied.

The twelve huts comprising the lazar-house were burned and an isolation hospital, with one end open to the fresh air, was built. A staff of male and female nurses who had had smallpox as children was recruited and put in charge.

During the medical party's stay there were only 19 deaths and 22 new cases, none of which occurred during the last week

Every now and then the ship would spend an afternoon on an organised fishing party. For a whole afternoon the war would be put on one side, and having landed as many of the crew as was possible, with all the boats and carley floats as well, the Gunner's party would drop home-made explosive charges. The boats and floats would circle like hungry seagulls and collect fish as they floated to the surface. Ashore, the Bosun and his party would be showing the assembled sailors how to lay out the long sein net from the stern of one of the cutters. They would leave one end ashore and then row out to sea in a wide circle before landing the other end further up the beach. Both these ends would then be hauled in while a noisy mass of sailors swarmed outside the float-line to seaward and 'kicked up all hell'. The fish thus captured joined the others and the whole ship's company would dine on fish and chips that night.

Such afternoons were inevitably rare, but what a boost they provided to the ship's morale! It was on one of these sessions that I saw what I took to be a monkey, running along the beach. As the poor soul got closer, I realised with a feeling of sickness that it was in fact a small girl I can well remember the feeling of frustration as I discussed this case with our young doctor. There was so much wealth in these Arab states but also so much poverty. We had had the chance to see both and I was thankful that we had also been given the chance to do something helpful.

Months later I received a letter from home with a newspaper cutting from the *Daily Mirror* or *Express* telling the story of our rescue mission. I felt proud to have played a small part in it. Needless to say it merely referred to 'a cruiser'!

Soon we sailed for Aden, then on again to Kilindini. We had covered a lot of miles since we left this tropic port and Frank and I decided to take a quick run ashore just for old times' sake. We had left as new mids; we felt now, as we walked ashore,

37

we were already old hands! Certainly the past months had taught us a lot. I remember we went to a bookshop and I have still got a couple of slim volumes with a pencilled note inside - 'Mombasa 1942'. Frank was a poetically-minded young man from Devon. My own hero was Rupert Brook, and during our time in the Gulf I had a great yearning to read about the fields and green countryside of home. We used to have long discussions about poetry but I always felt academically inferior and shy at producing any of my own efforts, having spent my school days concentrating on my sporting and athletic activities rather than anything academic. Poets I had always regarded as rather 'wet'!

Now we sailed to South Africa. As always in wartime only the Captain and a very few chosen officers had any ideas about our future movements. On our arrival in Simonstown we were berthed alongside a jetty well away from public gaze. The following after-noon the pipe 'Clear lower deck' rang out. The entire crew was mustered on the quarterdeck by divisions. The First Lieutenant called the ship's company to attention and reported them to the Commander. Then the entire crew were marched in single file off the quarterdeck down the after gangway on to the jetty. Here there were army lorries drawn up with an armed escort standing by them. Orders were given for the crew to form a single line, shoulder to shoulder. This reached from the lorries, up the gangway and down to the flat outside the gunroom. The Leading Hands, Petty Officers and Chief Petty Officers were spread out to watch over a small section of men as were all the officers. The back of the first Army Lorry was opened and a parcel, packed in wood, was handed to the waiting hands of the first man in the queue. It was so unexpectedly heavy he nearly dropped it! The parcel was a solid gold bar surrounded by metal-strapped wooden packing. Each was stamped with a number which was checked out of the lorry as it was passed from hand to hand up that human chain till it reached its destination in the gun-housing outside the gunroom. Here again each parcel was checked before being carefully loaded into its place.

This operation took considerable time. When it was finished we returned to our home to find a welder busily welding up the steel door that was also given a brand new padlock! From then on, for the rest of the time that valuable cargo was on board, a Royal Marine sentry stood guard, just to make sure no one got ideas of making off with any of those bars. Since each one must have weighed almost half a hundred-weight, we thought the precautions rather pointless but the Navy thought otherwise.

CHAPTER SEVEN - HOME RUN

At the time we sailed for home we did not know whither we were bound. Neither, thank God, did we have any idea about either the numerical strength or the positions of Hitler's U-Boats.

HMS *Dauntless* had no Asdics or any other means (except for sharp eyes) of warning us about the presence of submarines. While undoubtedly the Captain and more senior officers were kept informed about the latest news on this front, we, along with the rest of the crew, sailed along in blissful ignorance! A quick glance at the maps produced today, showing the various U-Boat distributions and the number of ships sunk at that time in the war, make me very thankful that we were kept in ignorance!

I suppose that because of our valuable cargo (£10,000,000 worth of gold bullion) we sailed alone on an odd route which took us inshore of the normal convoy routes. We steamed at our top cruising speed and arrived at Takoradi without incident. After taking on fuel, water and fresh vegetables we pressed on to Pointe Noir where the same routine was followed. Zigzagging northwards, we arrived at Dakar; here there were a number of French warships.

That first night in harbour I was Midshipman of the Watch and when time came for the 'sunset' lowering of the flag ceremony it was suddenly discovered that all the Royal Marine buglers had been allowed to go ashore. The Officer of the Watch was absolutely furious. Apparently the French were in the habit of making a great fuss at 'sunset'. They fired off guns and bugled their hearts out; the Commander had warned him that he wanted to put on a good show as we were the only British ship in harbour. Here we were, without even a single bugler available!

As soon as I heard of the reason for the panic, I approached the Officer with a suggestion. He told me, in very nautical terms, to 'get lost'! However, when it became clear that there was simply no other option, he sent for me.

'Were you pulling my leg when you said you could blow a bugle?' he asked. I repeated that I had played the said instrument in the school band but naturally was a bit out of practice now. A bugle was sent for and I was told to go and practice at once. In the meantime an electrician fixed a microphone out of sight on the quarterdeck from where I could see the Officer of the Watch and signalman without being seen.

Sure enough, at the allotted time, the French ships 'blasted off'. As our ensign was slowly lowered, a solitary bugler could be heard playing a nervous, but almost correct, 'sunset'. The Commander did not appear for this ceremony, being, I believe, entertained by some very generous officers at the wardroom bar! I am sure I must be one of very few midshipmen ever to have blown 'sunset' for real - and at least the Officer of the Watch bought me a drink!

Having topped up once more with fuel, we again zigzagged northwards; our next port of call was Casablanca. As we slowly steamed up the channel we were saluted by the ships lying alongside the wharves. One of these was the French battleship

Jean Bart. She had been hit by one of the 16-inch shells during our bombardment of the port and a huge section of her forecastle was now open to the world. As we steamed slowly past we could see her sailors, at their mess-tables, enjoying their evening meal; her foredeck had been lifted by the force of the explosion and was raised in a graceful curve several feet high. The jagged hole showed the thickness of armour plate which had been penetrated, rolled back like an opened sardine tin.

Several of us went ashore to buy presents for our families. I wanted to get some real French scent for my mother and a nightie for a girl friend. Having found the right sort of shop for our purchases we set about things in our schoolboy French. The scent did not provide any problems, but when it came to seeking a simple nightdress I ran into terrible difficulties. A mere male does not understand such simple things as female sizes! When the charming young French girl asked me this question I was at a loss. She disappeared and returned with another girl who was very well built around the bust. The first shop assistant placed her hands around her own 'top' and asked,

'Your girl - is she like me or like her?' Her right hand moved to cover the large girl's ample breast. My friends were bursting with laughter at my predicament and I knew the whole shop was watching me. My face was purple with embarrassment. 'Perhaps,' smiled my inquisitor, 'she is so-so - half and half - oui?'

'Oui,' I said, grabbed the tiny parcel and fled. Never again!

Soon, the long Atlantic swell and those cold, grey-green seas reminded us that our tropical 'holiday' was at an end. The news broadcasts, now that we were once more entering the war zone proper, brought home to us the reality of our position. No time now to watch flying fish skim away from our bow wave, every eye on watch needed to be alert all the time. One had to assume any speck in the sky could be the beginning of an attack. Lives depended on our preparedness - to see before being seen.

As we approached Scapa Flow my mind ran back to those weeks less than two years before when, as green ordinary seamen we had sailed away in *Shropshire*. So much had happened in such a short time. Scapa had not altered; the weather, even in June, was cold, wet and windy. We waited impatiently for orders to sail south. By the time they came and we had reached Chatham, we were not much browner than our colleagues who had been serving at home all the time. Our 'foreign service' faces and our bronzed bodies were rapidly returning to their natural, paler hue - we were fed up!

As soon as we docked we were invaded by plain-clothes men, anxious to relieve us of our cargo. A smell of burning paint indicated that a blow-torch was opening up the gun shield outside our mess and soon the reverse procedure to that employed at Simonstown was in full swing. The most relieved man, apart from our Captain, must have been the Royal Marine sentry! At last, too, the gunroom flat sweeper was able to use this space to store his mops and buckets and other cleaning gear.

The Captain now sent for each one of us separately. He went through with us the content of his report on our performance during our time aboard and asked us what sort of appointment we would like him to recommend us for. In my case I told him that I had volunteered twice before for Coastal Forces and very much hoped that this time my request would be granted. He looked at me and smiled. 'Despite a couple of close-run escapades,' he said, 'you took good care of me in your motor cutter. Let's see how you get on handling something a bit more powerful. I'm going to recommend you - and jolly good luck.' He stood up and, reaching over his desk, shook me warmly by the hand. My eyes clouded over as I grasped his hand and thanked him.

'At last!' I thought, and stumbled my way rather clumsily out.

There was an air of expectancy as we packed our gear. We all had 14 days of leave and suddenly realised that we would probably never see each other again. Frank and I had been together ever since we met at *Drake*. Due to the speed of life in those days, we lost contact - I wonder is he still alive today?

My father's school had been evacuated from Bath to Uppingham, so I made my way there. I arrived eventually, never having been to that town before, and went in search of my father. I found him doing corrections in a small room on his own. He was so surprised at my sudden appearance (I had not been able to contact him) that he nearly had a heart attack! We both put our arms around each other and cried with joy.

I remember he took me across the road to his local and with obvious pride introduced me to the assembled company. No pint of beer has ever tasted better. I was home. I had left as a callow youth and returned as a travelled young Naval Officer, treated now as a grown-up. I felt like a stranger when I met my young brothers (my sister was away nursing). My mother made a great fuss of me and for a short while I enjoyed my new found 'star role', but as the days passed I grew restless for the male companionship to which I had grown accustomed. When my new appointment arrived through the post I was thrilled. 'Appointed to HMS *St Christopher* for training' it stated. This was the Coastal Forces training base at Fort William in Scotland - at last I was to join the part of the Navy after which I had always hankered.

CHAPTER EIGHT - *ST CHRISTOPHER*

A journey from London to Scotland overnight in a blacked-out train in wartime has to be experienced to be understood.

It is hard to know where to start to describe things. Not only was every seat taken, but each inch of space in the corridors was filled by uniformed men and women plus all their associated gear. In some compartments the overhead racks also held sleeping bodies. The air was thick with cigarette and pipe-smoke. The dim lighting made reading almost impossible; the lack of heating was compensated for by human body warmth, but in the early hours the cold became intense. No food or drink was available; even a trip to the loo became such an impossible scramble that one 'held it'.

Such a journey seemed to last for ever. We arrived at Glasgow around breakfast time and made for the station Hotel. Pre-war it had been renowned for its marvellous breakfast menus.

'Kippers,' my new friend murmured in my ear as we tried the restaurant door.

'Two eggs and bacon with mushrooms to follow,' I replied. A rather scruffy waiter appeared. We sat down at the first table and asked for a menu. He looked at us pityingly and said, 'Don't you know there's a war on? Bloody sailors,' he muttered and asked if we wanted a cup of tea and some toast or not. We thanked him and ordered.

To our relief the train for Fort William had plenty of seats and six of us took over one whole compartment. This particular train journey must be one of the prettiest in the UK. After leaving the city and following the Clyde north, the line meanders its way through the mountains and lochs - we were enthralled. After some hours, we arrived at a small country station and stopped. Everyone left the train and made for the bar. Here were stacked great plates of freshly-made sandwiches. Each of us ordered six rounds; further up the counter were pint mugs filled with the local brew (because of the scarcity of glasses these mugs were made from bottles cut to size) - each of us ordered six pints. Weighed down with our 'loot' we returned to our seats. As we passed other compartments we could see that everyone was suitably supplied. Having had no food or drink for so long, everyone was famished. That little station was renowned for its marvellous service and I trust the people who organised this life-saving effort retired as millionaires - they deserved to!

By the time we arrived at our destination we were all in high spirits and, having found the hotels in which we were to be billeted for the next seven weeks, we had just enough energy to meet the other occupants and then turn in, dead beat but happy.

The seven-week course covered everything we would be expected to know on joining a coastal forces craft. The instructors were all experienced people and we listened avidly to our lectures. Wherever possible the experience was practical, and the ship-handling and navigation was carried out aboard MLs (Fairmile Motor Launches) as was the engine-room instruction. We lapped it all up; I had never before been with a group of students all so keen to learn.

Our off-duty activities were somewhat constrained by the weather. Fort William has one of the highest rainfall records in the UK and it did in fact rain at some time during every day we were there! The WRNS ran dances and these, and the traditional young officers' bar activities, took care of our non-working hours. A book had been started which recorded the various climbs up Ben Nevis by previous course-members and since it had become something of a tradition we decided we should also have a go. However, since none of us were inclined towards mountaineering we decided that we would go up by night - there was no record of such a journey previously.

After our final WRNS dance two of us returned to the hotel and changed. Full of beer, and our friends' good wishes, we ran the few miles to the fields at the base of the mountain. We had no idea how to find the path that led upwards to the summit, but argued that if we climbed straight up the side we should hit it at some point.

To start with we made fast progress in the moonlight and by midnight had not only found the path but had made very encouraging headway. However, around two o'clock in the morning we entered what appeared to be cloud. We stopped and decided that we would proceed one at a time; when the second lost sight of the first he would shout, the first would then stop while the second caught up and the same routine would be repeated. This idea worked well to start with, but then we realised that we could not see the path clearly enough and a couple of times nearly fell off the edge! We felt sure we were not too far from the summit but had no way of knowing where we were. Common sense prevailed, and with regret at having to call the effort off we turned our faces for home. The cloud was now very thick indeed and we had the utmost difficulty in retracing our tracks safely. Eventually, around five o'clock, we had moved below the cloud level and were able at last to trot down the steep path. A steady drizzle was now falling as we ran back to the town and our hotel. By seven thirty we were soaking in hot baths and just had time to shave and breakfast before going on parade. We had failed, but the girls were wide-eyed as we 'dined out' on our adventure at our final party!

CHAPTER NINE - *AGGRESSIVE* - HMMTB 602.

The Old Railway Hotel, Newhaven, had been taken over and turned into the officers' mess. As I entered the bar that first evening, I noticed paintings of coastal forces scenes by Peter Scott who was the Senior Officer of the Steam Gunboat Flotilla based there. Although I was a new boy, everyone was extremely friendly and in no time I was chatting away to the other young officers in the bar. The enthusiasm was infectious and the talk mainly about the various 'actions' which had taken place recently around the east and south coasts. I listened with interest and looked forward to the time when I could be involved in such exciting escapades - it was all rather like playing for one's school as a first team member!

While I was having my dinner, a young RNVR Lieutenant sat down beside me. He was very pleasant and asked me about myself. When he learned that I had just arrived, he asked me which boat I was joining. I told him that I was due to report to 602 the following morning and he was most helpful. It was only later I learned that he was none other than Mark Arnold-Forster, then Senior Officer of the MTBs at Newhaven, a very dashing and gallant officer, but one would never have guessed from our conversation that evening that he was anything other than a pleasant RNVR Lieutenant being kind to a new boy!

602 was part of the 51st(?) Flotilla, whose function was to work closely with the steam gunboats and the smaller MTBs. By 1943 our air attacks on the enemy rail and road links in France were beginning to take effect, so that any vital stores or equipment were being routed by sea via the channel. The ships carrying these things sailed in very heavily defended small convoys at night - 'port-hopping' - some eastbound from Brest and some west, going through the Straits of Dover.

My Captain, having explained what 602's role was, introduced me to the two other officers. I would be the fourth officer ('gash hand') and, while I would report to and work under the Navigator, I would also be required to assist the First Lieutenant. Such a 'dogsbody' position gave me the advantage of being able to learn what other officers' duties involved without being responsible for them - one could learn, too, from their mistakes!

I soon found out that the First Lieutenant's main job, in harbour, was to 'run the ship'. With 30 plus people to cater for, pay and generally look after, this was very much a full-time job and depended on the very personal co-operation of his right-hand man, his Coxswain. It was also his responsibility to report to the Captain that the ship was in all respects ready for sea and battle every time we sailed. To be able to do this he relied on a first-class Chief Engineer and his stokers, a senior gunnery/torpedo rating and his back-up of sailors, a telegraphist/flag-wagger and radar operator - in fact a whole small inter-dependent team. Interdependence always struck me as the vital clue to the team spirit, which was the hallmark of every boat in which I served.

In many of the boats the policy was to train everyone to be able to do the basics of everyone else's job; this had the great advantage of breaking down traditional barriers between different types of sailors (gunners, stokers etc.) and also gave each man a respect for the other's job. Officers were expected to have the same knowledge. It also paid off, of course, when key people were killed in action. There were many examples of boats being brought home which could well have become burnt-out wrecks had it not been for this training.

Intelligence reports, emanating from French Resistance contacts, or the RAF Coastal Command and photographic patrols, would enable the Base Staff to set-up offensive operations. These would be planned with the senior officers of the various flotillas to be involved. The afternoon of the operation, the Captain and Navigator of each boat would attend a briefing session, often backed up by a final quick briefing, if any last-minute information had become available. At these briefings the staff officer would discuss the 'strategic information' and the various senior officers would then detail how they planned to carry out the attacks from a tactical viewpoint. Being merely a 'gash hand' I only attended one of these meetings, for educational purposes, but remember finding it fascinating. The detail known about what the enemy was up to was astonishing. I remember being informed that the men manning a certain coastal gun site were all suffering from food-poisoning, so they should not worry us if we sailed closer in shore than was normally healthy!

I had just become accustomed to our harbour routine when we were ordered to intercept a small convoy in the Baie de la Seine. As was the custom, the boats all started their engines 15 minutes before they were due to sail. It was 1545. The noise of all those engines starting up at once was terrific; eight D-boats with four 1500-horse-powered engines each, apart from all the smaller MTBs, really did rock Newhaven harbour!

With the minimum of fuss and hand-signalled orders, each boat would slip its mooring lines and glide slowly into the open water; ropes and fenders would quickly be cleared out of the way and stowed safely. The crew, dressed in sea-going water-proof gear, would fall in 'at ease' at both ends of the boat with an officer in attend-ance. Each flotilla would then form up in order of their Captain's seniority and, in close line ahead, steam out of harbour, calling their crews to attention to pay their respects to the appropriate people by 'pipes' as they left.

This simple, disciplined start to an operation I always found so matter of fact that I began to realise very early on the true value of the traditional ways of doing things. These traditions had been handed down by generations of sailors in our Navy; we were merely the latest, albeit volunteer reserves, to continue them.

Shortly after clearing the harbour wall, our course was adjusted, and as the first spray flipped over our heads speed was increased and the crew were 'fallen out'. The gun crews were 'closed up'. Now every gun and sound-powered line was checked. Guns were test-fired on a safe bearing - again the noise was terrific.

Within a very short time, every boat was ready for action and the crew were sent to cruising stations for the long passage across the Channel. As soon as war was declared, both sides had laid ground mines over huge areas - these areas were published in the *International Notices to Mariners* to warn all shipping to use only 'swept channels'. Shallow draft vessels like MTBs would normally be able to sail over these mines with out being blown up, but prudence dictated it was better to use our own 'safe' routes.

Our Captain's seniority put us third in the line of boats now steaming at some 18 knots in line ahead. Station was kept so close to the boat ahead that, from our bridge, we could not see their transom; this meant that instant action would be demanded if anything caused the boat ahead to lose speed. Pride in being able to maintain such close station was part of the flotilla's tradition. No one wanted to receive the dreaded signal: 'Close up 602!'

I had taken up my position at the back of the bridge. At that time coastal forces did not have close-range voice radio sets; we had to use the backpack army sets with long aerials. The pack itself did not appear to weigh very much and I settled myself for what I knew would be an extended watch. We had checked our ability to talk to the other boats as we left harbour and now all I had to do was to listen in and repeat any signals or messages - my function seemed simplicity itself.

As the light began to fade the Senior Officer passed his orders by a tiny hand-held torch light to the next astern, who in turn passed it down the line. The order would then be executed, thus maintaining radio silence. As the sea became rougher and spray was constantly flying over the bridge, I found that it would be impossible to hear anything my Captain said because of the spray, wind and engine noise unless I kept one earpiece off my ears; the other needed to be kept in place in case any message was transmitted from the Senior Officer or other boats.

The static noise from this earpiece meant having a constant 'fuzz-fuzz' noise echoing round one's head. To begin with it was just an annoyance, but after several hours it began to dim my mind and by 0200 I found I was beginning to hallucinate! The wash of the boat ahead became a country lane lit by headlamps, and the exhaust fumes, curling away into the darkness, took on the shapes of passing bushes and trees. I knew I was imagining these things but I had to stick a long pin into my bottom to keep me awake; my eyelids just refused to stay open. This was dreadful! To miss a message might be understandable, given the noise, but nevertheless would be unforgivable. With the utmost difficulty I pulled myself together and then, at last, the boredom was relieved. The tiny light was flashing and, as we read out the coded message, I could feel the boat surge ahead as we increased speed.

Immediately the excitement cleared my head. As I glanced astern I could just make out the other boats as they too turned and increased their speed. The constant crashing as we pounded into the seas sent great clouds of spray flying in the wind, and I was forced to hold on to the armour-plating surround to save me from being thrown across the tiny bridge. Suddenly the 'fuzz-fuzz' was interrupted by a voice, I ducked down below the level of the bridge and placing earphones over both ears listened carefully. It appeared that Mark Arnold-Forster and his MTBs had made contact to the north and we were being placed to intercept or create a diversion, depending on how things developed. I passed this message to my Captain and continued to listen out.

'Flashing ashore - green 90,' a voice in the darkness sung out the report and I swung around to look in that direction. Sure enough there it was again - I wondered who it was and what message they were trying to flash. A few moments later we knew.

A great plume of water appeared off our port bow. It hung there, apparently stuck in time, then fell down in a welter of spray. The radio voice was talking again. This time an immediate course-alteration was passed and as we swooped on to the new course my ear, open to the bridge, picked up a most curious 'woosh, woosh' noise I had never heard before. Suddenly I realised what it was and felt very naked. We were being shelled by the large guns ashore.

The German coastal radar was not as good as our own and they may have had difficulty in picking up a single wooden boat, but with six or eight boats in line ahead and close station, we probably produced a relatively good radar picture, good enough anyway for their batteries to place their shells much too close for either safety or comfort! Our intention was to sink enemy shipping not to become casualties ourselves.

As the night drew on, more reports were received and we steamed to try and intercept the enemy convoy, but it had escaped before we were able to engage it, and another offensive patrol came to an end.

My first night of coastal forces action had ended. The war, I was to discover, would contain mostly nights like this, ending in frustration or simply in rather tedious routine patrols. The moments of excitement that did happen were often very short-lived. The winners were usually those who had managed to keep their concentration going at top level throughout their boring routine patrols - the crews who were most 'on the ball'!

First light at sea is a magical time, wherever one is and whatever the weather. No two daybreaks are the same. As we rolled our way home I suddenly realised that I could see the boat ahead and glancing astern those boats too were visible. A lightening on the horizon, and in the sky above it, was heralding the start of a new day - the happenings of the night were now history.

In his book, written immediately after the war, *Battle of the Narrow Seas*, Peter Scott has a coloured picture of one such dawn with a flotilla of short MTBs returning home. For me that picture recaptures so many dawns at sea; it really has to be experienced to be appreciated, for it is not just the wonderful colours of the sky and the cloud formations, or the reflections from the sea, but the very real tiredness of the sailors who are viewing these things, alone and in silence, that produces that particular brand of 'rejuvenation'. Such, indeed, were my own feelings as we made our way home. A solitary Coastal Command plane appeared on the horizon, the first rays of sunlight reflected off its fuselage, mugs of steaming cocoa appeared and cigarettes were lit. The tiny bridge suddenly became a quite different place. I was able to remove my headset at last and the backpack (so light the night before) that was now like a ton weight. My young legs were taut with the constant flexing required by the boat's movement. To relax at last was heaven.

Quite soon England appeared and the whole boat became a hive of activity. The First Lieutenant was discussing domestic details with the Coxswain, the Captain and the Chief were busy discussing engine-room requirements and in no time the signalman was hoisting our pendants ready for entering harbour. The crew fell-in either end of the boat. Another patrol had ended.

Back in harbour we were visited by various base staff. WRNS were then filling many positions previously held by male ratings. Guns, torpedoes and depth charges were all areas where these girls gave assistance and first class it was too. As often happens, since males do not like to be found wanting, the girls tended to keep the men on their toes in their various specialised subjects. It would never have done to know less than a girl!

About this time, on one of my visits ashore to collect the boat's mail, I was bewitched by a pair of deep blue eyes. They laughed at me as our hands brushed and I took the letters. Plucking up courage, I asked if I could see her back to her quarters at Seaford, a short rail journey away. To my delight she accepted my offer and that evening my heart missed a beat as she met me. I was very shy but her bright smile suddenly made me feel quite different.

While we waited she talked of her home town. I noticed, in the gloomy half light, what beautiful white teeth she had and how well her neat uniform and blouse fitted her trim young figure. As the train drew in I opened the door and we sat down. At Seaford she suggested we walk to the seafront. She chatted away as if we had known each other for years. I felt relaxed and happy as we sat down in a glazed shelter. The evening was chill and she moved towards me. I undid my great coat and spread it around her, drawing her to me. Rather shyly we kissed.

Suddenly, afraid that she would consider me too forward, I sat upright.

'What's wrong?' she said, her eyes teasing in the moonlight. I thought how pretty she looked, her naturally fair hair framing her impish expression. 'You silly,' she sighed as she snuggled up to me. Turning, she kissed me as I had never been kissed. Her left hand sought my right hand and placed it over her left breast. It was the first time I had ever felt a girl's breast. She kissed me again and immediately a great surge of emotion swept over me. Very gently I caressed her. I was terrified of being too rough - she was so fragile. We lay there in each other's arms, oblivious to the rest of the world. Suddenly I realised that she had got to be back at her quarters by 2230! I looked at my watch; it was 2200.

'Quick,' I said. 'We've only just time to get you back.' She sighed, tidied her hair and, putting her hat back on, stood up.

'Could we do this again tomorrow night, if you're not at sea?' she asked. My heart was beating so hard I thought she must be able to hear it. The pit of my stomach was aching with a desire I had never known before. My voice, when I replied, was higher pitched than usual and I blushed as I took her arm to walk her back.

'Why not? I'll pop in and see you during the afternoon, once I know for sure that we're going to be in harbour.' At the gate of the 'WRNery' I kissed her goodnight then turned and walked hurriedly away. I could not believe what had happened. This was something totally new and I felt that I was walking on air.

The following night, as we were not at sea, we met as arranged. But this time, having reached our shelter, we wasted no time with the small talk we had embarked upon the night before.

I was in love! As the weeks passed it became obvious to my fellow officers who ribbed me without mercy. One unforgettable night it was blowing a gale (which had kept us in harbour) and was pouring with rain. As I climbed down the few stairs leading to the wardroom I could hear the noise of a party in progress. Carefully I opened the door. My Captain was seated at the head of the tiny table. The small room was packed to overflowing and thick with smoke. As I entered, the Captain looked at me, held his hand up for silence and said,

'Do up your fly buttons, you randy young midshipman!' Without thinking I immediately looked down, only to find of course that everything was quite in order! The laughter could have been heard at the WRNery! I went bright red and stammered something incoherent. A glass of neat gin was thrust into my hand with the order to down it in one. Only too pleased to be doing something to cover my embarrassment, I swallowed it and a glow of relief embraced me.

Not long after this episode, I was sitting with the Navigator in the wardroom one afternoon, when a messenger arrived. He passed me a signal pad, which held instructions for me to join ML 309 immediately! Collecting up a night bag I asked the Navigator to inform my Captain and No.1 about this sudden 'pier-head jump' and left to find the ML.

When I arrived on board, the First Lieutenant told me how they had been exercising their guns on some wrecks that morning, as they made their way back to Newhaven. One of the depression rails had failed to operate properly and his Captain had received shrapnel wounds in his back! He had been told to take over as CO and I was to take over as First Lieutenant! 'We sail in half an hour to rendezvous with the east-going convoy currently mustering outside. I've a couple of things to sort out ashore, perhaps you'd get things ready for me to leave on my return.' And he left!

Naturally I had heard the expression 'pier-head jump' but up to then had never experienced it! I sought out the Coxswain and introduced myself. In less than half an hour I had to get to know my way around this small vessel and meet her crew. As I made my way below I heard the engines start up and saw the shore connections being disconnected. By the time the new CO returned we had 'singled up' the ropes and the crew were ready for sea. I reported the ship ready for sea (as I had grown used to hearing the First Lieutenant of 602 doing) and then fell in ahead of my new crew in the bows ready for leaving harbour.

As the swell entering the harbour lifted our bows, we were ordered to 'fall out and close up for sea'. After a quick round of the decks to ensure that all the ropes and fenders had been properly stowed away, I went to the bridge. Just like 602, every phone and gun was tested but, unlike 602, we were now joining a motley collection of coasters as one of their escorts.

A destroyer was flashing us and our signalman was answering with his hand-held Aldis lamp. 'Can you write this down, sir?' said the signalman. I grabbed a pencil and pad as the first wave broke over the forecastle and smothered us in spray. I waited. The signalman would sing out a couple of letters then would go silent. In the heavy swell running, we could see the destroyer when we were both on the top of a swell, but when we were in the troughs it was out of sight!

It took an eternity for us to receive details of our position in the screen, and once we had taken up our station we realised that the actual convoy speed was going to be very much slower than the theoretical speed. My new CO explained that all we had to do was maintain our position in the screen. However, as the petrol engines, even at slow ahead on one engine, would drive us forward too fast to keep in station, we would need to keep starting and stopping them. Such behaviour was not to our engine's liking and every hour it would be necessary to go 'half ahead' on both engines to 'blow' them out. Otherwise, if we needed to use what speed we had, the engines would be 'coked up' and let us down. Shortly afterwards he went below to catch a couple of hours' sleep before the night set in.

I was glad to have the chance to talk to the Coxswain and pick his brains, as I had absolutely no idea what the ship's routine was. Also, since this was the first time I had ever done any convoy work, I needed all the advice I could get. Fortunately, he was a fund of information and experience.

'See that ship with the barrage balloon.' His hand motioned towards a very dirty old coaster making clouds of black smoke. 'Take a bearing of her. Could well be that when we get under the Dover cliffs the only thing we shall be able to see tonight will be that bloody balloon!' I did as he bid me and sure enough, later that night, I was very glad I had.

As night fell and the weather got worse, it became increasingly difficult to see anything. Every hour we would increase our speed to 'blow out' the coke in our engines, take a wide circle round and try to return to our place in the escorting screen, but with all the ships blacked out it became more and more difficult to know exactly where we were and the only clue I had was the 'barrage balloon' riding high in the overcast sky. Later on, after one of our 'circles', I realised that we were heading towards a flashing green light-buoy! The sight of a mast and funnel with water breaking round them encouraged us to take immediate avoiding action! The chart was in the chart-house just below the bridge but I was too worried about leaving the bridge to venture below until my new Captain returned to take over, by which time we were fast approaching Dover.

For the rest of that night I was either on the bridge or in the chart-house. Because these boats were doing the same run every other night they became so used to the various courses that they tended to operate by memory. This may have been fine for them, but to me it was terrifying not knowing exactly where we were. In fact, the chart had been left on the chart-table so long that it was covered with cocoa stains and mug circles. It was almost impossible to read it! When I asked whether they had a new chart they thought I was quite mad.

'Don't need one old boy,' said the CO. 'You just follow the destroyer and his flock'! Which might explain the rumour that a ship had landed up off the French coast one bright morning - much to the amusement of the Germans!

By the next morning the convoy was still intact, though rather more strung out than the destroyer would have liked, and we spent our final hours, like patient sheep-dogs, trying to chivvy the older and more decrepit vessels to catch up. As they slowly made their way to the north, we sidled off to Ramsgate. There, once inside the tidal lock, we could confidently rest until the next tide would allow us to exit once more.

This was a completely new side to the war, which I had never experienced before, and like all new experiences it was fun. In future I would look at the MLs in a different light; their convoy duties demanded a different kind of commitment and team spirit. The inherent dangers were totally different to those experienced by the MTBs and MGBs. Their patience, and the time they spent at sea in all weathers, amazed me.

On our arrival I learned for the first time exactly how much work was needed to run even the small crew carried by an ML. When someone else is responsible for seeing that you have food and water, pay and leave, when someone else takes the ship away to top up with fuel or ammunition, when someone else looks after the paper-work necessary to keep account of all such happenings, it is never apparent. It only becomes apparent when the person responsible turns out to be you! My time as gash hand in 602 now proved its worth. While I had never had to do these things before, at least I had prior knowledge of the sort of things that a First Lieutenant had to do. I was very fortunate in having a first class Coxswain to guide me at every turn - without him I would certainly have struggled!

The weeks passed and the old Captain was reported to be making a good recovery. We made our way back to Newhaven one night and then back to Ramsgate the next. I was soon in danger of becoming as blasé as the other long-term officers and, while I was happy in a very happy little ship, I was relieved one day when the Captain returned and I was dispatched back to my old boat. The varied role of the 'DOG-boats' I found to be more interesting and I was delighted to rejoin my friends aboard 602.

I had not been back long when the Captain sent for me. He said that he had had favourable reports about my short sojourn aboard the ML and that it was time for me to become a Third Officer (Navigator).

'You are going to join a brand new boat commissioning at one of the best-known yacht-builders on the Clyde,' he said. I was very proud and rushed off to tell my friends. That night we organised a final farewell party and it was not until I came to kiss a certain little WRN goodbye that I suddenly realised just how much I was going to miss her. Some months before I had been concerned because a naval issue protective device I had been wearing had broken in use. After some heart-searching I had said that, should it be necessary, I would, of course, marry her. Her immediate response had shattered my ego.

'You don't think I'd marry you, do you?' she had said. 'Don't be so stupid. We are great friends and not too bad as lovers, but we would never do as lifetime partners.'

Although we were roughly the same age, she was so much more mature than I was. I have always been lucky with my friends and I have never forgotten her. She taught me so much and I shall always be in her debt. So I left Newhaven with sadness in my heart and a hangover in my head and set off for Scotland and a new challenge.

CHAPTER TEN - HMMTB 718.

James Robertson's yard on the Clyde had a reputation for building fine yachts. Charles Milner, our 'Sparker', rowed me from the shore in our dinghy. I felt immensely proud as I climbed aboard this lovely lady, pristine in her new paint.

The Captain, Ronnie Seddon, and the First Lieutenant, Guy Hamilton, had already been standing by the vessel for some time so the commissioning process was well advanced. Because of my experience in the ML, I knew much more about the First Lieutenant's job than I did about my new role as Navigator. In retrospect I now realise that neither Ronnie and Guy nor I myself understood this! The result was that I spent most of my time assisting Guy and precious little time preparing my own small department! Fortunately I had a first-class telegraphist in Charles Milner; he got the signals side sorted and took the young radar chap under his wing. A Northern Ireland sailor called Matchett was appointed as Navigator's Yeoman and between us we collected the various charts and other navigational paraphernalia and stowed it away. With the benefit of hindsight (and the experience I later gained) my department was disorganised tidiness!

Our commissioning was rushed through as fast as possible, partly because Naval Intelligence, for whom we were about to work, needed us in a hurry, and partly because all of us were impatient to get back to the job in hand. At last the formalities were over and on a beautiful sunny day we slipped our moorings and turned for our first passage.

'Course to steer?' It was my Captain's voice down the short voice-pipe joining the bridge to the chart-house.

'North 20 East, sir,' I proudly shouted back up the pipe.

There was a scuffling sound on the bridge and I could just hear the Captain say to the Coxswain, 'Steer South 20 West'. Then the sliding door into the chart-house was banged aside and the Captain pushed me out of the way. Grabbing the parallel ruler lying on the brand new chart he placed it along the carefully-drawn course I had just pencilled in, rolled it across to the printed compass rose and, jabbing his finger into my ribs, said, 'You have become a member of the Reciprocal Club, you dozy young clot. Now get your mind out of neutral!'

As he returned up the few steps to the bridge I could hear the Coxswain and other crew on the bridge chortling. Matchett was grinning beside me and I felt terribly ashamed. However, I had learned from the start a very valuable lesson; at sea it pays to check everything twice to make sure you are correct - mistakes at sea can cost lives!

Naturally this small incident did nothing for my confidence, essential for any Navigator, and I can still feel today my relief when, having been out of sight of land for some time, the predicted landfall appeared almost on time and roughly where I had said it would appear.

I suppose that one of the reasons I still get such a kick out of navigating at sea is the unpredictability of some of the variants which can affect a vessel's position. On land, one knows, within very strict limits, one's position, course and speed no matter what the elements do. At sea, although in coastal waters there are tide tables to assist the inshore navigator, these are not guaranteed and are only guidelines. Off shore in the North Sea for example, if the wind blows consistently from one direction for several days, it can set up a surface 'drift', which is not predictable and makes life more interesting for the navigator! I was to discover, in the not too distant future, just how interesting!

My memory of that first passage is of not daring to leave the bridge and chart-house area in case we got lost! It must sound stupid today - it does to me now - but I had the awful feeling that I had to *be* there. I suppose it was really a complete lack of confidence. Certainly no one was more surprised (or more delighted) than I was when the 'boom' vessel at Dartmouth swung aside to let us in. We sailed slowly up the Dart to moor alongside the old paddle steamer *Westward Ho*. I had made it!

It was now time for the Captain to muster the crew and talk to us. He started off by telling us what he expected of us and then, in very serious mood, he explained what our job was going to involve.

'We are now part of a small flotilla that works only for a department in Admiralty responsible for obtaining intelligence from occupied Europe. This will involve us in landing and collecting agents from various out-of-the-way places, also the collection of escaped POWs. Over the next few weeks we will be going to an area where you will learn how to handle boats that have been specially designed for landing men and equipment in surf and other difficult conditions.' He paused and looked around at the silent young faces. 'Sound interesting?' He paused again, and a general murmur showed he had our full attention. 'Now,' he continued, 'the price we have to pay for being selected for such work is the vow of silence! I cannot emphasise this point too much. It is not only vital for your own and my safety, which I'm sure I care about, but, far more importantly, the lives of many people right across Europe can also depend on your ability never to say anything about what you do to anyone - not your families, wives or even your mates in the Service - no one, is that quite clear?' He again looked around and a rather subdued 'Yes, sir,' echoed back to him.

'As you know, all mail is censored. Anyone found wanting in this area will immediately be sent back to general service as will anyone found disobeying these vital rules.' He turned to the First Lieutenant. 'Carry on No. 1,' and left the mess deck. The silence that followed his exit showed the effect his short talk had had on us.

Back in the chart-house Matchett asked me about the new job. I told him that all I knew was what the Captain had just told us, but it certainly sounded super. He grinned and agreed.

That lunchtime we were invited to meet the other officers in the flotilla. Some of them had been involved with DDOD(I) (Deputy Director Operations Division Irregular, Captain F Slocum) for some time, and we were most interested to listen to their experiences. However, these conversations only made us the more impatient to become operational and as soon as possible we sailed for the Helford River and the necessary training.

We carried two specially designed boats, one a smaller version of the other, but the underlying principles of handling these boats in surf conditions were the same. We were sailed to Prah Sands, a beach I had known on holiday before the war. Now we were anchored some half a mile off shore; a south-westerly had been blowing hard for some days and the waves were roaring ashore like galloping horses, their manes flowing behind them as wind-blown spume. 718 was rolling hard in the swell and the crew had great difficulty in man-handling the small boat over the side. Two sailors got in and I followed. We had been told how to proceed, but nothing is quite like the real thing! Seated on the stern coaming, with my legs holding me in position, I put all my weight on the long sweep-oar under my arm and steered the boat away from our bucking ship's side. The two sailors lay back on their oars and we slowly pulled towards the shore and those breaking waves.

As we approached the shore the swell steepened and shortened and I started to count. Off that coast one usually found the biggest wave arrived every 3 or 5 - which was it today? The men were still pulling in a steady rhythm and as the boat rose over the latest wave I could see the first of the breakers ahead.

'Hold it,' I said, holding my hand up, and I lay on the sweep-oar to keep our stern directly facing the oncoming waves. 'Hold water... back together,' I shouted above the roar, as a mighty wall of water came rushing towards us, its crest beginning to break and the wind blowing the spray in a soaking rain all over us. Our small craft stood on her head; for a moment I felt sure we were going to be tipped into the sea then, as suddenly, we were sliding down the back of the wave as it tore ashore sending great sheets of water and pebbles rushing up the beach. The sudden calm water was the signal for us to pull like mad!

'Give way!' I shouted as both men lay back with all their might and we shot ahead. The next wave raced towards us at the speed of an express train and with just as much noise. By now we were out of the very dangerous area and only had to keep stern-on to be able to beach our boat with the minimum of wetting - we had made it!

As we stood on the shelving beach my mind went back to the summer of 1938; I had surfed on this beach using ply surfboards. One of the guests had been the pretty daughter of a German Admiral. I wondered where she was - what a strange world!

My wandering thoughts were abruptly brought back to earth by my crew's laughter. Another boat had 'broached to' and the unfortunate occupants were thrashing around like so much flotsam. We managed to return to 718 without further incident and spent the rest of the day in practice until we were able to land both ourselves and passengers in safety. So much, I thought, for landing in daylight. At night it would obviously be much more difficult, especially as the nights chosen for our sort of work would have the minimum of light - no moon certainly!

Our chance to find out how difficult night landings were soon arrived. To my surprise it was not as hard as I had imagined. The same simple principles applied and once one's eyes had grown accustomed to the gloom, the lack of vision seemed to concentrate the mind on the immediate rollers, rather than on the others following, which helped! In fact, in a surprisingly short time, we were able to satisfy our teachers that we were safe to be let loose in an operational role. Having successfully carried out some night exercises, we returned to Dartmouth.

Ronnie Seddon, meanwhile, had prepared himself by accompanying one of the other boats on an operation as an observer. Such personal experience was invaluable, and on his return he briefed Guy and me accordingly. There were several things that we needed to practise; one was the simple action of anchoring in complete silence.

Under normal circumstances one would use a chain to anchor boats of this size. Obviously the noise of a chain rattling out some 400 yards off an enemy shore would not be helpful, so we carried a heavy grass line shackled to our CQR anchor. The anchor itself had a line bent to it from its balance point. This line was long enough to allow the anchor to be lowered below the surface without any splash. Anchoring needed to be carried out in total silence. Hand signals took the place of words. Only whispered comments were acceptable if any special situation required action out of the ordinary. Attention to detail was essential, just as essential as the silencing of the rowlocks and the ability of each man to do his own part of the total job without any orders or commands.

Soon we were proficient and waited impatiently for our first chance to prove it in practice.

CHAPTER ELEVEN - 718 OPERATIONS
'SCARAMOUCHE'

Our chance arrived on the 15th April. We sailed in company with MGB 502 for a beach in Brittany known as Beg-an-Fry, just north of Morlaix.

With one of the specialist navigators aboard, my own function was to watch and learn as much as I could. The trip over was uneventful and the boats landed to collect their passengers without any problems, returning to their respective mother ships in good time.

However, on our return in line ahead, while still working our way back to sea, three German patrol boats were sighted. They appeared to be steering on a parallel, but opposite, course and approaching very quickly. Both the MGBs crews were at action stations already and every gun aboard each vessel was trained on the enemy, now clearly visible.

Then the leading German ship flashed a challenge. Peter Williams, the Captain of 502, told his signalman, Colledge, to reply with a flashed KA - he understood this to mean in German, 'Wait I am fetching my Captain.' - but he was to do so in as clumsy a way as possible to play for time. After a short pause, the German ship flashed the same challenge again, and again Colledge sent his KA reply in his best erratic morse. By now the two vessels were no more than 150 yards apart and fast passing each other It looked as if the ruse had worked. Suddenly though, as the second enemy vessel was passing abeam, she opened fire. Both British crews, guns trained on the enemy, sat awaiting orders to return the fire. No such order came.

Meantime, in the relative safety of my tiny chart-house, all we knew about the happenings on deck was a laconic word down the voice-pipe from Ronnie Seddon when the three patrol boats were first sighted, 'Write out a sighting report and have Milner ready to send it if necessary.' This was followed a little later, after the sound of gunfire, by a message to the effect that, 'One of the silly bastards opened fire, which you could probably hear, but it looks like they've been shaken off and we're making for home'.

It was not until this incident was over that anyone realised that 502 had lost a sailor. Most of the flak had been seen to pass over their heads and aft of the bridge. It was not until the signalman was sent aft by his Captain to check things out that he came on the body of their young Oerlikon gunner, killed outright. A similar inspection aboard 718 showed that she had received a direct hit on her port quarter on the towing plate.

Undoubtedly both small ships had been lucky. Their bravado was seen to have paid off when we were informed that the German naval authorities in St Malo had reprimanded the patrol boat commander for firing on his own forces!

The self-discipline displayed by both crews enabled the same area to be visited again should this be required, but much more importantly, had our boats fought it out the Germans ashore would almost certainly have set up an intensive search of the whole area and the very brave people we relied upon to 'service' both the agents and escaping POWs would very probably have been picked up. Somebody once told me it took nine months to organise a safe beach, with its safe houses and safe routes and contacts stretching across occupied Europe.

Whether this is accurate or not, it does make the point that absolute discipline (the sort only each individual can achieve) was vital. Such discipline seems all the more praiseworthy when one realises that all our training had been to fulfil an aggressive role. Although we were required to remain 'the silent service', none-the-less our guns were exercised on every occasion possible, and our gunners prided themselves on their excellent performance.

502 had signalled ahead that she had received a fatal casualty. As we entered Dartmouth an ambulance blowing its horn was the signal for her to peel off to port and land her man. There was a quietness as we moored alongside *Westward Ho*. Although our first operation had been successful, we had lost a colleague. It was pure bad luck, but a family was missing a loved one and we knew it could so easily have been any one of us.

The First Lieutenant in each MGB was also the 'Boat's Officer'. This meant that if only one boat was needed, although we often embarked a specialist navigator, I could not get ashore. To obtain additional experience in this field I decided to volunteer for 'Spare Boat's Officer'. As soon as I learned about an operation being planned in which 718 was not to be involved, I would obtain permission from Ronnie Seddon and then call on the Captain of the MGB involved and get his OK.

A couple of weeks later, as Spare Boat's Officer, I had a grandstand view of the only real naval battle I ever witnessed. It was an experience I will never forget.

502 had sailed from Dartmouth to pick up an agent from a beach near Treguier. The trip across had been uneventful as usual. During our final silent approach to the landing area, I had positioned myself at the rear of the bridge, out of the way! The sky to the west was lit by what we took to be an air raid in the general direction of Brest. Such happenings were of only passing interest since we were fully involved with our own operation.

The night was very dark and, despite a swell, the boat was soon floating alongside without a sound. I watched as the crew silently boarded the boat and heard the first few strokes as the muffled oars pulled the boat clear of the ship - then nothing but silence. This was the worst part of any operation; until the boat returned we would have no idea whether or not there were problems - we just had to sit and wait.

The 'fireworks display' we had noticed during our approach now seemed to be getting closer. The Captain, handing me a pair of binoculars, told me to keep an eye on things and to report to him if there were any developments. Obviously an air raid on a static target could not move and yet this particular 'fireworks display' was moving in our direction. I steadied my glasses on the bridge surround. Out there in the inky blackness, beyond the rocks and the headland just visible, somebody was engaged in one hell of a battle!

'What can you see?' the Captain asked.

'Looks like naval gunfire, sir, but it's too far away at the moment to be able to be more specific.' He returned to the job in hand.

'Keep watching,' he ordered. A slight splash, almost alongside, indicated that the boat had returned. A few murmured comments drifted to the bridge and I could just pick out the men on the forecastle hand-hauling the grass rope on which we had anchored. As the anchor cleared the water the Captain turned the vessel to face out to sea and one engine was engaged at slow ahead. At less than walking pace, we left our anchorage; the second engine was engaged and we made our way slowly and with stealth towards the safety of the open sea. 'Operation successful,' I thought as we threaded our way out.

Suddenly, with no warning, we found ourselves illuminated by three perfectly placed 'star shells'. Every detail of the ship stood out as clearly as on a sunny day. The rocks, previously hidden by the darkness, now seemed very close indeed! Immediately following the explosions, there was total silence, then the signalman grabbed the Verey pistol (already loaded with the correct two-star signal) and fired it. High above our heads the twin colours lit the sky.

'Shall I repeat the signal, sir?' he enquired of the Captain.

'For Christ's sake, yes!' was the instant response. As the second twin stars spluttered their way downward and went out, we all wondered what would happen next.

I was still trying to make some order out of the constant flashes to seaward, but even with binoculars it was impossible to establish the numbers or types of the vessels involved.

'What can you see now?' the Captain asked. I realised that my reply would be quite inadequate.

'It's very difficult to establish anything in detail, sir. The ships involved are having one hell of a battle and there is no doubt that their progress up the Channel is closing our own course.'

'Keep watching and report as soon as there is any development.' The Captain was concentrating on our own safe passage. I lifted the glasses and continued my eye-aching search.

All this time we had been creeping slowly seaward. What no one could under-stand was why the shore batteries had not blown us out of the water. Surely they must have seen us in the star shell illumination. A shadowy shape crept into my line of vision away off our port bow. I dropped my binoculars, rubbed my eyes, and returned the glasses to the same bearing. Sure enough, it was becoming clearer; it was a destroyer steaming flat out and crossing our bows. I could now see her bow wave.

'Red 20 destroyer steaming left to right across our bows,' I reported, in what I hoped was a casual voice. The Captain swung his own glasses on to the bearing.

'Well done,' he said, and we could hear the engine-room telegraph signal as he stopped the engines. We lay wallowing in the gentle swell.... a loose halyard clicked against the mast...out to sea the battle continued unabated. The enemy destroyer was quite obviously only interested in making for safety, much to our relief! As soon as it was out of sight, the Captain proceeded once more. The Navigator gave him a new course to steer.

'Course North 40 East'

'Steer North 40 East, sir,' the Coxswain repeated to the Captain and I could feel the deck tremble as the engines increased speed.

Owing to our unplanned delay, we were still too close to the enemy shore for comfort when the first rays of a new day dawned. Would the Germans discover us during their early morning air sorties? A lone MGB was a sitting duck - we all knew that! However, Lady Luck had favoured us all night and as the English coast appeared over the horizon we realised she was still with us. In actual fact she had been even kinder than I realised.

It seems that one of the passengers that night had run up to the bridge when he heard the star shell explosions. As he reached the top of the ladder, the hammer of his revolver caught on something and fired! The bridge was full of people and it was a miracle that no one was hit. I suppose it must say something for my own concentration that I knew nothing about this incident until told about it afterwards!

Subsequently we learned that HMS *Black Prince* and four destroyers, three of them Canadian, had caught up with three German Elbing-class destroyers. Theirs was the battle we had witnessed, albeit unwillingly! I think this must have been one of the few occasions when an MGB returned empty-handed. The Boat's Officer, having waited for an hour without any sign of anyone turning up, was recalled to the ship. It was not until some time afterwards we learned that the unfortunate agent had been picked up by the Gestapo. They had shot him that very afternoon.

The final paragraph of that night's action was not written until a few days later. Coastal Command photographs indicated that the Germans were hurriedly trying to repair and refloat the destroyer, which had beached herself. After various bombing attempts had failed to achieve her destruction, it was decided to allow the Dartmouth MTB Flotilla to have a go. Tom Cartwright led his Dog boats over without incident; evidently our enemies were so involved in their salvage work that no one noticed them until Tom's first torpedo blew the stern off the stranded vessel! The flotilla returned, delighted with the result, but frustrated that Tom's first fish had done the job. They had gone all the way there and all the way back just to watch their Senior Officer fire a torpedo!

CHAPTER TWELVE - 718 OPERATIONS 'CYGNUS'.

To the west of Dartmouth a large area of Devonshire had been taken over as a 'Battle Area', the inhabitants being evacuated for the duration of the war. It was here that the invasion forces were trained (especially the Americans) using live ammunition. Driving the lanes of Devonshire then, it was a common sight to see great quantities of stores lying under tarpaulins, awaiting D-day.

Berthed up the river Dart were a host of enormous Tank Landing Ships carrying their full complement of tanks and men. April saw three American PT boats arrive to join our flotilla, and I see from my old Navigator's notebook that on the 12th of May we exercised with PT 72 and PT 199 at Prah Sands.

After explanations about how to land our special boats in surf conditions, we set off with the new PT boats' crews for the shore. There was a good surf running and our crews all landed without difficulties. Unfortunately the Americans had failed to listen to the instructions they had been given. The sea shows no mercy. Predictably and unceremoniously their boats were up-ended and they were thrown into the cold water. By the time we had helped them to collect their oars and boats, they had learned their lessons from the best teacher of all - personal experience!

During this time I spent quite a lot of time with one of the PT boat's CO. He was a charming man. I accompanied him when he took his boat to run over the 'measured mile' and watched as he exercised his gun crews. To my amazement he had no means of talking to his gun crews by sound-powered phones. This meant that they were not under any sort of control and I felt this could be disastrous in our sort of operations. When I mentioned this to him he was most receptive. He also greatly admired our Oerlikon guns. It was nevertheless a surprise, only a week later, to find his engineer fitting such a gun in place of the one he had. It appeared that he had 'acquired'' the Oerlikon for a bottle of Scotch! As an engineer in civvy street, he had designed and had built (by their workshops ashore) a very neat 'mounting' about a tenth the weight of the Admiralty pattern one. He also had his bridge steel-plated and (after D-day) produced electric sanding machines (things we had never seen before) to remove the paint from his upper decks - he was a great guy!

One morning, just before D-day, I was standing talking to him on our bridge when the LSTs, which we had seen sail the previous evening, began to enter harbour. The first had a huge hole where its bows should have been and the Bofors gun in its eyes was pointing drunkenly straight down into the water. The second LST had also been shot up and it soon became obvious that they had suffered a real mauling. The American was visibly shocked when I told him that E-boats had done the damage. Up to then they had shown little respect for the fighting ability of the German E-boats. They had come from the Japanese Pacific where they had distinguished themselves valiantly, but the Japanese did not have any equivalent to the German E-boats and I think they found it hard to realise that this was a very different arena. The events of that tragic night have now become public knowledge and a memorial at Slapton Sands records them, but at that time security was tight and it was not generally understood just what had happened

It was now mid May and I was waiting to catch the boat to go ashore to meet my new WRN girl friend when Ronnie Seddon jumped aboard.

'Where do you think you are going?' he enquired. Grinning, I replied that I had a red-hot date and moved to board the boat. 'Not tonight you haven't,' he said as he restrained me. 'Get the charts out to take us to Holyhead. I'll be with you in five minutes.' And he disappeared to his cabin. Disappointed at having to 'stand up' my WRN - there was no way I could get word to her - I made my way to the chart-house and began to get the necessary charts into some sort of order. Soon Ronnie appeared.

My notebook states that we sailed at 0623 on the 24th May and passed the boom at 0630. The normal notes record our progress during the day and at 2330 we passed Holyhead breakwater, securing some five minutes later alongside. Ronnie and I left for the Base at 2340 and at 2345 Guy took the ship away to fuel. We returned at 0330!

My own needs were soon satisfied. We needed additional charts to take us to the Shetland Isles, but they had to cover both the route round the West of Scotland, via Cape Wrath, and the route via the Caledonian Canal and Inverness to the east. Having completed my various tasks, I waited for Ronnie Seddon to reappear. He had gone off to see the Duty Officer and obtain up-to-the-minute instructions. The weather, which had been increasingly beastly as our journey had proceeded, was now becoming a real problem. It appeared that the RNO (Resident Naval Officer), a Senior RN Captain, had refused to allow us to sail!

Ronnie, who knew but could not explain why we had to sail, asserted that it was simply imperative that we be allowed to sail at once. Because four straight RN stripes have rather more authority than two wavy Navy ones, it now became necessary for Ronnie to ask permission to use the Captain's telephone. He spoke direct to our bosses in London. After a short discussion between them and the Captain, Ronnie was in-formed that he would be allowed to sail at 0630. Relieved and pleased, we made our way back to the ship, which Guy had taken away to be refuelled. I see from my notes that we turned in at 0330.

Although the weather was uncomfortable we made fair progress up the Irish Sea. I see we challenged three cruisers around 1100 hours and were steaming at 21 knots when, just after lunch, the Chief Motor Mec appeared on the bridge. We had picked up contaminated fuel at Holyhead, which was why both the starboard engines had suddenly stopped!

As we rolled our way northwards, the engine-room personnel had a wretched time combating the water in the fuel lines and had no sooner cleared one line than another would cause trouble. Eventually, just before 1800 we secured alongside at Oban. Having signalled ahead our trouble, there was a petrol tanker lorry ready and waiting on the jetty. First the contaminated fuel had to be pumped out of our tanks, then new clean fuel had to be pumped in to replace it. The engine room staff wasted no time and we were under way again by just after 1900. Half an hour later we were tied up to a buoy at the southern end of the Caledonian Canal and at 2200 we started the long business of 'locking'. At each lock, men would jump ashore and assist the local lock-keepers to wind the windlass handles to open the lock gates. The locks had never been worked so fast and we were making great progress when, at 2300, the lock-keeper at a particular lock told us that we could go no further. We were astonished. There was a war on and here we were in a hurry to get ahead. The dour Scot knocked out his well-smoked pipe on his horny hand and spat into the swirling water. 'See you tomorrow at 5 o'clock,' he said, turned and was gone.

At 0445 on the 25th our engines were running and all was ready to proceed. True to his word, the old lock-keeper appeared and we made our way through the ladder of locks without further ado. As soon as we entered Loch Ness, Ronnie put all four engines to full ahead and we streaked up this famous Loch. It was a lovely day, and we all enjoyed the wonderful scenery. We did not need a chart for this part of the passage and I was on the bridge along with the others. Quite suddenly we reached the end of the Loch and as we entered a bend we saw to our astonishment a narrow canal ahead with another lock at the end of it. Immediately Ronnie pulled the four levers back to 'Stop'! However, our wash overtook us and went ahead like the Severn Bore. Two old lock-keepers, chatting on the lock walkway, looked up in total disbelief! What in heavens name was a great big MTB doing approaching them at such speed?

The wall of water, whose momentum had been increased by being contained within the narrow canal banks, rushed towards them at a frightening pace. One dropped his pipe and the other his cap as they ran off the walkway to safety. The wave hit the solid lock with an enormous thud; spray was hurled into the air. The resultant suction, as the wave retreated, dragged the two lock gates open, snapping their retaining chains like cotton. By now Ronnie had 718 stopped alongside and he went ashore to face the two angry and frightened lock-keepers. History does not record the conversations that took place. Suffice it to say that Ronnie could be very charming. Somehow these two disgruntled Scots were persuaded to help us get the show back on the road, although it was a rather sheepish group of sailors who stood on the bank ready to help. It was 1430 when we secured alongside at Inverness.

Once again the engine-room staff de-fuelled and then re-fuelled. Even so we sailed at 1730 for Lerwick. Apart from altering course to investigate a white flare, which the bridge reported as having been dropped by an aircraft, the trip continued without further incident and we berthed alongside at Lerwick at 0415, our lines being taken by a very wet and wind-swept RNVR Lieutenant. He came down to the ward-room and informed us that Captain Slocum was due early that same morning and there would be a briefing at 1030; a car would be alongside to collect Ronnie and me at 1000. After a quick cup of tea, we thanked him for meeting us and, as he left, we turned in.

It was 69 and three quarter hours since we had left Dartmouth. Of this we had spent 51 and three quarter hours under way. This meant that we had covered the 900 odd miles at an average speed of just over 17 knots which, considering our fuel problems and the rather unkind weather, was a very creditable performance. Morale was high, and as Ronnie and I were taken by car to the briefing, Guy took 718 away to re-fuel once more. He also collected an extra 1000 gallons (in jerry cans) as deck cargo! This was the first time we had had such a cargo and when Ronnie and I returned we gazed in amazement at the great stack of cans carefully lashed in place.

On top of the other work needing to be done, the engine-room staff also had to do their routine 50-hour engine maintenance. Thus Saturday passed into Sunday and around 1500 hours we sailed for Norway.

We were making for a rendezvous near Batalden Island, about 80 miles north of Bergen, to collect eleven people who were in grave danger. Also embarked for this trip was one of the specialist navigators, 'Tich' Salmond RNR, and some Norwegians in case they were needed on our arrival. The weather was overcast and miserable, good from our point of view, as it would make us more difficult to see from the air.

After some hours the Chief Motor Mec appeared on the bridge. He had sufficient space now to take the 1000 gallons stored in jerry cans on deck, so when all was ready he would like to start to get that job out of the way. Guy and the Coxswain had already worked out how they intended to carry out this exercise. First a 40-gallon drum, which had had a deck-fitting braised into its base, was screwed into the port fuelling deck fitting. Then a line of sailors, swaying to keep their balance as the ship rolled, passed jerry cans from hand to hand in a constant flow. When they arrived at the open-ended 40-gallon drum, they were opened by two sailors who, having emptied the contents into the drum, passed the empty cans on to a second line of sailors to the stern. There stood a man with a large, pointed, copper hammer. His job was to hole each drum in a couple of places (copper so no sparks!) and hurl it over the side.

As we proceeded, a line of gradually-sinking cans stretched into the distance. This was the first time he had tried out this scheme and it worked well. Obviously the ship's motion made it difficult for the men to keep their balance and, as inevitably some petrol was spilt, the deck became very slippery. However, the job was completed and, by stretching a canvas dodger over the area, contamination of the fuel with water was kept to a minimum. Despite these precautions, and the action taken by our engine-room staff, we still suffered occasional engine stoppages throughout this trip.

Early in the morning of the 29th, 'Tich' Salmon reckoned we were within 20 miles of the coast. Speed was reduced and the engines were silenced. Fog had set in and it was decided to risk using our radar to see if we could obtain a fix based on the highest peaks (strongest echoes) on Batalden Island. These were the days before we had any accurate navigational aids and the previous day, when I had been discussing things with one of the Norwegian navigators back in Lerwick, he had astonished me by telling me that sometimes they had been up to 50 miles out because of North Sea drift! I could not imagine how Ronnie would react to my landing him even half this amount out! But the warning had been timely and I did not forget it.

The fix put us rather closer than we had thought and a new course was set to make the 'pin-point'. We crept slowly in. On deck visibility was still very poor. The Norwegian Pilot, who had been sleeping in the Captain's cabin, was shaken and took over the wheel. We started the echo sounder and the Pilot, peering into the gloom, steered us into the murk. When we were about 500 yards off the shore the fog lifted a little. There, inshore, could be seen a small motorboat making its way towards us, towing a dinghy.

'Come on the bridge,' Ronnie ordered me. 'Go to the port quarter and challenge that boat.' He waved at the small motorboat I could just see through the haze. Wavering a moment I queried,

'Challenge, sir?'

'The password given at the briefing - Churchill,' he said, and I ran down aft just as the two boats came alongside. Leaning over the side I caught the motorboat's painter.

'Churchill,' I whispered, as loud as I dared, passing the painter to a sailor. To my amazement both boats' passengers started to give a great cheer. We hurriedly shut them up as they were hauled over the side, seven men, three women and a small child. My request to Ronnie Seddon that we might be allowed to tow the lovely little motorboat back with us received a swift and nautical response! One of the Norwegians, wielding an axe, scuttled her; the noise in that deserted sea was deafening and we were all very relieved when the job was done and we set sail for home.

It took us another nine hours to sight land but we were now safe with our precious human cargo - the operation had gone like clockwork and we were all thrilled to bits. It can now be told that no one was more surprised than our masters! Apparently they thought the likelihood of the operation being successful was very slim indeed. Perhaps the bad weather and bad visibility helped.

Having landed our Norwegian friends and generally tidied things up, I went ashore to the base and fell fast asleep in a lovely hot bath - I came to, shivering with cold and had to run another one to get warm again!

Because of the tough time the crew had been through, Captain Slocum told Ronnie to find his way back to Dartmouth in his own sweet time. So it was not until 0830 on the 31st May that we set sail for Stornoway. It made a wonderful break to be sailing in daylight on our own without any worries about deadlines to be met or an enemy to be seeking to kill. However, even this passage produced a floating mine around lunchtime. We attempted to sink it by gunfire, but time was short and the swell made things difficult so we reported it and sailed on, arriving at Stornoway around eight o'clock that evening.

0800 on the 1st of June found us heading for Northern Ireland. By 2130 that night we were tucked away in Spenser dock at Belfast. My Navigator's yeoman, Matchett, was in his home port. We tested the local brew and returned to the ship in a horse-drawn cab. Leaving Belfast at 0830 we made Holyhead by 1430 and I must admit it seemed much more than nine days since our last visit.

Everyone was now talking about the coming invasion of Europe. We sailed for

Newlyn at 0400 on the 6th June. As we made our way down the Irish Sea we sat in shirt-sleeves on the bridge. A battery-driven radio (hard to come by then - ours was a comfort provided by the Windmill Theatre in London) was giving almost constant news broadcasts and it seemed quite unreal to be listening to eyewitness reports of the happenings of that momentous day. We berthed at 1730; our own small success seemed insignificant in comparison to the tremendous news. But there are some Norwegian folk alive today who might not have been, but for our insignificant little journey!

We left Newlyn at 0915 and returned to our berth alongside *Westward Ho* at 1400 on the 7th. This trip had proved we were at last worthy members of our flotilla. New boys we certainly were, but we had now proved ourselves, the only boat from the 15th to operate off the Norwegian coast - and so it continued to be.

CHAPTER THIRTEEN - 718 OPERATIONS
'REFLEXION.'

The excitement and activity caused by D-day made us feel left out of things. So when, a week after our return from the Norwegian trip, we were briefed to land three agents in Brittany we were delighted.

The 'pin-point' was Bonaparte Beach, Plouha. (So insists Jean Trehiou one of the agents landed that night.) The trip over passed without incident in reasonable, though overcast weather. The bridge did report an air raid in progress in the St Malo direction as we made our approach, but there had been no problems and, at 0200, 718 was anchored some 1200 yards off the shore as planned.

I watched as Guy and his two-man crew (Leading Seaman Dellow and Able Seaman Rockwood) boarded the small boat. Silently they helped the three agents into the boat and stowed their gear. With a wave to 'let go' they were off, and the muffled swirl of the first few oar strokes disappeared into the blackness. As soon as he had the boat settled on its run to shore, Guy tested his hand-held walkie-talkie; the reception was very crackly but at least we were able to converse. Then the waiting began.

On these operations the waiting while your mates were away was always very tense. After a while Ronnie checked the bearings on which he had anchored his vessel. They had altered, which meant that the anchor was not holding us in the position where we had anchored. Whispered orders were given, and the forecastle party could be heard easing out more of the grass line on which we were anchored. When Ronnie considered the anchor would have had time to gain a new hold and the extra line had its effect, he again checked the bearings. There was no doubt; we were being swept along by the strong tide. He had no option but to restart the engines and steam silently and slowly back to the position from which the boat had been launched.

These unwanted activities helped to occupy the time, but now the waiting started once again. There had been no sound from the shore, nothing except static from the walkie-talkie, and there was still no sign of their return. The minutes slowly ticked past. Ronnie manoeuvred the ship to maintain his position, constantly checking the bearings. Where were they? What had happened to so delay them? Time was rapidly running out. We would have to leave shortly because the dawn was already threatening in the eastern sky. I asked Ronnie if I could take the other boat inshore to try and find out something. Quite rightly he refused.

Despite the risks, he then took a slow and silent sweep inshore. With dimmed light, signals were flashed towards the beach and then, in case they had rowed past us while we had been regaining our anchor position, we flashed out to sea. There was no response and no sign of any boat. Earlier we had switched on the echo sounder. Its regular 'click, click, click' had sounded loud in the confines of the silent chart-house. We could think of no other action to help resolve the mystery; there was nothing more we could do. Slowly 718 turned for home.

Words cannot fully explain the awful feeling in each man's breast. We had grown into a very close-knit family and to have to leave now, not knowing what had befallen our mates, was intolerable. None of us will ever forget that long return journey, and none of us was more directly affected than poor Ronnie Seddon. Not only had he been forced to leave Guy Hamilton (who had become his best friend) but also two men from the crew, which he had moulded into such a warm and close unit. His face, normally cheerful, told the story. He looked totally drained and very tired. Once close to the English coast, he gave Milner a coded message to send by W/T to Ted Davis at Dartmouth. It read simply 'Reflexion not completed - three missing.'

It was a strangely silent crew that tied up the warps of 718 as she returned to her place alongside the old solid *Westward Ho*. Ronnie immediately left for the shore to report in person. I took over the routine role normally filled by Guy. It felt very strange, but the things that needed to be done, still had to be done. Our team was now three short, so duties would need to be re-allocated. A quick session with the Coxswain soon sorted out both these and other more normal routine problems. Life, we suddenly had to realise, did not stop!

On his return, Ronnie sent for me in his cabin. 'I'd like you to take over as No 1,' he said. 'Thank you, sir. Until we get Guy back I'll do my best,' I replied. There seemed nothing more to add, so I left him to write his official report and went about my now official duties.

For the second time in my short Coastal Forces career I had made a 'pier-head jump'. Overnight I had moved from Navigator to First Lieutenant but this time it involved my friend and my own crew. About one thing I was determined, when Guy returned I wanted him to find his boat in even better shape than when he left.

Having been officially accepted by my Captain, I had a meeting with the Coxwain and we discussed the situation in depth. I could not have wished for more co-operation than I received from both him and the rest of the crew. They were superb. Meantime the authorities had decided that, for security reasons, it would be preferable for 718 and 502 to sail for Helford. My notebook shows that we sailed in company with 502 at 0915 on the 17th June. My own last entry is of a course alteration at 1005 to N75W - I can only assume that Ronnie had told me to forget navigation and concentrate on my new duties as First Lieutenant. Certainly the next entries are in a different hand and follow a different pattern - a new Navigator had taken over by the 19th.

Now came the real waiting period. To rebuild morale and keep minds occupied, we began a series of exercises with 502, based on Helford. The weather was beautiful and both boats had a marvellous time. This was made possible by the news from Guy Hamilton that they had been picked up by the Resistance and were safe! The relief was almost tangible and Ronnie became his old self.

Unknown to us, Guy had managed to have a message sent to Ted Davis. It read, 'Safe. Beach clear for future operations. Hamilton.' So plans were made to collect these 'loafing sailors' as soon as the dark nights returned.

For security reasons, it was 503 that was to be allowed the satisfaction of retrieving our missing mates. Ronnie was allowed to travel with them; I was obliged to wait. I shall never forget the morning when we watched 503 return. I am sure that I was not the only sailor with unwanted but happy tears streaming down my cheeks. There they were, three unshaven, smiling faces, Guy's face looking different somehow - we did not know that he had acquired a broken nose in his travels!

They were all rushed off to be de-briefed along with the other returned escaped POWs. It was going to be some time before they once again graced our decks, but they were back; that was all that mattered.

In the middle of July we were sailed to Gillingham for slipping, refit and a spot of leave. I remember we were all amazed at the mass of shipping as we passed the Isle of Wight. The passage was without incident and the only item worth recording occurred during our refit time.

A certain rating discovered a Nissen hut, which housed a stock of the most beautiful RAF all-weather zip suits. It must have been a coincidence but after our refit, on our way down Channel, some of the officers and crew could be seen wearing very similar, very smart, outfits, which were the envy of our friends for the rest of the war.

My trusty notebook shows I was once again Navigator from Southend to Shoreham 4/8/44.

'1140 - Slip from Chatham and proceed to Southend.

1405 - Slip from Southend and proceed to Shoreham.'

If I recall, the day was fine and sunny once we left the Thames estuary and, apart from holding the almost traditional 'shoot' on various wrecks as we passed through the Goodwins, (I seem to remember they also had some practice against the odd flying bomb in the Straits of Dover) nothing of interest occurred. The log shows we anchored briefly off Shoreham, but eventually berthed alongside at 1930.

On the 7th August we slipped from the inner basin at Shoreham and sailed for France. This was our first trip using the D-day traffic system - it was marvellous. Once you were in your own lane all you had to do was follow the buoys, which led you all the way to whatever part of the beachhead you needed. From then on all one needed was a good pair of binoculars.

On this first trip we left our berth at 1322 and arrived some five hours later; we had averaged just over 25 knots. We lay alongside MASB 36, another member of our flotilla. Around midnight the Officer of the Watch reckoned both ships were dragging their anchors, so we slipped from the MASB and anchored separately. The next morning we passed the Mulberry entrance at 0813 bound for *Westward Ho* in Dartmouth. We made good speed till around 1500 when we ran into thick sea fog. When it was time to turn north for the entrance to Dartmouth I had started the echo-sounder. As Ronnie slowed down, the lookout stationed right in the bows shouted that he could hear people talking on the beach! Certainly the echo trace was getting very shallow! We turned out to sea and started all over again. This time we were successful, and as we passed the boom Ronnie called me on to the bridge. I gasped. Astern one could see a great white wall of fog swirling back on itself to form a blanket - inside the harbour it was bright sunlight!

The voices the lookout had heard were those of the families bathing on the sunlit beach round the corner from the harbour. I heard after that some of the shore staff were watching our efforts on the shore radar, gin and tonics in hand, taking bets on how long it would take us to 'find the hole' without assistance!

718 was home again, her original crew complete.

The crew of 718

CHAPTER FOURTEEN - 718 OPERATIONS
'KNOCKOUT'

On the 12th of September we sailed, in company with MGB 318, for L'Aberwrach. By 1555 we were secured alongside a destroyer, HMS *Londonderry*. The immediate area was clear of Germans, though there were still pockets of resistance along the western seaboard of Brittany.

There was an official photographer on board with an aircraft-type camera. We sailed at 0900 on both the following two days to enable him to photograph those parts of the coastline needed by our boss back home. We also had time to climb over the destroyer that Tom Cartwright had sunk on the rocks, and investigate the huge gun emplacements ashore.

Our evenings were spent being entertained ashore by some of those very brave people with whom we had worked. Prized wines, which had been hidden, now appeared to accompany meals the like of which I have never seen since. Both the quality and the quantity of those superb dinners, cooked and served by the ladies of those households in a style only the Bretons know, defy description. For hungry young sailors, who were still suffering from severe rationing, these dinner parties were experiences never forgotten!

August had seen the US Third Army capture Cherbourg and they were now fighting their way into the Brittany peninsular. The Resistance fighters needed arms and ammunition to enable them to take the battle to the enemy. Thus it was that 718 sailed alone to Benodet, loaded with a cargo of just such supplies.

In addition to the naval photographer, we carried other 'observers', hitching a ride on their way to a meeting with an FFI Colonel at Quimper. The weather was hazy as we passed Brest and the photographer was further frustrated by fog until we reached the Baie de Trepassier. Here he was able to start his programme.

The FFI at L'Aberwrach had told Ronnie that there was still a pocket of German resistance, some 500 men with two 75 mm guns plus other smaller pieces, sited half a mile west of Audierne Light. But since the cliffs would restrict the arcs of fire of the 75mm guns, a course was chosen to enable the photographer to continue his work. It was something of a surprise, therefore, when we were fired upon between 1100 and 1115. No damage was sustained and our own guns responded with interest. As we sailed on, we carried out a further bombardment of some enemy gun positions ashore, some of which could be seen to hold imitation guns! No further opposition was encountered.

Late that afternoon we tied up to a buoy in Benodet harbour. Another D-boat was on the same mooring buoy. Having unloaded our supplies into a small store boat and said goodbye to our 'observers', we went below to the ward -room. Here a large map covered the table and Ronnie and the CO from the other D-boat were deep in conversation with a couple of very rough-looking French Resistance men. Guy, who was a fluent French-speaker, was involved in the interpretation of this conversation and all

I could do was to try and follow the general gist of what was being discussed.

Apparently the buoys that we were using had been, until very recently, used by E-boats. Quite naturally, they had been strictly out of bounds to the locals. Now, of course, their Allies were occupying them and so they reckoned they were free to come aboard with impunity. And they did. Within half an hour of our arrival it was impossible to move aboard. Even the shyest man on the mess deck, who would have turned his back on his male colleague before removing his pants, was now forced to stand naked while his mate threw his clothes to him, over the heads of the admiring mass of assembled French, and some photographs taken at the time indicate that the crush of people here was as nothing to the position below decks! No Navy Day drew such a crowd!

At 0645 the following morning our engines started. We were preparing to leave, as arranged the night before with the CO of the other D-boat. Suddenly, his unbrushed head appeared. 'Ronnie my dear old boy! Terribly sorry, I forgot to tell you I'd given my chaps all-night leave.' And he waved an apologetic hand.

'Let go forward, let go aft, hang on to your fore-spring, fender forward.' The familiar orders kept pace with Ronnie's engine movements. 'Let go fore-spring.' There was a splash as the final rope was hauled aboard - we were off again.

Our task now was to carry out a bombardment of the gun positions so carefully discussed the night before with the local FFI men. This was to cause a diversion to enable them to mount an attack at the same time from the shore. That much I had gathered, though in all fairness an MGB was hardly in the 'professional bombardment' business. Still, if our Captain was prepared to drive our small ship into someone else's back yard and try to punch him on the nose, we would do our best to support such an action, even on a beautiful sunny day when it would have been much more appropriate to pipe, 'Hands to bathe'!

I was dispatched with a pair of binoculars to the after six-pounder. This was of the old type and was manned by both a layer and trainer with the usual back-up loading numbers. This gun's great feature, as I was soon to discover, was that it had a most comforting old-fashioned gun shield.

Slowly we slid towards the sandy beach over a silken blue sea with not a ripple. I still felt a bathe was more appropriate than a bombardment. The sun shone from a cloudless sky. Our very tall photographer was standing on the seats lining the wing of the bridge to get an even better view. For my part I was scanning the immediate shoreline to try and find a likely target. I heard Guy on the power phones tell all guns to train on to a bearing and search for likely targets. Suddenly he ordered the forward six-pounder to open fire. Then he ordered all guns to fire independently. My six-pounder was aimed and ready.

'Fire!' I cried, feeling rather like an old-fashioned sea dog. My gun's crew rapidly went through their well-rehearsed routine.

'Layer on, trainer on, *fire!*' I found myself joining in as if on a training exercise. Through my binoculars I could see our fall of shot and we trained left a bit. Suddenly, as I was searching for the latest fall of shot through my glasses, a huge splash filled my eyepiece. Thinking that my own gun's crew had depressed their gun I shouted for them to get their aim up and returned to my study of the target area. Once again my field of view was interrupted by another huge splash. I removed my binoculars and glanced behind me at the bridge. As I did so, all the figures on the bridge disappeared from view, including the tall photographer who seemed to dive into the deck. Looking back to the shore, it was plain now who was responsible for those large splashes. Even as I looked, more flashes and splashes appeared. It was then that I recognised the comfort of the gun shield!

718 spun round and, at full speed, turned her smallest target area (her stern) to the gunners ashore. Since my six-pounder was fixed to the stern, my gun's crew and I could do nothing but continue to fire, which we did. But I would be the first to admit that I had no idea whether or not we were landing in the right place to do real damage. Ronnie's official report states that '...Local control of the 6 pdr by S/Lt Townend was most effective and greatly increased accuracy of fire.' I am proud to think that he thought to say so, but I am not sure that the enemy would have agreed!

However, as we rather hurriedly left the area of conflict, Ronnie ordered us to make smoke. The CSA canisters in the centre of our transom had valves that should have been free to be opened by a strong hand but, despite our overwhelming wish to do as Ronnie had ordered, none of us could get the valves to budge. Finally, a stoker with a wrench achieved this task, and at once a glorious plume of white gas was swirling in our wake. As soon as there was enough of a screen, 718 turned behind this white wall and edged her way to seawards; then she sallied forth once more at speed to lay another wall of white and, just as the guns were getting her range, she dashed back behind her newly-laid protective screen. This cat-and-mouse game continued until we made the protection of the far headland. Once safely round that, Ronnie stopped and an inspection was carried out to establish exactly what damage, if any, had been sustained.

When I looked over the stern I was surprised to see a neat shrapnel hole. This was happily sucking in water each time our gentle roll placed it under the surface. A tingle was sent for and I was lowered over the stern with a hammer and some copper nails to make good the damage. Apart from being submerged (much to the amusement of the onlookers) every time we rolled, the job was soon completed and I am proud to say it was still intact much later when we were placed on the slipway for repairs.

Meantime Guy and the Chief were carrying out a detailed survey of the boat. Another piece of shrapnel, or a shell, had caused a hole on our starboard quarter about a foot above the waterline. This too received its tingle, but there was nothing to be done about the damage caused by the 20mm semi-armour-piercing shell which had pierced one of our special boats and gone on to whiz around the Oerlikon bandstand before attacking the metal framework of the deck petrol-stowage. We had always been a lucky boat and certainly that day the good Lord must have been keeping an eye on us.

The worst outcome of all this was the possibility of petrol fumes from the damaged fuel tanks leaking into the boat. That meant a 'no smoking' order below decks until we could be sure there was no danger.

We made our way back to Dartmouth with mixed feelings. It had been great to feel that we were helping the FFI by our bombardment (we were told much later that the FFI had wiped out that pocket) but at the same time we were all very much aware of the danger we had been in. An MGB on a beautiful sunny day in a calm bay well within your range is the sort of soft target any artilleryman would relish. I can only assume that the Germans were so surprised by our cheeky behaviour that they could not believe their eyes. There must have been some reason for our good fortune.

In the ward-room, Guy and I wondered how Ronnie was going to talk his way out of this one. Because of the damage we had sustained we would naturally have to be slipped and we were genuinely concerned. As it turned out he ended up by being highly commended. Rumour has it that certain of the observers, who were well-connected and highly-respected officers, spoke up for him. We were all delighted, especially Guy and I. Guy's birthday is on the 23rd of September and mine on the 22nd. The way things had happened enabled me to get home for my 21st birthday.

In the event I spent the day at sea, fishing in a small boat off Fowey. On our return, the Coast Guard 'held me'! I had no fishing permit. What was I doing? My efforts to persuade him that a serving RNVR Officer on leave should surely be allowed to join his mother for a day's fishing (she had a permit) were in vain. All he would say, rather grumpily, was that I had been warned and had better not try it again.

The next day I took over while Guy dashed off to celebrate his birthday with his Windmill girl friend in London. I was just a simple country boy; Ronnie and he were much more sophisticated and I loved to hear about their London parties.

In fact it may have been at that party that he and Ronnie arranged for the Windmill folk to take their next rest period at Torquay. Anyway, one lovely Saturday it was announced that at 1100 we would be invaded by some of the raving beauties from the latest production. Everything was polished and everyone was looking his best when the boat came alongside. The girls in their summer dresses looked delicious and, as I led them down the ladder to the ward-room, their scent filled the air. They had never been aboard such a small craft before and were amazed how civilised we were! Naval size gin and tonics were poured and as soon as the Coxswain had issued the men with their rum ration the whole party moved forward on to the mess deck. I had volunteered to act as Officer of the Day and having seen everyone 'looked after' went on deck to smoke a cigarette.

The party was a huge success and, after lunch, it was suggested that I might like to row a few of them up the river. Naturally I was pleased to do so, until I found that the only takers were the two male dancers! Too late to back down, I had a rather awkward hour's rowing. It seemed to me that my passengers were rather more interested in my own 'lovely shoulders and strong arms' than they were in the scenery! I cut short the exploratory row by an hour. When I entered the ward-room earlier than expected, Guy was quite upset!

Later on, when we were operating from Shoreham, the girls stayed at Brighton. They took their 'adoption' of 718 seriously. They raised money on the stage and presented the boat with presents; any of the crew who called at the stage door on their way through London would be well looked after - they were super people. At least two of the girls, Joan Rock and Charmian Innes, became stars later on in life.

CHAPTER FIFTEEN - 718 'TROT BOAT SERVICE.'

A month after our 'fun run' to Brittany we were sailed to Shoreham. The intervening weeks had been occupied with repairs and various exercises.

My log records that we went to Ostend on the 13th of October and returned to Shoreham on the 14th. On the 21st we sailed over to Dieppe, returning on the 22nd. Back again to Dieppe on the 24th, returning on the 26th. It seemed that our new role was to be a fast, reliable 'Trot Boat Service' for various VIPs. This was not our scene and we were all delighted when Ronnie returned one morning with the news that we were off to Aberdeen.

Obviously it had been most interesting for us to be able to see for ourselves the invasion beaches, also to see the amazing organisation behind the constant supply of food, arms and ammunition for all the forces now fighting deep in Europe. But, this experience apart, we were all glad to be doing something more in line with our own training.

Before passing on, though, there was a purely personal incident that might amuse the reader. It really started back in Dartmouth a couple of weeks before. I had gone on deck one evening for a final cigarette. It was sometime after 11 o'clock. The blackout ashore was complete and only a few stars lit the sky. Some shouting ashore caught my attention; voices were calling for a boat. Thinking that perhaps some of our crew had missed the last liberty boat I quickly undid the painter holding our dinghy astern and rowed ashore. The voices turned out to be American. They had indeed missed their last boat and were now stranded. Could I possibly help them out? Naturally I piled them in and pulled back to a large towering LST. When we arrived the Senior Officer invited me to come aboard for a cup of coffee. Thinking it would be interesting to have a look around, I accepted and left our dinghy, looking very small indeed, secured to the bottom of their long ladder. Half an hour later I returned to row myself home. The sight that met my eyes left me speechless. In my absence, somebody had given orders to 'fill that dinghy with stores'!

Having thanked my generous American friends I paddled very carefully back and slung the various boxes and sacks on to our deck before turning in.

Next morning, I was woken by Guy. Both he and the Coxswain had already questioned the crew. Which American stores had been raided and by whom? When I told him my story there was real relief that they were totally clean and could be safely stowed away. 'Thank God,' was Guy's comment. 'I thought we were due another visit from the local police!'

The 'sack' mentioned held half a hundredweight of best American coffee. In France they had not tasted proper coffee for years. It is the story of this bag of coffee that I wish to tell. On our last run to Dieppe, Ronnie (unknown to me) arranged for me to be taken by car to the Abbey at Fécamp by a French-speaking member of the shore staff. So, with the bag of coffee in the back of his vehicle, we set off. As we drove he was telling me about the black market and the fortune my bag of coffee would fetch

Shaken at the apparent prospect - black market deals were certainly not what I had in mind - I made my feelings known. He looked at me and grinned. 'Just wait till we get to the Abbey,' he said.

When we arrived I slung the bag over my shoulder and, feeling somewhat conspicuous in my naval uniform, followed my friend into a large open area rather like a cinema foyer. He approached one of the small glass windows and, speaking fluently in French, asked to see the Abbot. After more than a few drinks and some extended negotiations between my friend and the Abbot, we left with a great selection of bottles of genuine Benedictine. I had not realised that this was the Abbey where the liqueur was made!

We loaded our valuable cargo into the car and set off for Dieppe. True we were slightly behind time but my gallant driver was so pleased with himself and in such good humour that he overdid the speed. As we approached a wide bend, we slid on the mud left by our tanks, turned over, and finished upside down in a ploughed field.

Opening my door, I fell out. Just in time I reached inside and rescued a bottle gurgling its contents on to the roof. It was an almost full bottle; just the neck had been broken. My friend appeared from the other side of the car. Across the field, approaching at a steady plod, a pair of beautiful horses was ploughing. In a flash my friend ran over and in his most eloquent French begged the farmer for help. Within minutes the farmer had his team unshackled and with their help had towed our poor car back on to the road. I was so happy I presented him with the bottle in my hand - his eyes lit up and he took an enormous draught. As we left he could be heard singing the praises of the British Navy to his patient horses. I doubt they ploughed more furrows that afternoon, but I bet he remembers that incident too!

Now my friend saw it was urgent to find a garage with petrol. In his haste he drove past the next one, braked hard and fell out to find the owner. Time passed and he still had not returned. I looked around; a small group of Frenchmen were looking at me and chatting. It would save time if I backed the car closer to the petrol pumps. I moved into the driving seat. The pumps were not visible from where I sat. With my eyes on the group of watching Frenchmen, I slipped the car into reverse and very slowly let out the clutch. Ever so slowly I eased the car backwards towards the pumps. I watched the Frenchmen and they watched me. Suddenly there was the most appalling crash of breaking glass. I stopped the car and got out. In disbelief I was looking at a fallen petrol pump. I had been going so slowly that when the car met the pump there had been no warning bump. It had just very slowly pushed it over! At that exact instant my friend returned with the garage owner. They too looked in disbelief! My attempts at an explanation and apology were cut short by my fluent French-speaking friend. I have never discovered how he persuaded that Frenchman to 'fill us up' rather than 'fill me in', but he did!

We arrived back at the jetty just as the last ropes were being readied to be let go! But the look on Ronnie's and Guy's faces, when they saw the 'cargo' being loaded aboard, told me that all our small problems had been worth while.

CHAPTER SIXTEEN - 718 OPERATIONS 'AQUARIUS'.

Our passage to Aberdeen was broken by stop-overs at Lowestoft and Immingham. Having left on the 29th October, we arrived on the 31st.

Our briefing told us that we were to collect four agents from a 'pin-point' on the Island of Skarvoy near Egersund. To assist us we embarked a Norwegian Quartermaster who knew the Egersund area well.

Early on the morning of the 2nd November we sailed, the now familiar deck cargo of additional petrol lashed in place. During the afternoon this was transferred into our tanks. Although clouds covered the whole sky, the weather was fine; the barometer, however, was dropping. We needed to take avoiding action a couple of times for floating mines, but otherwise a nice steady 17 knots took us to Norway.

As darkness fell, Ronnie reported that visibility was extreme. Above the cloud-cover a full moon was shining; every now and then a break in the clouds would send shafts of silver to light the sea below. The bridge picked up the outline of the Norwegian Coast some 30 miles ahead and Ronnie slowed to 14 knots on two silenced engines. All seemed to be going according to plan.

Then, at around 2200, Ronnie reported down the voice-pipe that they could see an enemy convoy some seven miles away steering in a northerly direction. 718 lay stopped and silent. All eyes on the bridge were now firmly focused on those ships.

An escorting M-class turned towards us. As it became apparent that their course was closing on our position, Ronnie turned about and slowly steamed away, offering as small a silhouette as possible to the enemy. We assumed that the Germans must have picked us up on their radar and were not really surprised when the M-class minesweeper fired star shell in our direction. These shells illuminated the sea between us and the trawlers, which had left their convoy position to investigate in our direction, making their job even harder! Ronnie increased speed just enough to ensure that these trawlers did not close on us. After a little while the armed trawlers were recalled to their stations. Round one to us!

718 now turned back towards our rendezvous and stopped. Once more we lay wallowing in the gentle swell. I heard Ronnie say something to Guy and then the sliding door was pushed aside and he came into the chart-house.

'Where are we now?' he asked. I pointed to our position. 'And where is Stavanger?' I pointed to the chart. We knew that if the Convoy Commander had reported his suspicions to the folk ashore it was possible that a reconnaissance aircraft could be scrambled to take a look. We did a few fancy calculations based on the distance it would need to fly and using a speed of 150 knots. He glanced at his watch and returned to the bridge.

Shortly after this he almost chortled down the voice-pipe that they could hear an aircraft's engines. We stayed stopped. The engines were running to supply power to our guns, but we would not be showing any wash to prying eyes. We could hear voices on the bridge but could not hear the actual conversation. We waited. The door slid aside again and Ronnie, like an excited schoolboy, borrowed my pencil and drew an outline of an aircraft.

'Dornier reconnaissance,' he explained, 'flew right over the top of us at no more than 5 or 600 feet.' I glanced at Matchett and smiled - we found it difficult to share our Captain's enthusiasm! He retired to the bridge to continue his vigil.

We waited a little longer to make sure that the aircraft was not going to return, then, on silenced engines, began our approach once again. With the help of the Norwegian Pilot, Ronnie now made his way across the convoy route and in to the designated 'pin-point'. We were much later than had been planned. In fact the delays had placed us right on the time limit for leaving.

'You can come on the bridge now.' It was Ronnie's voice down the voice-pipe. I slid the door aside and quickly mounted the few steps to the bridge. It was an incredible sight. The bright moon was lighting the shore assisted by Hestnes Light-house which, switched on for the benefit of the convoys, swept every five seconds in a searchlight-style arc over the area. Clearly visible, only a very short distance away, were the four agents, and Guy's boat's crew wasted no time in collecting them. In less than 15 minutes it was all over.

As the boat was recovered, the four agents came to the bridge. Ronnie shook their hands and dispatched them below.

'Steer West,' I said very seriously looking at my Captain. He grinned and turning to the helmsman said,

'Steer West.' Laughing to myself I returned to the chart-house. Once below, I entered the various details necessary in my log and ruled off a more accurate course. We were still feeling our way out to sea when I heard the engines increase speed and felt the boat heel as we made a sudden alteration of course to port. At moments like that you did not ask your Captain for information, you kept an eye on the compass in the chart-house, the rev counter and your watch. Then was the time to run a 'guesstimate plot'! You followed what you could see happening and when all was over you made an inspired guess as to where you had finished up!

In our case this proved not to be necessary, for shortly Ronnie told us that we had run into another convoy, this time south-bound, and he was playing at being an E-boat. As soon as we had run into this convoy he decided that the only course of action open to him was to turn to port and, travelling at top speed, cross the convoy's path, and hope that they would think we were one of the Egersund E-boats. As I have already said, 718 was a very lucky boat and Lady Luck did not desert us on that occasion either.

Once clear of the immediate danger, Ronnie told me to go below and see that the agents were being made comfortable. The steward had made up two berths in Ronnie's cabin and two in the ward-room. When I entered the ward-room they were tucking into a plate of sandwiches. I unlocked the wine cupboard and took out a bottle of Scotch whisky. Half-filling four tumblers with the neat spirit I handed one to each man. They looked at me and smiled broadly. I indicated that I could not join them as I still had work to do and they downed their 'medicine' in one. I explained that two of them were to sleep in the Captain's cabin and a couple, one huge and one small man, left the ward-room.

Having settled the first two I went over to the Captain's cabin to ensure that they too were quite happy. My eyes nearly popped out of my head because the top bunk, level with my eyes, held a small molehill of armaments! On the peak of this pile was lying the tiniest automatic I had ever seen. Without thinking, I reached out and picked it up. The huge Norwegian turned to me.

'You like?' he said, more of a statement than a question. I blushed at my bad manners and mumbled that I could not possibly, and hurriedly replaced the gun. A massive paw thrust the tiny thing into my outstretched hand and, in a voice that would brook no argument, announced 'You like - you have!'

Grasping my tiny weapon I beat a very hasty retreat back to the safety of my chart-house. Matchett told me that the captain had asked if I had returned so I called him up the voice-pipe to report that the agents were suitably comforted and on their way to nod land. I did not dare say a word about my encounter with the Norwegian Bear. In fact it was years before I dared tell anyone about it, but for the rest of my time in the service I always carried that little gun with me. I felt it was a good luck charm - certainly it seemed to work for me.

As mentioned earlier, the barometer had been falling during our trip out and now the weather turned distinctly unpleasant. Because of the various interruptions to our planned programme we were still much too close to Norway for comfort as dawn broke. We knew the Germans were in the habit of flying sea-search patrols at first light and we thus were obliged to put as many miles as we could between us and their air fields. Fortunately the bad weather had also brought a fairly thick cloud-cover, but any aircraft flying just below this would certainly be able to see our wake as we crashed our way through the ever-heightening seas. Ronnie had a dilemma. For the sake of the men and the boat we needed to reduce speed. For safety we needed to maintain speed. As in many such cases, compromise proved a problem. The weather decided that we had to reduce speed and that was that! Apparently, in his unofficial report, Ronnie stated, 'weather next twelve hours, the bottom - or worse!'

It is hard to describe what it is like to be at sea in bad weather in a small boat of this sort. To start with, each man aboard was stuck at his work station, wherever that happened to be. The engine-room staff were stuck in a small space full of hot, extremely noisy, smelly, petrol engines; they would normally be dry and warm but having to hold on for dear life to avoid being thrown around like rag dolls. If they were prone to seasickness, then their fate was even worse, there was no 'out'! The same conditions prevailed for the W/T and radar operators who were cooped up in even more constricted spaces. Instead of the engine-noise (which they only heard second-hand) they had their own noises to contend with and the hot, sickly, electrical smells produced by their own equipment. They too had to suffer any seasickness where they sat. The constant smell of your own vomit in a bucket beside you for hours on end in a bucking tiny cabin was no pleasure either.

On deck everyone would be both extremely cold and soaked to the skin. The constant washing down by both spray and solid green water left the face caked with salt and the eyes sore and red. The gunners, in their turrets, would be so stiff, after hours of sitting in the same cramped position, that they found it hard to stand upright when eventually they were able to be relieved. Their loading numbers and those on the bridge, or elsewhere, who were obliged to spend long hours on their feet, found the constant balancing-act required to stay put gradually wore down even the fittest. At least those on deck, though cold and wet, could be seasick without having to live with it!

I was always eternally thankful that seasickness never bothered me and was always truly sympathetic towards anyone who was so afflicted.

As the morning wore on, it became less and less likely that we would be sighted. I relieved them on the bridge while they took a much-deserved rest. The difficulty of keeping a steady course required so much wheel work by the helmsman that it became necessary to change them at most after half an hour. Remembering that these were extremely fit, strong young men, one can begin to comprehend just how demanding steering a bucking, swaying 130 tons of boat under those conditions really was!

Like all rough passages at sea, ours eventually came to an end. We tied up in Aberdeen almost 36 hours after we had left. 718 had taken a considerable hammering, as had the crew, but we had achieved what we had set out to do, and we all felt extremely proud - not to say relieved!

On the 21st November Ronnie received the following signal from Admiralty: 'It is desired to congratulate you on your execution of Operation Aquarius which appears to be a copy-book example of a faultlessly executed Operation.'

During these rather extended periods of 'watch on, stop on' operations, we were given some sort of pep pills, which we could take to enable us to stay awake. Until 'Aquarius' I had never bothered to take any of these but I did take some during that operation. The effect really was quite dramatic; shortly after taking one, my mind became very clear and the nagging tiredness totally disappeared. However, the down side of taking these things was that afterwards, when the good effects had worn off, a tremendous sleep would ensue! I felt one hundred per cent while we were at sea and afterwards for the first few hours after we berthed. Then it hit me. Fortunately we were not sailed south until the 5th!

I see from my notebook that we had force 5 to 7 south-westerly winds on our passage to North Shields and arrived at Onslow Quay at 1755. We were on our way to Lowestoft the following morning in similar weather by 0800. This passage too was without incident. 1800 that evening saw us snugly secured alongside the north wall.

Lowestoft was Ronnie's old base; it was from here that he had rammed an E-boat while commanding ML.145.in 1943. We spent a couple of days here before sailing once more on the 8th. The wind now had veered to the west and eventually to the north-west and dropped to force 2, so we had a much more peaceful run to Newhaven where we secured at 1705 that evening. Over the past ten days we had steamed almost 2000 miles. But now we were back to the 'trot boat runs'.

Christmas that year found us in Shoreham Dock. Ronnie, as the custom has it, swapped places with the youngest rating aboard, Weaver our radar operator, who wore Ronnie's Lieutenant's uniform with panache. Having had Christmas at home, I returned to look after things with a care-and-maintenance party over the New Year festivities. As soon as we were on our own I mustered the half dozen men on their mess deck and we discussed the routine, which would be run until after the holiday. It turned out that not one of the men left aboard could cook! Since we had inherited a lot of extra rations, apart from parcels from home, I decided that I would take over the cooking duties and they would do the spud-peeling and washing-up afterwards.

The days passed quickly. Guy and I had drawn up a list of jobs that needed to be done over the leave period, and the men set to with a will. We only needed to keep a fire party on board so the non-duty men spent their time ashore. There were no problems and on New Year's Day we celebrated in great fashion - they even complemented the chef! It is the only time I remember, in this country, swimming on New Year's Day!

At 1030 on the 28th we sailed with eight 'passengers' for Dieppe. The party was over! Having arrived at 1330 we collected eleven new 'passengers', and at 1900 returned to Newhaven, arriving at 2215. After this trip I started a new navigator's notebook. I feel sure that I took this book with me when I left 718, but it has disappeared.

HMMTB 718 - Norway

CHAPTER SEVENTEEN - 509/2009 'VICTORY IN EUROPE'

The war in Europe was now entering its final stages - the news was good. At Dartmouth moves were afoot to restructure the 15th Flotilla ready to sail to the Far East to continue its operations out there. At the time, of course, we had no knowledge of such plans. However, one morning I was sent for by my Captain.

'How would you feel about taking over as First Lieutenant?' he asked. Naturally I assumed that Guy was being given his own ship and that I would take over from him.

I replied quite simply, 'Great, sir, when does Guy leave?' To my utter astonishment he said that Guy was not leaving, I was! He then explained that Peter Williams was being promoted to Commander and taking up a shore job at Admiralty. Mike Marshall was being promoted to Lieutenant Commander and taking over as Senior Officer of the Flotilla and that he had recommended me to Mike as his new First Lieutenant. He would be commissioning a new Camper and Nicholson boat being built at Southampton. I thanked him very much and returned to the ward-room in a daze.

While the appointment was a great honour, I had grown so fond of 718 that being taken from her now, after all we had been through together, was like lovers being separated.

Guy was sorting out some paper work when I entered. He glanced up. 'You look like you've just been shot. What did Ronnie want?' I repeated what I had just been told and added in a rather pathetic small voice,

'Trouble is I don't really want to leave 718.'

Without looking up Guy said 'Don't be so wet!' Then, smiling in his most charming manner, added 'Welcome to the No. 1 Club. You'll be the youngest member, but as Senior Officers we'll have to watch ourselves!' He stretched out his hand, and as we were shaking the Quartermaster knocked on the door.

' 'Scuse me, sir, but 502's CO wants a word with you.'

Mike Marshall was a pre-war England rugby forward. He had scored a magnificent try against Scotland at Twickenham and when the war arrived he was commissioned into the RNVR from Oxford University where he had just got his degree. His background and character fitted him perfectly for Coastal Forces and he had had a very successful tour of duty as Captain of MGB.607 at Yarmouth, as the DSC on his chest proclaimed. His performance since joining the DDOD(I) Flotilla was reflected in his current promotion, and also in a bar to his DSC. He was not only much admired by all, but also a hugely popular man with a puckish sense of humour. Though he was as strong as an ox, he was essentially a very gentle man and terrific company. Nevertheless, it was a very nervous young man who knocked on his cabin door.

'You wanted to see me, sir?'

'Sit down,' he said, waving his large hand. 'Ronnie has told you about the new boat building at Campers in Southampton. I'm looking forward to you joining me there. I'm going to stay at the Dolphin Hotel and I want you to meet me there at the bar at 1845.' He gave me the date.

As arranged my taxi dropped me to keep this appointment, and, having checked in to Reception, I made my way to the bar. There was Mike with a pint of bitter at his elbow. As I approached he rose and said,

'What will you have?'

'Half a pint of bitter please, sir,' I replied. He looked down at me and smiled.

'You've just made two mistakes. We're ashore now and my name is Mike. Also, since you are my First Lieutenant, you will drink pints!'

I grinned sheepishly and, taking the mug, drank to the health of our new partnership. Much later that first evening, as we made our separate ways to our rooms, I realised that I was going to have to learn how to cope with 'pints' - it was with the utmost difficulty and concentration that I found my keyhole!

The following morning we took a taxi to the boat yard. Here we were met by Charles Nicholson who showed us around. As soon as I set eyes on 509 I fell in love with her. She had the most beautiful lines, round-bilged like a baby destroyer with a flare, which indicated that she was built for speed. Campers had a worldwide reputation for building superb and expensive yachts. It was soon very evident that their craftsmen had used all their skills in building this small vessel. She was so well finished; no millionaire was ever as proud of his new yacht as we were of that boat. She was a picture.

That first day, Mike and I inspected every inch of our new vessel, my notebook at the ready. By that evening I had a list of items that required action. As the days passed, this list was reduced and other items took their place. Now a very tall young officer joined us, Sub-Lieutenant Snaith our Navigator.

My Coxswain, CPO Mould DSM, was one of the most experienced Coxswains in Coastal Forces and we knew each other well from the time he was Coxswain of 318 at Dartmouth. He was a terrific man and just the right sort to weld our new crew together. The other vital appointment was the Chief Motor Mechanic. CPO Rawlins was a delightful chap, first class at his job, a man who ran his department with the minimum of fuss. In a remarkably short time the new crew became a very happy family.

I had designed a special cabinet to hold bottles and glasses for parties in our beautifully fitted ward-room. This was presented to us at our commissioning party by the yard. The front of this cabinet, when unlocked, opened flat supported by two brass elbows. As it was opened, a light came on inside, lighting up the bottles and glasses reflected in a mirror at the back. It was much admired and lent an extra touch of class to a very classy lady!

Trials completed, we sailed to join the other boats, which were all being re-sited in Aberdeen. The ward-room was right aft in 509 as were the officers' heads. As we steamed at a steady 20 knots up the East Coast, I went aft to relieve myself. Imagine my surprise when, as my feet touched the bottom of the short ladder leading down to the ward-room flat, I saw my towel float past me! I opened the ward-room door to be met by a rush of water. As the ship pitched in the short head sea, the wave rushed back again. I ran back to the bridge and told Mike what I had seen. The engine-room immediately started the pumps, but it soon became apparent that they were not reducing the water level. A line of sailors started to bail out with every bucket we could muster, one chap even using the loo as a means of pumping out the water!

Mike signalled ahead to Immingham that we needed assistance and, as soon as we berthed, a fire-tender put a large hose, like an elephant's trunk, through one of the engine-room portholes. In half an hour we were sucked dry. Only then were we able to discover what had caused the trouble. The pipe which took the waste water from the tiny officers' bath was connected to the outlet by a threaded nut. This should have been wired after being tightened. It had not been wired and had been shaken loose by the vibration, eventually coming off altogether - hence the inflow of water, so simple and yet so potentially devastating!

However, this slight hitch gave us the chance of a couple of days in Immingham to dry out! While in Southampton Mike and I had bought a 1935 Norton 500cc motor-bike, the TT model. This now stood proudly on the jetty (maintained and tuned to perfection by our ex-garage engine-room staff). Mike now phoned Stella, his wife, and warned her to expect us. Leaving the boat in the Navigator's capable hands we set off for Robin Hood Bay in Yorkshire where Stella and her two small daughters were staying. We shared the driving during the journey but, as it became very cold, I had the better of things. I could shelter behind Mike's bulk, but he overhung me. As a result, when we arrived, he was almost frozen solid! But the welcome we received soon thawed us both out. They were such a very happy family. Stella was obviously head-over-heels in love with Mike and he was so gentle as he played with his two small children - the war seemed a million miles away.

After the kids had been tucked up in bed, Mike told Stella that he was planning a party to beat all parties in Aberdeen. We knew that victory was not far away and he told her to get everything ready so that when the time came she and the kids could join us. We left the following morning after a real Yorkshire breakfast and sped back to Immingham. We sailed at once for Aberdeen.

On our arrival we were delighted to meet up with the other boats and looked forward to the arrival of 718 on her way down from Lerwick. Anticipation filled the air. Victory was imminent.

The morning of VE day Mike and I went ashore. We listened to Mr Churchill's speech on a radio in the Hotel's laundry as they had closed the bar, then made our way back to the harbour. Hooters were hooting and sirens were blaring, and as we arrived at the jetty some idiots were firing two-star flares across the harbour and, to our dismay, our Navigator was manoeuvring 2009, with two other boats attached, in the middle of this chaos. As we watched, he nudged his charges very gently back alongside. We took the ropes thrown by the duty watch and very thankfully went aboard. It was then that we learned that a signal had been received shortly after we had left, ordering the minesweepers, which had been moored inside us, to sea immediately.

Poor Navigator! He was the only officer on board the three boats and had no option but to slip all three together to let the minesweepers out. All was well until the fools started to fire those flares. Fortunately none of them had landed aboard!

That evening the party started in earnest. Everyone went wild. A very well known Scottish comedian was staying at the hotel and he was called on to do his stuff as the whisky did the rounds. Mike phoned Stella and the general relief coaxed even the most sober citizens to let their hair down. At last those long blacked-out years were at an end. No more nights of terror. Life could get back to normal once more - and we were all alive! The joy was almost tangible.

MGB 2009 and MTB 718 alongside - Norway

CHAPTER EIGHTEEN- 2009 TRAGEDY STRIKES

Now that the VE day celebrations were over, life returned to normal. 718's crew had been given 72 hours' leave after the battering they had received on their way down from Lerwick. 2002, 2003 and 2009 were carrying out their usual harbour routine tasks. A signal was received from London to the effect that 2002 was to be sailed to Gothenburg on the 11th May with important passengers. Immediately there was great excitement; this would be the first visit to Sweden since the victory and a super party would naturally be planned. Jan Mason, the Captain of 2002, had been called to attend an investiture at Buckingham Palace, as had Ronnie Seddon and Guy Hamilton. (All three had been awarded Distinguished Service Crosses.) Mike Marshall was ordered to take 2002 over for the trip.

The First Lieutenant aboard 2002, 'Dinger' Bell, had damaged his arm during the celebrations and I asked him if I could take his place. 'You must be joking! This is the one big trip I'm not going to miss,' he said. We were all jealous of those lucky enough to be involved and there was much good-natured banter as we slipped their lines and waved them God speed.

The following afternoon I went to the base and asked if they had received any signal from 2002. I knew that Mike would have sent some sort of cryptic message on their arrival. The Duty Officer was unconcerned. 'Probably too busy being entertained,' he said. I was worried. It was not like Mike to fail to report his arrival, but there was no other senior officer I could discuss my worries with - they were all in London. I returned to the base the next morning. There was still no news and I began to 'kick up hell'. I asked for permission to sail 2009 to carry out a search of the likely area. This was refused, but they said that an aircraft search was being flown and they would let me know if anything was found. Still no news.

The waiting was intolerable, but as a mere Sub-Lieutenant there was nothing I could do. As soon as Ronnie arrived by train I met him at the station and told him of my frustration. He immediately went to the base and on the 18th May 718 and 2009 sailed to carry out a search, backed up by further aircraft searches. We saw plenty of floating mines (sinking some by gunfire) but found only floating wreckage. Other wreckage was found ashore near Lista Light. It now became apparent that two survivors had been picked up by a Norwegian ship from a carley float on the 16th May. They were in a very poor state, having been adrift for four days, and were in hospital. Their report told that 2002 had struck a floating mine in the early hours of the 12th. It had exploded under the bridge and only the after end had floated for a very short time after the explosion.

With heavy hearts we returned to Aberdeen; we had all lost so many close friends. In wartime we had all grown accustomed to accepting losses as inevitable; they hurt just the same but were never unexpected. After the recent celebrations and the relief of having come through alive, this disaster was a tremendous shock, remembered by all of us, even today.

In 2009 we had lost our Captain and our Sparker, who had been asked to go along to back up the telegraphist on board. I was distraught and angry that the base staff had refused to allow me to take 2009 to search earlier when I had asked permission to do so. In retrospect, they were probably correct in that they did not know what had happened. We all guessed correctly at the time both the probable cause of the problem and the rough position it would have happened. The search area we eventually patrolled was exactly the area I had asked to be allowed to investigate. Our guess was based on the fact that we knew a Naval force with minesweepers had crossed to Norway on the 11th May. Since we also knew the Germans had mined the Skagerrak very heavily, it was highly likely that floating mines would be a major danger to any vessels sailing in those waters. There is no doubt in my mind that had 2009 been allowed to sail, we could have found the survivors earlier. However, I can also see that 2009 would have been at the same risk as 2002 had been and that the base staff did not feel such a risk to be justified.

One thing our search with 718 proved conclusively, to us at least. When searching sea areas, small craft like ours had a very much better chance of finding wreckage or survivors than even low-flying aircraft. Such a statement would be confirmed by the number of times during the war that survivors reported seeing aircraft that have been searching for them, but have not spotted them. Perhaps today, with modern radar, the situation is different.

My immediate personal problem was to write to both families from 2009 who had lost their men folk. My Sparker I had only known a short time, but Mike's widow was terribly difficult. In the end I sent off a letter but arranged to meet her in London to hand over his personal possessions.

We met in the foyer of a well-known hotel. I led the way to the bar. She was very composed and, although conversation was stunted she put me at ease. Slowly the alcohol did its work and by the time the meal was ending we had, despite the odd tear, covered the ground we both wanted to cover. I saw her back to her station. What else could I say to try and comfort a young widow with two small daughters, whose very gallant husband had been killed after surviving so many battles during the war?

When the train drew in, I helped carry her things into a compartment. Quite suddenly, without thinking, I put my arms round her and gave her a brotherly hug and a kiss. Embarrassed at my own show of emotion I stammered a 'good bye'. With tears streaming down my cheeks I ran back to the safety of the platform. A few moments later the guard blew his whistle and Stella, leaning out of the window, gave me a wave. She was off to her children in Yorkshire. I was to return to my ship in Aberdeen. I was lucky enough to find a seat for my return journey and, aided by a large flask of Scottish whisky, slept like a baby!

My arrival back on board reminded me that whatever else happens in life, however important, the ordinary daily routine which makes ships work, just continues you are there or not! All I had to do was to 'slot back in' as if I had never been away. 2009 was to get a new captain and I wondered who he would be and how he would fit in with the ship's company.

CHAPTER NINETEEN - 2009 LIBERATED NORWAY.

Our new Captain, Lieutenant Bourne, arrived and we sailed for Norway with 718. Our task was to photograph specific parts of the Norwegian coastline for our bosses in London.

One lesson the war had taught the folk in Whitehall was that the quality and quantity of detailed information held about our immediate neighbours' coastlines in Europe was negligible. Obviously it is absolutely vital to have such information available, if one is to be able to plan the sort of operations that we had been carrying out. There had been many occasions during the war when the planners had had to resort to old holiday post cards and snaps, even to visiting Thomas Cook's the travel agency, because they had nothing on file!

The passage over was uneventful apart from avoiding the many floating mines (sinking them by gunfire when possible). It was indeed strange to be sailing without our guns' crews being closed up in broad daylight, and of course wonderful not to be carrying all those jerry cans full of petrol. After our first taste of naval peacetime routine, we arrived in Norway in a relaxed holiday mood.

At that time of year, in those latitudes, the sun hardly sets. We were all very fit young men, but even we found the energy and fitness of the local people quite remarkable. At almost every small village we visited we would be challenged to a football match and between the crews we could field quite a reasonable side, but they always beat us. Then the locals would organise a very energetic dance in the village square starting around 1900; again, between the boats we could produce enough musicians for a small band, which proved extremely popular. These dances would go on until after 0300 the following morning. The locals would then walk or row back to their homes to grab a couple of hours of sleep before returning to wave us goodbye as we sailed at 0900!

Because of the speed of events prior to VE day, the German troops in Norway had been left stranded. I well remember on one occasion I was walking my Norwegian girl back to her farmstead around 0400 when, as we rounded a rocky corner, we came face to face with a fully armed German sentry! My pretty Norwegian companion flounced past, her face a picture of disdain. For my part, as her gallant escort, I was much relieved that he had made no effort to stop us, and was even more relieved when he let me through his position on my return, again without question!

The folk living on the west coast of Norway, like the folk who live on the west coast of our own island, are traditionally seafaring and small farming folk. They have enjoyed personal freedom for centuries and are fiercely patriotic. Unless one has personally experienced occupation by an enemy it is almost impossible to imagine what it was like for these very brave people. To have been occupied by German soldiers was bad enough, but to have the added worry of the Gestapo made life even more unbearable and extremely dangerous. The tremendous relief these people felt, now that they were free, put our own joy into perspective. We might have had to endure the hardships of a country at war with all its heartbreaks, but we had never had to give up our freedom, never had our towns and villages full of enemy soldiers.

Everywhere we went we were given a tremendous welcome. We all felt proud of the work we had done, happy in the secret knowledge that our previous journeys to their lovely country had helped to restore their freedom. However, this was tempered by our embarrassment at being treated as heroes - in our eyes, they were the heroes not us.

Gradually we worked our way south through the leads and arrived at Bergen. Here were gathered thousands of German POWs. Our own army people were at their wits' end to find useful work to keep the less militant prisoners occupied. Soon after our arrival we were approached by a young Major and asked if we could help. I discussed this request with my Coxswain, CPO Mould. His eyes sparkled; in his mind's eye he could see every piece of paintwork washed and repainted, every piece of brass-work polished and glowing like gold.

'I suppose we could use a hundred for a morning, sir.' I glanced at the Major.

'How many crew do you have?' I told the Major we had around thirty. 'In that case I suggest we send you no more than twenty prisoners. The work needs to be seen to be useful and physically hard. Also, please explain to your sailors that the work has to be supervised, and there is to be no fraternisation.' I nodded and the Coxswain nodded too. 'Fine! I'll have them alongside at 0900 tomorrow morning.' As he left, he repeated over his shoulder, 'Supervised and no frat.!'

Promptly at 0900 the next morning a young British soldier, with a rifle slung over his shoulder, called his group of POWs to a halt on the jetty below us. The Coxswain sent our Leading Seaman ashore and he marched them in single file on to our forecastle. There each one was put under the supervision of one of our sailors and set to work.

Having watched them arrive, I had to go ashore, returning around 1200. As I walked up the gangway I was surprised that there was no sign of our working party and sent for the Coxswain. He too had been tied up during the forenoon. Together we inspected the various tasks he had delegated to be done. Every task had been completed impeccably and a lot of extra work had also been done. We made our way on to the seamen's mess-deck. There we found the entire crew and their POWs enjoying mugs of tea and swapping photos of wives and girl friends!

I turned and Mould followed me. Once out of earshot, I looked at Mould and said, 'Looks like the no frat. message has not got through to the crew 'Swain ?' His old weather-beaten face broke into a smile.

'Well, sir, they had worked so well the blokes asked if they could give them a break.' He paused as the truth emerged. 'I had a look at what they'd done and told 'em to take 'em below for 15 minutes. They're only kids most of 'em anyway.'

This was quite true - seeing them all together on the mess-deck it had struck me that they were all about the same age. I did not have the heart to say more about it 'Fine, 'Swain, but for goodness sake get them back on deck and seen to be working

2009 during sea trials in 1947.
She was the first boat in the world to be fitted with gas turbines

before the gallant Major returns.' I turned to go aft and he turned to go forward. No harm had been done.

One of the problems for people in Coastal Forces (the RAF experienced the same problems with their Fighter Stations) was that our war tended to be treated rather like a game of rugby. There were rules which each side would obey and only the odd one would ever think of 'fouling'. No quarter was ever asked by either side and the killing was very real, but hate was a word we found almost impossible to accept. Even at the end of the war, by which time photographs of survivors being murdered, unarmed POWs being shot and the horrific reports about the concentration camps were being printed, it was still hard to find anyone in Coastal Forces who actually hated the enemy.

For our troops in the field it was much easier to understand just what they were fighting; they not only saw these things personally and had experience of the awful atrocities as they fought their way into Europe but could see for themselves and talk to the people they were freeing. For them it was much easier to feel hate. But, the British character being what it is, even the most battle-hardened soldier was often more angry than hating.

Eventually our duties were completed and we returned to Aberdeen. Peacetime routine gave us time to land sports teams daily and I remember we were involved in a local athletics meeting where the locals put our efforts to shame! After the constant activity of wartime we found life routine and dreary. Despite our best efforts our crews were getting bored. So, when news arrived that we were to be sailed to Portsmouth where the boats would be 'paid off', we were disappointed but not surprised.

For the last time we made our way out of the harbour we had come to know so well, down the east coast and through the Straits of Dover. No dangers now, we were just more mariners going about our daily duties. We drove 2009 up to Fareham Creek, and there, along with a host of other much-loved boats, we left her. As I rowed my old Coxswain ashore for the last time, our gear weighing down the dinghy, we paused to take a last look at the boat, which had been our home. 'Never sailed in a more beautiful lady.' Mould had put into words my own feelings exactly.

We were both feeling sore inside having had to say farewell to our crew, men we might never see again. Partings I hated. In fact, I had letters from almost all of my crew after that parting, asking if the crew could be kept together to commission a new boat to go out to the Far East together. I felt immensely proud.

Unfortunately their Lordships had other ideas for all of us.

CHAPTER TWENTY – 'DWELL A PAUSE.'

I had never met the expression 'dwell a pause' before joining the Navy, but it does describe the next brief period of my life. Having 'paid off' 2009 I was sent on indefinite leave. I had assumed that their Lordships would be unable to continue the war without my help for very long! In the event, after six weeks without news from the Admiralty, I was becoming more and more impatient. Even the locals in the pub were saying, 'You still home?' So I decided to go to London and find out for myself what plans were being hatched.

I found my way to the Admiralty and eventually found an officer who was dealing with Officer Appointments. He looked harassed, with a desk full of papers.

'What can I do for you?' He spoke in between answering telephone calls.

'I've been on leave for six weeks and want to get back to sea,' I replied.

'You must be mad. Why don't you leave me in peace and go home?' When he found that I was serious and stubborn he tried a different tack. 'You'll have to go overseas,' he said. I grinned.

'Where to and when can I start?'

'Ever done any mine-sweeping?'

'Good heavens, yes,' I answered, praying that he would not ask me for any further details of my experience. As a safety net I added, 'Mind you it was back in 1941 so I'd need a refresher course to bring me up to date'. He was examining some papers in front of him.

'OK. If I fix for you to attend the next course in a week's time, you'll be able to sail for the Far East on completion.' I thanked him for all his help and left.

My knowledge of mines was limited to the old-fashioned moored mines that we had swept in my days aboard HMS *Night Hawk*. All the ships I had sailed in (not Coastal Forces craft) had been equipped with paravanes to deal with these mines. I knew that they were also protected by miles of wire surrounding their decks to negate their own magnetic fields because we had had to steam over a 'de-gausing' range on occasions. It was not until I attended the minesweeping course that I learned about all the nasty things the German boffins had invented to blow us up!

Ground mines were so named because, unlike the moored variety, they stayed on the ground. In the areas we would be sweeping, they had been parachuted from aircraft. They lay on the bottom, sinister canisters waiting for a ship's magnetic field to activate their switch, then 'bang' as the ship passed innocently overhead!

As the war progressed and ships were fitted with the means of reducing their own magnetic fields by being 'de-gaused' the boffins installed a second means of activating their horrid tin cans. They reasoned that since every ship's propeller makes a noise, why not introduce a mechanism that would blow up when it heard a strong enough noise-signal. Now they had a mine that could blow up a ship even if it was magnetically safe! Perfect! No ship could steam around in total silence! However, because in most convoys the most valuable cargo would be stationed in the centre, a counting device would also be added so that the escorts could pass over safely. In essence this knowledge was the basis of our course. We now understood how the mines worked, what protection ships could be given to lessen the likelihood of their becoming victims and how we were to set about sweeping these rather nasty objects.

I paid my last visit to my local pub, said my good byes to my family and entrained for the Clyde. Passage had been arranged for me in a Woolworth aircraft carrier. Having reported aboard, I met Bill Dalziel. He was a Lieutenant RNVR who had also served in Coastal Forces, the DSC on his chest indicating that his past had included very active service. We immediately became firm friends and used the short time available prior to sailing to sample the local Officers' Club.

The night before sailing, I went to telephone my mother to wish her a final farewell. As I entered the small booth, the 'phone rang. I picked it up and a soft, female, Scottish voice asked if Lieutenant G.... was available. Telling the voice to hold the line I made enquiries around the Club. Bill joined me with the pint of beer he had bought for me.

'Hello,' I resumed our brief conversation. 'Terribly sorry, but apparently he has had to go to sea.' There was a pause and then the voice said,

'Oh dear! I was so looking forward to meeting him and being introduced to your Club.' As Bill listened to this conversation, his eyes twinkled.

'Tell you what, why don't you walk down and I'll meet you. Bring a friend and we'll make up a foursome.' I replaced the 'phone, collected my greatcoat and left. Shortly afterwards the four of us were involved in a great farewell party. I never did get round to 'phoning my mother that night. I gave my mother's number to my girl friend who promised she would do so the following morning for me. I must admit I was more than surprised when my mother told me later that she had received a call from a very nice Scottish girl who had apparently met me!

A few days after sailing I had reason to have a personal chat with the charming RNVR Ship's Doctor. After a rather cursory glance at my most personal possession he turned away and said, 'You've just overworked it, old boy, that's all!' I was extremely relieved.

The voyage took us through the Med to Colombo, a sunshine cruise that under different circumstances would have been great. As it was, in retrospect, we really did not make the most of it. I suppose we were impatient to get back to work and, being passengers along with a host of other service personnel, did not create the right atmosphere. Bill was going out to take command of a minesweeper and I was going out to take over as a First Lieutenant. We had already decided that, if at all possible, we would both be appointed to the same ship.

Colombo is the most beautiful place, situated in the most beautiful island. The Gaul Face Hotel was the most beautiful hotel in Colombo .While awaiting our next 'lift' from Colombo to Singapore, Bill and I spent most of our time at this lovely hotel or on its beach.

It started the first night we were ashore. Looking round the bar that first evening we noticed a group of very pretty WRNS being entertained by some young officers. The band was playing, but since they were not dancing we decided to ask two of the girls to dance. To our delight they accepted, and because we were free during the following daytime, and guessed that their escorts would probably be working, we invited them to join us at the Hotel Beach the following afternoon. When they turned up, Bill and I were entranced; in swimming gear they looked simply stunning! Lady Luck was certainly smiling on us.

Christmas was fast approaching and Bill and I had already planned how and with whom we would be spending it. The days passed without any sign of a ship to take us onwards; we were enjoying a marvellously romantic time in a very romantic island. One evening, after a candle-lit dinner, we were dancing when the band struck up a tango. Bill took his partner firmly by the hand, but I started to lead mine away from the floor.

'Why can't we dance?' pouted my partner. I went slightly red and owned to the fact that I couldn't do the tango. 'Don't be so silly. Come along, it's easy. Hold me and I'll show you.' Feeling nervous, I took her in my arms. At once she took complete control and to my amazement I found myself being swept around the floor. I had never danced with anyone like this before. She was like a shadow, so light on her feet, her lithe young body in perfect harmony with the music. All at once the band reached its crescendo. To my astonishment, she threw herself backwards in a graceful curve drawing my body over hers - then silence. Everything stopped. It was with some difficulty that I regained my equilibrium, but it was the noise of clapping which suddenly brought me back to my senses!

Red-faced and sweating, I walked behind her to our table - as I held back the chair for her to sit down. Bill said, 'Where did you learn to dance like that?' Her reply startled me.

'Oh!' she said in an off-hand manner. 'Before joining the WRNS I worked at the Windmill Theatre.' Small world indeed! Certainly, we thought this Christmas was one we were going to remember for many years, the first peacetime Christmas in wonderful surroundings and with two such charming and beautiful partners. Dreams are made of such stuff, especially when you are free, fit and in your early 20s!

The following morning dawned bright, hardly a cloud in the azure sky. After breakfast we were sent for. 'You are to join the troopship lying in the Bay by 1300,' they said. We could not believe it, not even time to say our goodbyes. With leaden hearts we packed our gear and made our way as ordered.

The ship had been converted for trooping duties and the crush was unbelievable. When Christmas day arrived we were totally depressed. Even the loudspeaker announcement that we would all receive an extra can of beer was greeted by such comments as 'Big deal!' We had so much looked forward to this day. Our own innate decency and our patience had made the anticipation of the Christmas Party especially exciting. In the event, fate decided that that particular romantic interlude would remain platonic!

CHAPTER TWENTY-ONE - BYMS 2006 OPERATIONS.

Ever since mankind traded by sea, Singapore, because of its unique position in south east Asia, has been the hub of the trading wheel whose spokes reach out in all directions. We were looking forward to exploring this most interesting city and were impatient to get ashore. Here East had always met West and the population was the more fascinating for being so very cosmopolitan. The Japanese occupation forces, who had treated civilians and service people with great cruelty, had only recently been overcome and there was still a great feeling of relief ashore.

A taxi took Bill and I to the offices where Captain M/S was housed. A young Staff Officer checked our details against a list in front of him.

'Lieutenant Dalziel, you are to join BYMS 2006. You will be taking over from the present Captain who is returning to UK for demob.' He continued to search his list. 'You,' and he turned towards me, 'Sub-Lieutenant Townend, should not be here!' Bill and I looked at him in utter amazement. What on earth did he mean? 'According to this list of appointments, you should, right now, be sitting in the naval base at Trincomalee. You should never have been sailed to Singapore!'

I felt anger welling up inside me and decided that I had nothing to lose by venting some of it on this Staff Officer. 'With respect, sir,' I began. 'You have just told me that somebody has been stupid enough to sail me all the way from Ceylon to Malaya by mistake. Is that correct?' The Officer shuffled his papers and looked decidedly uncomfortable.

'It seems so,' he said. I pounced.

'Then I'm sure you would agree it would only compound such crass stupidity to try and sail me back again?' He looked at me and I glared straight back into his eyes with a stare that should have told him that I could be a very stubborn customer in situations like this one. He was obviously lost for a solution as he studied his papers. 'Tell you what, sir. Lieutenant Dalziel is taking over 2006. Why don't you alter my appointment to BYMS 2006, additional for training? With all the older COs going home for demob the First Lieutenant in 2006 will soon be promoted to a command and then I can take his place.'

Such a simple solution appealed to the Staff Officer. It would get him off the hook and could be justified to Admiralty. He reached for a pen and altered some of the typed words on his papers. 'That seems to me to be a simple and sensible solution, Sub. OK, I'll have a car take you both down to the jetty where 2006 is lying.' He shook our hands and a young WRN secretary saw us out. Once outside, Bill and I shook with laughter. It had taken us all our time to contain ourselves. What a gift! Owing to some idiot's mistake, we were going to be able to join the same ship. Perhaps fate had not been so unkind after all!

The naval driver dropped us off opposite a trot of very scruffy minesweepers. Leaving our gear on the jetty we boarded the first. There was no sign of a gangway sentry or Quartermaster as we found our way over the deck to the next one. This one turned out to be our new ship and, if possible, was even scruffier than the first. We had never been aboard such a vessel before. A sailor, stripped to the waist, indicated the ward-room.

Bill opened the mosquito-netted door and walked in. I followed. Two officers were sitting talking. As we arrived they both stood up. After the introductions the taller of the two, the First Lieutenant, disappeared to arrange for our gear to be brought on board. The day was hot and the Captain poured us cold drinks. He wished to leave as soon as possible because he was hoping to catch a Trooper due to sail in a couple of days for UK. Bill and he then started the 'take over'. By lunchtime the various papers had been signed, where they were available for signature! The longer the conversations continued, the clearer it became that the ship had been allowed to become a floating wreck!

Permanent stores lists, which it should have been a formality to spot-check before signature, were either missing or were totally wrong; the whole thing was a shambles. Some of the more desirable items, like binoculars, were missing, and it became quite obvious that the only solution would be for the base staff ashore to come on board and do a complete audit. After a couple of telephone calls Bill released the Captain from his responsibilities to enable him to catch his boat home. After he had gone we would have to set the wheels in motion to sort things out!

Even a landlubber would have had no difficulty in noticing that poor old 2006 was in a state of decline far in excess of her years. Naturally, too, the crew's morale was at an all-time low! Everywhere you looked there was either filth or machinery that needed attention. For Bill and I, who had so recently left boats which were kept like peacetime yachts, and whose crews brimmed over with pride and self-confidence, this came as a culture shock. Neither of us had ever seen anything like this before.

Quite shortly, another Captain was demobbed and Bill immediately transferred his First Lieutenant to that ship to take command.

When the base Stores Chief arrived with his Stores Assistant, I took them forward to the 'eyes'. When the first item to be checked, an anchor, was missing, he agreed with me that they had a job on their hands!

Two things needed to be done very quickly. First the ship had got to be docked to replace planking that had been attacked by the dreaded torredo worms, to be cleared of the weed which hung from her hull like a forest, and repainted with anti-fouling. At the same time the whole of the engine-room machinery needed to be overhauled and given a clean bill of health, as did all the associated sweeping gear, winches and all. Every space 'tween decks needed scrubbing out with strong disinfectant prior to being repainted. All the upper deck and superstructure needed scrubbing or chipping before being red-leaded and painted. The work involved was going to be tough and would take time.

Having had a chance to assess the total dismal picture, I spent an evening discussing with Bill how we should proceed. The most worrying thing was the total lack of pride in our crew; things had been allowed to get worse for so long that they had all given up hope. Even the long-suffering and patient Chief Engineer was convinced that spares were quite unobtainable. Bill told him,

'You tell me what you need, and I promise I'll get them for you!'

The Navy has a different routine for ships serving in the tropics. Tropical routine allows the crew to start early in the morning and have the afternoons off. Bill and I decided that until further notice our crew would revert to normal UK routine. As can be imagined, I was not the most popular First Lieutenant afloat when I broke this unwelcome news to the crew. We were in dry dock at the time, but the result of the extra working hours very soon became apparent. Each day saw 2006 take on a new look.

By the time we left that dry dock, Bill was able to report to Captain M/S ashore that 2006 was fully operational for the first time for months. To anyone reading this who has served in a ship, it will come as no surprise to learn that our ship's company was now completely different to the one we had taken over so recently. When we rejoined the flotilla, spotless and gleaming, our sailors were smartly turned out and smiling. Now we reverted to normal tropical routine and our football team was soon beating its opponents. It is a truism that there are no bad crews, only bad officers. 2006 was a good example.

We were now able to join the other operational boats that were currently clearing the approaches to this great port. The job entailed sailing early each morning in line ahead to the 'fishing grounds'. A line of dan buoys would have been laid to show the Senior Officer where the sweeping would begin. He would then dispatch each boat to its allotted station and off we would go.

Sweeping in line abreast, the small flotilla would work its way down the line of dans, switch off their magnetic 'tails' and turn in unison back to the new starting-line, all together switch on their sweeping gear and set off on their return journey. Sweeping of this nature really becomes very dull indeed if one is not blowing up mines. The sort of mines that had been laid here had counting devices built into their firing gear. This meant that each area of channel needed to be swept a further *twelve times* after a mine had been exploded! Thus, by the time the Senior Officer was able to report to Captain M/S that the area was safe for shipping, we were all utterly sick of the sight of that particular piece of sea!

However, sailors need 'sea time' and for our own crew this first trip under new management was just the tonic they needed to finish off the work already started. Obviously chance decides, during a minesweeping operation, which boat will blow up a mine. But the right to paint a mine on one's funnel is a much-prized privilege in such small boats and we now needed that bit of luck to give our crew their prize.

With the main routes to Singapore now open, Captain M/S was able to answer the cries for help from further afield. The Siamese were desperate to open up their river to Bangkok. Already there were the wrecks of merchant ships littering the lower reaches and a few of our flotilla were chosen to solve their problem. We were all terribly excited. Sweeping in such a constrained area as a river was much more interesting

**Typical Bangkok houses beside the river,
only 70 yards from where we were minesweeping**

than being stuck out of sight of land, and to be able to go ashore each night in such an exotic place as Bangkok would be wonderful.

We fell in love with this city as soon as we set foot ashore. Members of the Siamese Navy met us and made us most welcome. Only recently had their hated Japanese occupiers left and we were treated as heroes. They arranged for an officer to accompany me on my sweeping ops. We would sail very early each morning and return each evening. Our efforts were soon rewarded and at last our crew were able to paint their mines on our forward funnel. (We had two funnels, the newer boats only one!)

Shortly after our arrival, we were entertained by a Siamese called Joey who had acquired a car (one of the few then about). He spoke good English and seemed to know everybody and everything. He took us ashore and introduced us to a fabulous restaurant, which had everything under the one roof. This became our headquarters. The meals that they served us were out of this world. A group of us, ten to twelve strong, would go ashore each night at the end of a day's sweeping. A quick shower on our return, a couple of gin and tonics and we were off.

We soon learned from Joey that the best way of organising our evening was to board a local bus 'en masse', wait until all the locals had got off, then negotiate with the driver and his conductor a price to hire them as a private taxi service for the rest of the night! These buses were charcoal-driven and every now and then the conductor would have to get off and refuel with logs. I can still smell the strange fumes they made, along with the gorgeous smells emanating from the restaurants as we passed their doors. The restaurant would put us into a room on our own, a bottle of Siamese whisky on the table and a patient, petite young lady would help us to order our meal. This would normally consist of twelve or more different courses - if Joey was with us probably more, since he would insist we try all sorts of exotic dishes which we would never have dreamed of trying. I still have the menu from this restaurant - it has over 300 items on it!

All too soon we were recalled to Singapore; the job had been begun but, as each monsoon can alter the path of the river, we would need to return again.

Bill was now due for demob and, to my delight, he recommended me to be appointed to take over command. At last I had made it!

My first command – HMBYMS 2006

However, the base staff were still trying to sort out the mess that Bill had taken over. I signalled Admiralty to the effect that I was happy to accept command but that the paper-work would need to be completed by the base staff in due course.

Not long after this we were once again sailed to Bangkok. One of the problems which was beginning to become recognised, even in our Parliament (apparently it had made headlines in the press in UK) was the fact that some of the servicemen being sent home for demob. had contracted VD. A certain lady politician called for all returning servicemen to be made to wear yellow armbands to warn off any females. Understandably the gallant chaps who made up the returning warriors were not exactly tickled pink by such suggestions! Nevertheless, as captains, we needed to give this matter some thought, especially as one quite sensible proposal had been that men so afflicted simply would not be repatriated until they had been cured!

We held a small council of war in one of the ward-rooms. What action did we think we could take to try and make sure that none of our sailors, or officers, should be put at risk? There were several facts of life we reckoned we had to accept: first that any of us (we were all about the same age as our men) could be persuaded, without too much trouble, to accompany the very beautiful young local ladies to bed: secondly that the effect of a couple of drinks and a super meal made such free offers a temptation only a hard-nosed saint could possibly refuse. Having correctly and quite honestly assessed the position what the hell should we do?

After a lot of discussion it was noted that the Merchant Navy ships did not appear to suffer from quite the same trouble. Their crew could take their girl friends back on board. This had several advantages. First it discouraged the sailor from accepting offers of accommodation, which he might otherwise do - there was no point as he could use his own quarters for free! Secondly, and just as important, the sailor who was tempted, but so full of booze that he could not be selective, could rely on the sober sailors of the duty watch to discard unsuitable ladies, thus saving considerably more than his 'face'!

One of the captains present was ex-Merchant Navy. He was also much older than most of us. I felt he had made two very strong points, but what on earth would their Lordships say if they found out that we were entertaining such ideas! Everyone had another very strong drink. In my mind's eye I could see the headlines in the *Daily Mirror* back home. 'Young Naval Officers run amok - Minesweeping Brothels latest thing!' Somehow we needed to come up with an answer.

In the event, the older Captain took his entire crew ashore to a well-known and respected house of 'ill repute'. He arranged with the 'lady' who ran it to parade all her young females in front of his crew. Then and there he made each one pair off with a girl of his choice. Madam assured the Captain that each girl had a medical to prove she was clean each week. The Captain, in his turn, assured Madam that if any of his men caught anything he would come ashore and personally 'cut her throat!' Then, turning to his crew, he told them that if any of them dared to go with any other girl for the whole time they were in Bangkok, he would personally see that they were stopped demob as potentially unclean - was that quite clear?

Each captain tackled this problem in his own way. I am sure that their Lordships, back in London, let alone those sitting in Singapore, would have been horrified had they known what we had arranged, but the facts speak for themselves. We had, from then on, virtually no VD problems. The steps taken may have been a bit extreme, but the results were impressive. It may be a step in the right direction to issue everyone with free 'French letters', but it is not possible to guarantee they will be used. The same rules applied just as stringently to the officers. In effect, the young ladies who made us so welcome became our wives during our visits to Bangkok. In the case of the older Captain, when we sailed for the last time, he suddenly had to turn back. I signalled to find out his trouble. It transpired that when his steward had gone to tidy his cabin he had found the Captain's 'wife' hiding in his wardrobe!

During our second spell in Bangkok some of the officers were invited to the passing-out ball for doctors. It was held in the most beautiful surroundings. The dance-floor was covered by several huge shell-like roofs, supported on pillars and open to the lovely tropical gardens in which they stood. This was one of the annual social events and the dresses of the ladies present were only outshone by the beauty of those wearing them. We were all absolutely entranced. The partners who had been arranged for us all spoke some English and we were having a stupendous time. Tommy, my First Lieutenant, was a very handsome, dark young man, a real lady-killer. I was not therefore surprised when my partner, towards the end of the evening, started to spend more time with him than me. After the penultimate dance I approached Tommy who was having a fit of giggles in a corner.

'Well you might share the joke,' I said in a rather bad-tempered voice. He looked at me and burst out laughing.

'That demure little thing you have been looking after so well all evening,' he spluttered and dissolved once more into helpless giggling. 'When I danced with her just now, because she asked me to, she asked me how old you were.' I was puzzled. 'It's your beard that has her so worried. In her country, only very old men grow beards and yours would indicate you must be ancient indeed.' He again started to giggle. 'She held me tight and whispered, glancing at you, "too old, too old, no good"!' First thing next morning that beard was shaved off!

Our operations were now coming to a successful conclusion. One evening ashore Joey took me on one side. Could I take him back to Singapore with me? I was caught off guard. I explained that as naval ships we could not carry civilian passengers without permission and I did not see Captain M/S taking kindly to such a request from a very junior Lieutenant! He looked miserable. He had been such a good friend to all of us. I put my arm round his shoulders and told him I would have a think about things.

The following day, while we were sweeping, I asked Tommy to come to the bridge. I told him about Joey's request. After a little while we decided that we might be able to sign him on as a ward-room steward; we already carried a 'dhobi wallah' who was a great favourite with the crew. That evening when we returned Joey came aboard. We sat him down in the ward-room and told him about our idea. He was jubilant. Of course he would be very happy to be our steward. When should he join us? I decided the later the better and we tied up dates.

In fairness to Joey, no one could have acted out the part better than he did. We naturally felt very embarrassed, but he took to his new position like a duck to water. On our arrival in Singapore he wanted to present me with a massive silver cigarette-box. When I explained that I could not possibly take anything from him, he was almost tearful. I thanked him for all his help in his native Bangkok and hoped that one day we would meet again.

I was not, I must admit, totally surprised when told one day that he had failed to return from shore-leave the night before. Perhaps I was very wrong not to have informed the Military Police but he had been such a good friend to our whole ship's company I decided that he should be allowed to disappear into that great melting-pot, Singapore. Often since, I've wondered if he became one of the new millionaires; most certainly he was an entrepreneur.

CHAPTER TWENTY-TWO - BYMS 2006 OPERATIONS 'NEXT STOP BURMA'

Lieutenant Whale was the Flotilla Electrical Officer, an RNVR boffin who understood all the things ordinary upper-deck idiots like me did not understand! He had chosen to make his home aboard 2006, which was not only a nice compliment but invaluable.

It meant, for a start, that all our electrics worked. It also meant that if we were able to 'find' items other people did not want, like gas fridges, he was able to convert them. He, Tommy and I became firm friends.

While we were in Bangkok our original Coxswain had been sent back to Singapore for demob. The drafting people had signalled me that they were sending us a replacement. I informed them that I intended to promote one of my able seamen to Leading Seaman and that he would take over as Coxswain.

'Newfy', a Newfoundlander, was immensely strong. He had sailed with his grandfather off the Grand Banks in a schooner, fishing for cod, from the age of six. He was an excellent seaman and the crew all respected (and feared) him. He was the man that I rated up and made our new Coxswain. When I sent for him to tell him, he was speechless.

'But Skipper, I don't know anything about all the papers and things a Coxswain has to do,' he said. I explained that the First Lieutenant would look after that aspect of things and he would gradually learn. He would concentrate on the things he did understand. This appointment worked like a charm. I do not remember ever having any 'defaulters'; Newfy would sort out any problems in the time-honoured sailor's way. If the First Lieutenant's help was needed, this he would seek, otherwise he would administer summary justice of his own; I never had any complaints from my crew either.

By now 2006 was a very efficient and very happy small ship. It was while we were lying in Singapore that we noticed an MFV (Motor Fishing Vessel) lying alongside, being paid off. Some of these vessels had been sailed out to Singapore for harbour duties and the rumour was that they were to be sold. Our enquiries indicated that we needed to apply to the shore staff in writing. If Flag Officer Malaya decided that our reason was valid, he would make the necessary recommendations to Admiralty.

I undertook to make the case to FOM since none of us had any money! Tommy said that his father (a wealthy banker in Brazil) might be prepared to fund him and wrote accordingly. The case I made was based on the fact that there was a shortage of small trading vessels in that part of the world and we felt we would have no trouble in obtaining cargoes. I indicated that we would start by trading locally to build up some capital before gradually trading our way via the Dutch East Indies to Australia. We would use the same techniques to work our way round the Australian coast to New Zealand and then, island-hopping, across the Pacific to Panama. Having spent sufficient time in the USA to build up more capital we would then return to UK.

It was not possible to produce anything more than an outline idea. We thought that the whole trip would take us between two and three years to complete and we felt that the sale of the boat in UK would help to repay any finance still outstanding. To our delight, Flag Officer Malaya forwarded our ideas to Admiralty with a recommendation that we should be allowed to purchase. Apparently he added some comments to the effect that he was very pleased to see that the spirit of adventure was still alive in the younger generation! All we could do now was to wait for the reply from Tommy's father - everything rested on his willingness to help us with the initial purchase money.

Meantime we were being readied to join the other sweepers making up the first division of Force 11 to sweep off Burma. One morning, on my return to the ship, I was surprised to see a 16 ft clinker-built boat lying on the jetty beside our gangway. Tommy told me that they had found it lying in the dockyard looking a bit lost and he and the Coxswain thought it should be given a good home!

By that evening it had been repainted to match our own colour scheme; it swung happily from our ropes, davits out over our stern. It was now fitted with our own patent self-releasing gear and a smart new canvas cover and looked just like a yacht's tender, which of course is what it was to become.

At that time Singapore dockyard had all sorts of things just lying about. We found some brand new, uncrated outboard motors that the Japanese had left behind. Beauties! One of these was soon being 'tested' by our engine-room staff who pronounced it to be in excellent condition. We now had our own motorboat! In peacetime such thieving behaviour would be unthinkable, frowned upon at best. More likely it would call for Court Martial action. In the wake of a world war such as we had just been through and since we were still very much involved with the action, such entrepreneurial activities for no personal gain were accepted - so long as one did not break the 11th commandment.

In due course we sailed in company with the other boats for Penang. When we anchored, the Chief asked the First Lieutenant if he could strip down one of the flexible couplings that connected the main engine to the shaft. He needed to replace some broken parts. Since we had been told that we would be anchored overnight the First Lieutenant agreed. The Chief had just begun to replace these parts when we received new orders, which meant sailing immediately. The Chief was sent for. How long would it take him to connect up his machinery? He replied that it would take too long to replace everything but we would be able to sail on one engine in 20 minutes.

Accordingly I signalled the Senior Officer with the news that I only had one engine so that my maximum cruising speed would be reduced. He replied that he would set the speed of the group accordingly.

We started up our good engine and as our anchor came home I turned 2006 to fall in astern of the next ship. The Senior Officer now passed the course he intended to steer and increased speed to the intended cruising speed; we acted accordingly. Not long after this, we heard a dull thump but thought nothing of it till the Chief arrived on the bridge. He was sweating and obviously far from happy! Turning to the First Lieutenant he said,

'You're not going to believe this, sir.' Tommy looked at him quizzically. 'I told the duty stoker to secure that bloody coupling before we sailed. I had to go to the other end of the engine-room and forgot to check it. He thought that tying it up with a heaving line would do!' The Chief was almost in tears. He repeated, as if he still could not believe it, 'I ask you, sir, a bloody heaving line!'

Tommy went down to the engine-room with the Chief to have a look and report back to me. It appeared that the coupling, having been turned by the pressure of the water on the screw (propeller) had snapped the heaving line and been sucked back against the after engine-room bulkhead with considerable force. This caused the thump we had heard! We did not appear to be making any water through the stern tube and the Chief had managed to stop the shaft from turning. Assuming no other problems arose there seemed no point in my worrying the Senior Officer with any further signals. We would have to await a detailed inspection.

On our arrival at the new anchorage the Senior Officer signalled all ships. He would be hosting a meeting to explain our future programme to all captains. We were to attend at 1030 the following morning. There was no time to be lost. We needed to have a look at our shaft under water now. Stripping off, with a heaving line round my waist, I dived over the side. Because of the very strong tide running, it was necessary to hang a rope over the side with a weight on the end. By holding this rope we could haul ourselves under water and swim under the stern to view the offending shaft.

However, it soon became clear that, without proper diving gear, we would not be able to stay under water long enough to achieve anything. We racked our brains for ideas. That night the engine-room staff adapted a service gas-mask by blanking off the filter and braising a brass connecter on to it, thus enabling compressed air from our air-bottles to be delivered direct to the diver via a long rubber hose. First thing next morning the mask was tested. I climbed over the side and lowered myself down the ladder step by step. Once in the water I put the mask on and hauled myself down the standing rope until I was looking up at the offending shaft. Magically, I could breathe without any trouble, the compressed air bubbling past my cheeks in a steady stream to the surface above. I let go of the rope and swam upwards under our stern. Steadying myself against our hull, I squatted in the A frame holding our drooping starboard shaft.

I wondered whether it would be possible to fix up an arrangement of blocks and tackles in such a way that we could pull the shaft back into its position using our very powerful after winch. Releasing my hold of the A frame I worked my way back to the rope and shot to the surface. The mask was a great success and everyone wanted to have a go. Having explained my ideas to Tommy, I left him and the Coxswain to collect and set up the necessary gear on deck. I would place the strops and connect the gear under water later.

At 1015 I boarded our motorboat. We then collected the other captains and

105

secured alongside the Senior Officer's ship in time for his meeting at 1030. After he had told us his plans, he asked me when my engine would be ready? I could not keep our secret any longer - he had to be told. After I had explained what our problem was (understandably he was pretty upset since he needed every ship) he asked me how soon I would know the outcome of our pulling exercise. I promised to signal him no later than 1600.

The other captains were intrigued by our diving mask and came aboard to have a look. We needed to get cracking quickly, so our motorboat returned them to their ships as soon as we decently could. Once they were gone I undressed and went back over the side. The water was lovely and warm. The tide was still strong and it took a time for us to link up and connect the various pieces of equipment and secure the strops. Eventually all was ready and I surfaced to give Tommy the OK to start to take the weight on the winch. Very slowly he started to heave in and the wire became so taught that it was 'singing'. Tommy held his hand up. I dived again and the gear under water was bar-taut but the shaft had not moved an iota. There was nothing further we could do - we were beaten.

Reluctantly I surfaced and handed the mask to Tommy. Calling the signalman, I headed for the bridge. 'Make to the SO,' I said as he joined me. 'Much regret our efforts unsuccessful. Can sweep OK on one engine only. Very sorry for this inconvenience.'

We had been concentrating so much on our problems we had failed to notice that the sailors in the other ships were fishing over their sterns. A huge cheer drew our attention to the ship anchored next to us. We were just in time to watch as a very active shark was gaffed and lifted over their side! Almost at once, another thrashing shark was hooked by the ship anchored on the other side of us.

Because the 'pulling' idea had not worked, all we needed to do now was to unbuckle all the gear underneath us ready for our new orders. Before the shark incidents I had been badgered by both officers and crew volunteering to dive; now, however, I found I was on my own! I dived under the stern, tucked my legs round the shaft to gain a purchase while I undid shackles and unwound strops. I was as jumpy as a kitten, seeing vague sinister shapes out of the corner of my eye and feeling a tightening in my tummy every time a piece of weed floated past. Where before I had been quite happy to float around on the surface, now I had to make a conscious effort not to be seen to be in a hurry to leave the water. None of us wished to be thought 'chicken'!

It was now obvious that my ship would have to be dry-docked. So it was decided to tow me to Rangoon. The passage was uneventful and we were released where the muddied waters flowing from the mouth of the Rangoon River spread a great brown stain on the Gulf of Martaban - the flotsam, even in those days before the plastic revolution, was incredible in its diversity and dirtiness. The stream ran out of the river at some six knots and, on only one engine, it took us time to make our way up the river to our dry dock. This dock turned out to be not much longer than we were and almost at right-angles to the river. With two engines to manoeuvre the ship into place this would not have been too difficult. However, with only a port engine and the dock on the port side of the river, it made for quite an interesting ship-handling situation. As soon as I put the engine into astern the bows would swing hard to port. The tide in the river meant that I would have to start well upstream of the dock to allow for being carried down by the tide. If my astern order did not have time to take effect I would ram the dock end; if our entrance to the dock was not exact, we would be swept broadside on to the dock wall and damage our port side!

I had a discussion with Tommy and he mustered all available fenders in readiness. I would position my ship across the tide and drift slowly down. At the crucial moment I would put the wheel hard to starboard, ring down 'half ahead' to give us steerage way and to start our bows swinging to starboard. As we entered the dock, swinging to starboard, I would stop engine and go full astern; this should stop the swing to starboard and halt our progress. It would be vital for the heaving-lines to land ashore first time to enable warps to hold us at once. In the event, luck was with me. The plan went without a hitch. It is on those rare occasions that one is able to say conversationally down the voice-pipe to your Coxswain, 'Thank you, 'Swain. Finished with engine,' and leave the bridge while the ropes are still being rove and secured. Your own crew are always the sternest critics of your ship-handling abilities, but when things go right, as they did on this occasion, they 'swank' on your behalf to any onlookers. In this case there were officers from the Burmese RNVR who had come to welcome us, and thanks to Lady Luck, their first impressions were very favourable.

CHAPTER TWENTY-THREE - RANGOON AND BACK

By the time the dockyard staff had got us lined up, moored and a gangway aboard, I had had a quick shower, changed into clean whites and was ready with a large gin and tonic to welcome our Burmese hosts on board. They turned out to be quite the most charming and generous hosts one could have wished for. They explained that, because of the danger from Dacoits, we would all be transported ashore to their base, along with our crew. Only sentries would be left aboard to keep their own sentries company and to patrol the ship at night. Accordingly Tommy and a Burmese RNVR Lieutenant worked out a rota with the Coxswain and soon everyone, sentries apart, was being driven to the RNVR base. Having settled into our very comfortable new quarters we were invited to join them at their bar, and so began a most interesting evening.

At this time much of Rangoon was out of bounds to all troops. However, the Burmese RNVR were able to take us, as their guests, into some of those out of bound areas for an evening meal. The street they took us to that night was extraordinary. Each side of the road was covered by street traders cooking their curries over open charcoal fires on flat iron plates and in local cooking utensils. Archways of flowers, lit by bulbs, gave the whole place added atmosphere and scent in the warm evening air. The mixture of smells was unique; I can still smell it in my memory today.

Our hosts chose a table and we all sat down. Very cold local beer was produced and, as we took in the local scene, our hosts ordered our meal. They asked us if we liked hot curries? Wishing to be polite we naturally said that we did. We talked and shortly each of us was presented with a small saucer containing finely-chopped green and red vegetables in a vinegary sauce. Following our hosts' instructions, I placed some of this mixture into my mouth and started to chew it. The cucumber was crunchy and the vinegar started my juices flowing. Suddenly I realised what the other red and green things were - they were raw chillies! I reached for my beer and our host smiled at me.

'Hot?' he queried. I looked at him in amazement.

'Those are raw chillies!' I spluttered. My colleagues were by now also spluttering with tears running down their cheeks. He started to laugh. Then he explained that to get our palates ready for the curry he had ordered for us, it was necessary to eat this mixture first. I have never had a hotter curry in my life than we had that night. Nor have I enjoyed an evening more than with those kind folk. They were excellent company and we all slept like babies after their hospitality. It is true that the following morning we found the strength of the curry did indeed burn our bottom ends, almost as much as it had our mouths and throats the night before! Certainly I have never seen fit young men sweating so profusely as we had done that night.

The same trucks that had brought us to the base the night before returned us to the dockyard. Tommy and the Coxswain organised the crew as I walked along the dockside to see what was being done to sort out our shaft problem.

What I saw amazed me. In the dock bottom there were gathered two gangs of men split equally, and each man was holding a large rope wound round a battering ram of solid steel, the same circumference as our propeller shaft and probably twenty feet long. A large brass bolt had been fixed over the starboard propeller boss and the two gangs were swinging their battering rams ready to bash that brass bolt. It looked, for all the world, like a film clip of a medieval attack on some castle!

As I watched, the gang leader got them all going in unison, and suddenly there was an enormous clang as metal hit metal. I honestly thought that my poor ship was going to shed all her props and fall sideways into the dock. The shock of those blows sent a shiver right through both her and me! Then, quite suddenly, it was all over. A cheer arose from the dock bottom as they dropped their battering ram. I could see that the offending shaft had sprung back into place, and even more amazing was the fact that my poor ship was still upright on her chocks.

By the time I reached the deck, my long-suffering Chief Engineer appeared. His grin said it all. 'For God's sake, you weren't down in the engine-room while they bashed that thing home, Chief, were you?'

He just looked at me in pity. 'Course I was, sir. Wouldn't want them to bust anything would I?' The noise down there in that small space must have been like the sound of a hand-grenade going off, but then no upper-deck officer can ever hope to understand engineers can they?

We used the time in dock to check the various under-water fittings, paint whatever we could while we had the chance to do so, and to 'do' Rangoon while we could be shown the sights by people who lived there. Soon we were once more afloat with both engines fully operational.

It was time now to return to our flotilla as fast as we could, but not before we had thrown a thank-you party for the Burmese RNVR who had proved to be such delightful hosts.

On our return trip I decided it would be a good opportunity to practise 'exercise abandon ship'. Accordingly, one lovely morning, as we creamed our way across a glassy, deep-blue sea, I sent for Tommy and told him my intentions. Forewarned, he pressed the buzzer and we watched as boats and rafts were hurriedly lowered, lifebelts were quickly donned and the crew jumped into the warm water. The time it took was much longer than we would have liked but it was the first time it had been practised. We sent for the Coxswain and told him that we would try the exercise again since it had taken far too long for the crew to react. The message was passed to the crew.

That afternoon we practised it again and this time things really happened much more quickly. I was slightly puzzled, watching from the wings of the bridge, to see the Coxswain jump over the side and disappear for a considerable time. On questioning him afterwards it transpired that he could not swim! He felt he had to set an example, he said!

We were welcomed back to our minesweeping duties, which involved helping to clear Burmese ports like such as Tavoy and Mergui and their sea-lines working south.

On one famous occasion ops were stopped to allow Lord Louis Mountbatten to inspect and address us. There had been complaints from home that the demobilisation of men serving in Burma was being delayed - this was done in service number order. The term 'forgotten Army (or Navy)' was being used by the home press.

True to naval tradition, paint pots, spit and polish were at once produced. A guard was mustered with its blanco, white belts, webbing and rifles. A hastily-built dais (covered with the white ensign) was erected on the jetty. The officers and crews paraded as they would have done in any naval port in UK. Almost to the minute a jeep carrying Lord Louis arrived. Typical of the man, he took in the scene at a glance and saw the trouble these sailors (almost to a man reservists) had taken to welcome him. He inspected the guard and complimented them on their turn out. He then turned to our Senior Officer.

'It's too hot to keep your men standing waiting for inspection - if you don't mind I'd like to talk to them.' Our Senior Officer called everyone to attention and delivered the Admiral's message, then stood the parade at ease. Meanwhile the Admiral had mounted the dais. He made a movement with his arms and asked everyone to 'Gather round so you can hear me without my having to shout. Some of you may have very low demobilisation numbers and are rightly wondering why you have not been sent home already. Two things I want you to know. Firstly the minesweeping job you are doing is vital for Burmese trade; secondly that I am personally trying, through my staff, to ensure that suitable reliefs can be arranged as soon as possible to ensure your return to UK and your families. I hope you will do two things for me. First, trust me in my promise and secondly, recognise the importance of the job the Navy is committed to do through you for the Burmese Government. Finally,' and he turned to our Senior Officer, 'I can see from here the trouble all your ships have taken to prepare for my visit. I'm impressed and only wish I could repay that hard work with a visit to each ship. Unfortunately my schedule does not allow me to do so. Thank you for your minesweeping work, which is so important, and congratulations on your turn-out today.' He turned to the Senior Officer, 'Please carry on,' he said.

Our Senior Officer shouted to the assembled crowd of officers and men, 'Three cheers for Lord Louis'. The jetty resounded to three honest and hearty cheers. I am sure that I was not alone in listening to Lord Louis for the first time. The fact that he had taken the trouble to visit such a tiny band of sailors on the Burma coast really made an impression on all of us. Even today, fifty years after the event, I can still feel the magic of his personality and how it affected both my crew and myself. Nelson and other great leaders had just such qualities. So often today, young historians seek to debunk such men. They should have been there at the time to really understand how men felt then.

Our sweeping ops continued and in due time my demobilisation relief arrived. I was determined to drive my small ship down river myself for the last time to meet

110

the larger vessel that would collect us for passage home.

However, small ship tradition demanded that the Captain attend on Coxswain and petty officers mess to say a personal goodbye, before attending on my mess-deck to do the same to my long-suffering sailors. Thus my day began by entertaining all my fellow officers in our ward-room. Since it was going to be my ship that took all the demob officers and men to the collecting vessel, inevitably there was an air of excitement.

Soon after 'up spirits' had been piped (in those days rum was issued) I was invited by my Coxswain to his mess to share his tot. I had chosen him to be Coxswain, my right-hand man after my First Lieutenant. So leaving my No.1 to entertain our guests I went forward. Neat naval rum is a very strong spirit and, on top of chilled gin and tonic, fairly lethal. Having done my duty in the POs' mess I was conducted to our mess-deck where I was treated by the mess-deck comedian to a lovely mixture of abuse and genuine male 'goodbye'. Obliged again to share so-called 'sippers', a half-pint of rum-and-water given up by each of my crew and having to be drunk in a swallow or three, I was then required to make a speech. By this time I was feeling terribly sentimental about my first command and my wonderful crew. To my horror, I found they had produced another glass of rum, so, instead of being able to say my goodbyes as I had hoped, I now had to extend my farewells. It was shortly after I had managed to escape from my mess-deck and return to the ward-room that the Burmese Pilot arrived on board.

On his arrival I shook hands with all our guests in the ward-room and we said our farewells. I chatted with the Pilot and received the various automatic, prior-to-sailing reports from engineer and First Lieutenant. I accompanied the Pilot to the bridge. I knew, from my Coastal Forces days, that every officer and man was watching me. I remember telling my First Lieutenant in what I hoped were clear statements. 'Let go forward, let go aft, fenders forward. Slow ahead port (down the voice-pipe to the Coxswain), stop port.' The stern began to leave the jetty. 'Half astern starboard. Let go fore-spring No 1.'

I heard him say, 'In fenders and get fallen in.' I stopped the starboard engine and continued to swing my small ship around with her engines to face her down river. We left with waves and cheers from our colleagues and I turned to the Pilot and said,

'She is all yours now, sir. My Navigator will assist you - I need to go below for a while.' It was with great difficulty that I managed to negotiate the various ladders from the bridge to the upper deck and indeed the deck to my cabin. My bunk - at last a refuge!

Much later that day, to be exact that evening, my Navigator shook me to explain that we had reached the entrance to the river and made light-contact with the collecting vessel. I awoke with quite the worst hangover I have ever experienced. The odd thing was that I immediately shook off the effects and at once went to my bridge and took control as if I had been there all the time. Even more odd, everyone else also accepted this fact.

We anchored, and a boat from the collecting ship arrived alongside with the replacements and their gear. It took a little time for me to be able to hand over my ship to the new CO since he was obliged to sign for everything aboard on Admiralty forms, and the four-stripe Captain aboard the collecting ship became impatient and signalled his impatience accordingly. The rum must still have been running in my veins, for I replied to the Senior Officer's signal to the effect that I was handing over my ship in accordance with King's Regulations and Admiralty Instructions. He had no reply. Until I repaired on board his ship I had no idea that, through his binoculars, he could see us drinking gin and tonics in our ward-room.

We were carried to Ceylon and left to be collected by another naval vessel sailing via the Suez Canal and the Med, home to UK.

Explosion of a mine at sea – distance 300 yards – showing the wash from the magnetic sweeping 'tail'

CHAPTER TWENTY-FOUR - RETURN TO UK
DEMOB AND A FALSE START

Our return to UK involved being passengers in two quite different types of ship.

The first was an ocean-going floating dry-dock, a most interesting vessel with a small merchant ship and its own small tug secured in her womb. She took us first to Calcutta, where because of mob violence we had to stay aboard, then dropped us off at Trincomalee in Ceylon (as it was then called). Here we trans-shipped to a Landing Ship Tank (LST). This too was in its way fascinating.

Being passengers, our main problem was one of boredom, and I have to admit that we spent most of the time in the ward-room bar. Laboriously she pushed her way westward across the Indian Ocean, up the Red Sea, through the Suez Canal into the Med. The call at Gibraltar was fun, as I had never been there before, but soon we were buffeting our way through green seas in the Bay of Biscay, making our way to the English Channel and home.

My homecoming began with unpacking all the little presents I had collected on my travels. Like sailors from the past, I felt a real explorer as I explained the finer details of what they were. Suddenly my mother looked up and smiled broadly. She had opened what she had taken to be a box of silk stockings. However, as a joke, my Navigator had packed a box of a gross of naval issue French letters!

'You must be expecting a good leave,' she said as she slid the box out of view.

Having duly reported to Admiralty, I returned in my demob suit and riding mackintosh. Job-hunting now had to be the priority. I decided to apply for a government grant to attend University to study medicine; I wanted to be either a GP or a vet.

While waiting for a response, I received a cryptic telegram. 'AM OFF TO THE PACIFIC. WILL YOU COME?' It was signed by my Navigator. The telegraph boy who had brought the message was waiting. He handed me a pad for my reply. 'YES' I printed, 'WHEN?' and signed it 'JOHN'. He grinned and pedalled his bike back to the village Post Office. The news would be gossip in the pub tonight.

Not long afterwards, I received an invitation to call on my Navigator's father at his engineering works outside London. It appeared that he wanted to set up a trading station in the Pacific Islands. With this in mind he was seeking a suitable yacht to sail out there. His son had volunteered my services to skipper the yacht and set up the expedition. After the excitement of my wartime life, civvy street was already beginning to pall and this seemed too good an opportunity to miss. So I set to making contacts and seeking information. I obtained the various large-scale charts needed to plan such a trip and was making good progress when I was told to go to Paddington Station to meet the Boss. He had bought a yacht at Cork in Eire and we were to go over to collect it.

As I made my way on to the platform at Paddington I nearly fell over Newfy, the Coxswain from my minesweeper. We shook hands and embraced.

'What on earth are you doing here?' I enquired. It appeared that he too had been kidnapped by our Navigator and was going to Cork to collect the same yacht.

The trip over in the old *Innisfallen* cattle-ferry was unforgettable. A good strong south-westerly threw the poor old ship every which way. The passengers, huddled in the tiny bar, were hurled back and forth. It was cold. The air was strong with stale stout, and a mixture of smoke and sick. The cries of babies mingled with the noise of the wind and beaten spray. The moaning of the old ship's rusty plates complemented the moans of the sea-sick passengers praying for death. Newfy and I wedged ourselves into a corner, slept fitfully and swapped cigarettes. At first light the old ship turned into the shelter of Cork Harbour; we went on deck and gazed at our first view of Ireland. With the new day dawning and the sun breaking through, we were enchanted.

The warmth of the welcome from our host cemented our first impressions. This was a magical country with magical people. Our host drove us to Crosshaven where the yacht was moored.

Colleen is Irish for a girl. As the car drew up opposite the yacht, I thought how aptly she had been named. Fifty-four foot over all, she was sleek, tall-masted and beautiful. The owner rowed us out, and Newfy and I decided to move aboard at once; the new owner decided to book himself into the local hotel.

Eire had, of course, been neutral during the war, though many fine Irishmen had come across and joined our forces. The shops ashore were very friendly to Newfy and I and allowed us to purchase whatever food we needed without ration cards. I learned later on that the Irish method of dealing with ration cards and coupons in the country areas was quite simple. Everyone gave the shops all their coupons and the shops balanced their books in their own way. This common-sense method did away with any black market.

That weekend the old owner invited his cronies and their wives to join *Colleen* for one of the Cobh Club races. The day dawned bright and I spent the forenoon ferrying the folk aboard. The stores they brought with them would have fed an army for a week and the amount of liquor was staggering. Around noon we set sail and meandered our way towards the start line. The sun shone, the party was in full swing by the time the race started and it was not too long before the old owner announced that it was far too nice a day to waste it racing. 'We'll away down to Kinsale,' he said.

The new owner asked sensible questions like, 'How about people's cars and their families left ashore?' In amazement the old owner replied,

'They can see us going west sure, can't they?' And off we sped to Kinsale. This was the life!

After several trips of this nature to enable the new owner to see how the ship behaved and handled, the deal was sealed. We had a final farewell party in the local Yacht Club, our first meeting with Gaelic coffee and the ritual of singing for your supper. The ex-owner's brother, an accountant in Cork, and a charming Catholic priest were to accompany us as crew to Penzance.

Just after three o'clock on Tuesday afternoon, the 10th of June, we slipped our moorings and waved to the folk assembled ashore. The old engine pushed *Colleen* into the light south-easterly winds and by half past six we were four miles west of Ballycotton Light. By eight that evening we had set a south-easterly course to take us to Land's End.

It had been decided that Newfy and I would take one watch and the two Irishmen would take the other - the Boss, as navigator and captain, would stand no watches. That night and the following day *Colleen 's* crew fell into their routine easily. The log I kept at the time shows we needed to pump the bilges at eight that evening, and it noted that the weather was freshening from the SSE. Although it was logged as blowing freshly all night, it was not until the forenoon of the 12th that we suffered any real upsets. By 11o'clock the wind was gusting force 7 to 8 from the SSE. When we tried to reef the mainsail, the throat-block jammed solid. Having tried everything else without success, Newfy volunteered to go aloft. He hauled himself up the rigging, grabbed the topping lift and, by jumping up and down on the offending spar, we managed to shift the choked block and lower the mainsail; the sudden movement left Newfy suspended in mid air, hanging to the topping lift and being blown like a flag. A lesser sailor would have been lost overboard, but when he eventually arrived back on deck and I embraced him in relief, he just grinned and said it reminded him of his days off the Grand Banks with his grandfather. The log merely notes that we were virtually lying hove to at midday when we tried to talk to a passing merchantman by flag-signal without response.

The uncomfortable motion caused by the ESEasterly winds, the constant battering and very wet conditions, caused the Boss to take to his bunk. Below was a shambles; anything which had not been lashed down, or properly stowed, was rolling around on the deck. The constant washing down had found leaks never suspected during the quiet cruising trials. Although both Irishmen suffered sea-sickness they never failed to keep their watch.

Trying to produce even a boiled kettle on the old primus stove proved a major headache. So it was a real relief when, around eight that evening, the winds eased and we were able to get the primus to work once more. However, my major concern had been the two estimated positions that the Boss had noted in the log.

According to his note in the log at 0400 that morning he had estimated our position as being 52 degrees 25' North and 6 degrees 50' West, which put us some-where ashore in Waterford! At 1700 he had left his bunk to note that his new estimated position was 49 degrees 40' North and 6 degrees West. Having been relieved from my watch, I decided to rework our passage on the chart from my own log entries, and thus obtain my own estimated dead reckoning position. Armed with this 'guesstimate' position'' I shook the Boss in his bunk. When I told him what I had done, I suggested he allow me to take over until he felt better. He agreed so I went back on deck and explained to the rest of the crew the action I had taken.

They all accepted the situation and we set a new course to close the North Cornish coast. The wind now dropped away and we wallowed our way onwards through the evening. As I turned the page of the log to start a new day I suddenly realised it was the day sailors have always hated - Friday 13th. However, the morning watch started well when we raised the 'loom' of Pendeen light only to run into reduced visibility, but it did at least mean that my dead reckoning had not been too far out. The mainsail ripped shortly after 1000 but we spoke to a French fishing boat, which confirmed our position, and by 1300 the mended mainsail was hoisted again. By 1545 Pendeen Point was one and a half miles abeam to port and we were sailing happily down the Cornish Coast. The sun shone from a blue sky with cotton wool clouds and for the first time since we had left Crosshaven everyone was in good spirits. Friday 13th was turning out to be a better day after all. Even a tanker, which looked as if it was going to run us down that evening off Land's End, had missed us.

The ESE steady breeze which had blown all day began to increase, and by 2100 it was gusting to force 6. Once again we battened down the hatches and prepared for a rough night. By midnight the wind had veered to SSE and was increasing all the time. As so many sailors in the past have discovered, the south coast of Cornwall, with winds blowing one on to the lee shore, is a most uncomfortable place to be under those conditions. We were about to find out just how uncomfortable and dangerous.

The previous days of almost constant seasickness, bilge-pumping, lack of sleep and proper food, had made the crew tired. The new gale with its stinging wet spray and green water bucketing over them was the last straw. Suddenly to find themselves being driven on to a lee shore, without the ability to sail away from it, numbed their minds. The engine, a 1918 ambulance engine, which had been converted and installed pre-war, was impossible to start. I decided it was time that the Boss took the tiller.

I shook him in his bunk. Once he had woken I explained the position and told him that it was his job to man the tiller during what might well be a rather short morning watch. All the crew were mustered on deck. He looked ghastly and I felt for him, but once attached to the tiller, washed by the cold sea-water flung over him, he came to and steered. The crew trimmed the sails and waited - there was nothing else we could do.

It is hard to describe what was going through the minds of those silent sailors. Having discussed it after the event, the deepest impression seems to have been the noise and fierce movement, the noise of the raging wind in the rigging, the snapping sails, the noise of the crashing waves as they rushed at us, broke over us, and rushed onwards. There was the noise of the flying spray and, away to port, the constant deep rumble of those same waves as they thumped into the massive Cornish cliffs, sending great white pillars of water to be blown on inland. Our bodies, aching from the effort of holding on and bruised from the battering, slithered hither and thither with each new swell. *Colleen* pranced about like a wild thing, throwing anything not firmly lashed overboard.

I can remember going below to check something and silently saying a prayer. I also remember wondering whether it would be better, when the time came to jump, to keep my trousers on to protect my legs from the barnacle-infested rocks or to remove them to make it easier to swim. It was interesting to learn afterwards that everyone admitted they had prayed that night.

Without any warning, suddenly, the gale ceased. The wind veered, allowing *Colleen* to steer out to sea away from those fearful black cliffs. The change was so sudden, unexplained and dramatic, that for a couple of minutes no one on board could take it in. Then Newfy and I simply ran up the rigging shouting like madmen. The two Irishmen, on deck, did a jig and the gaunt figure of the Boss, previously slumped over the tiller, sat up.

Never before or since, in wartime or in peacetime, have I ever experienced anything like that moment. Cynics will claim there was a quite simple meteorological reason for our delivery but for those five tired sailors it was, and will remain, a miracle.

Slowly *Colleen* crashed her way seawards. Now the noise and green water surging past in the darkness was exciting rather than fearful. We had been allowed to survive. I went below and tried again to light the primus. Everywhere water slopped back and forth, but by wedging myself solid I was able to boil a kettle and take hot drinks to those still on deck. First light had never looked so good and, despite the weather, good-natured banter relieved our pent up feelings.

The log shows it took another four hours for the wind to reduce in strength as it veered to the south, worked its way to SW and by 1500 was a gentle force three. Eventually, battered but safe, we anchored in Falmouth at 2100, launched the dinghy and pulled ashore to clear Customs and pass the word we had arrived. A note states that I produced boiled spuds and stew for the first proper meal we had had for days. Everyone turned in with full tummies and thankful hearts - and slept.

The following day dawned bright. Everything was taken on deck to dry out and the job of sorting out below decks began. I found the reason for the blocked toilet was a signal-flag; the lesson to be learned, never stow such things where they can cause such upsets. There were many lessons to be learned from that short trip, to the great benefit of my future seafaring.

That night the Boss invited us all ashore for a meal at the Royal Hotel; the comment in the log was 'pleasant but rather lacking in substance.' We had forgotten that rationing in England was rather more rigid than in Eire!

My folk drove down from their home near Kingsbridge and collected the two Irishmen. Having heard how we had been feted in Ireland, they entertained them royally before seeing them off to Cork. The Boss left Newfy and I a long list of jobs he wanted done, to which we added more of a technical nature after a full inspection of the gear. He entrained for London saying he would return when the boat was ready to sail to Dover.

Over the next weeks Newfy and I worked from morn to dusk to put right the damage done by our passage and to renew various fixed and running rigging which, while satisfactory for a quiet sail, was certainly not satisfactory for more demanding weather.

In the event the Boss did not return and we sailed *Colleen* to Dover, with following winds and no problems, on our own. No problems, that is, until we found it impossible to start the old engine to enter Dover harbour. The wind was blowing force 8 from the south-west. With staysail and mizzen we entered the harbour. After circling to find a suitable anchorage we found a spot in the lee of the harbour wall and anchored, only to find ourselves dragging. Without an engine this was worrying. The log reading shows we had covered 266.5 miles during the 54 hours we had been on passage, an average speed of almost 5 knots, despite various sails having split and much of the passage under just staysails and mizzen.

Once the gale subsided we went alongside and I telephoned the Boss at his London Office to let him know we had arrived; a couple of days later he came aboard.

Colleen

My Father had asked me at Falmouth about my 'conditions of employment' agreement with the Boss. Since I was not interested in the monetary situation, (I was carried away with the idea of the coming exciting expedition and its logistics) it had never even occurred to me to enquire about this aspect of things. I just took it for granted that the Boss would treat me right. It came as a shock, therefore, when Newfy raised the subject quite separately. This conversation had really made me think, and he was adamant that I should tackle the Boss when we met in Dover. It appeared that the Boss had employed Newfy, after negotiation, on much more favourable terms than he was offering me, the Skipper and organiser of the whole expedition.

Thus, when the Boss arrived and we were sitting over a mug of tea in the after cabin, having gone through the work we had carried out in Falmouth and described our passage, I raised the subject of my remuneration. Immediately he flew into a rage, furious that Newfy and I should have discussed such things. I felt very uncomfortable but pointed out, realistically, that if he was inclined to treat me like this when we were in UK, how was he going to treat me when I was the other side of the world? He was furious and I offered my resignation then and there.

It was a tremendous disappointment to have to leave a project on which I had set my heart, and Newfy, whom I felt I had let down along with the Boss's son, my old Navigator who had suggested it in the first place. However, there was now no turning back. It was with great sorrow that Newfy and I parted. *Colleen* sailed on to Burnham but I don't believe she ever made the Pacific Islands.

Because of the priority for me to obtain a job I lost contact almost at once with both Newfy and my old Navigator. I have often wondered what happened to them and to *Colleen*.

CHAPTER TWENTY-FIVE - BACK TO SCHOOL.

The sudden collapse of my plans to sail out to the Pacific was a great blow. Such opportunities do not occur very often in life. However, it was now vital to obtain an ordinary job and settle down to the challenge civvy street had to offer.

My father suggested I attend on that long established schoolmasters' agency, Gabbatas Tring, in London with a view to obtaining a job in a Prep School. This I did, and the following week I received a host of details from Prep Schools all over the country that were looking for young masters. Dad and I were busily sorting these out when, out of the blue, I received a telephone call from Mike Marshall's old Headmaster in Yorkshire. After the briefest of conversations, the voice said -

'If you were good enough for Mike to appoint you as his First Lieutenant, you'll do me. Report up here the day before term starts so I can introduce you to the other staff'.

'Yes, sir', was all I could think to say.

My father had been teaching since leaving the RAF, just after the First World War - it seemed that I was doomed to follow in his footsteps. However, my application for a University place was still being considered and this seemed to me to be the best way to try and get back into the learning groove.

Looking back today, fifty years on, I am amazed at the confidence I must have had to take on such a job. I had left school in a hurry to join in the war. I had never really done any work, so my examination results were passable - just. It is true I was an above-average athlete and games player but I had no training in teaching at all. This was the 'deep end' indeed.

My nervousness at the first meeting with the Headmaster was, if possible, increased further when I met the other members of staff. They were all so self-assured and assumed that I knew what to do and where to go. That first day in front of all those boys - wearing a black gown along with the other masters - I felt totally lacking and as I tried to sleep that first night I wondered just what I had let myself in for.

The School produced a small school diary giving important dates, like school rugby fixtures and the names and qualifications of all the staff. Because I had been a last-minute selection my name was omitted. As well as myself, there were three other masters who had served in the forces, one in the Army, one (a contemporary of Mike Marshall's) in Bomber Command and one in the Navy. They were all older than I was and all qualified to do their jobs.

My home was to be a small bedroom at Catteral Hall, the Prep School. This doubled as a study where I would prepare my lessons and do my corrections. I was to teach English in the Prep School and to the bottom form of the Public School, Giggleswick. I was also to teach Geography, which I loved, and History, which I hated. I was to help the Head of the Prep School with the soccer - since he had never played soccer. I had represented Lancing (and been coached by a professional from Brighton and Hove Albion) so I knew that here I did have something to offer. In fact that term was the first time Catteral Hall had ever beaten their arch-enemy, and I felt so proud. I worked very hard to try and ensure the Headmaster did not regret his confidence in my ability, which, I felt, would have let Mike down. His widow had a small bungalow on the outskirts of the village and when Mike's parents came over to see their grandchildren they took me out in their car, which was marvellous. My only transport was an old 'sit-up-and-beg' push bike - the faithful old Norton was still at home in Devonshire.

I had already arranged to spend the next term at my old Prep School in Hampshire. A week or so before we were due to break up I was summoned to the Headmaster's study. In front of him I always felt like a small boy. He was a big man in every way and I knew about his achievements at that school. He was truly a very remarkable man and I held him in the highest regard. He motioned me to a chair in front of his desk, lit his pipe and looked me squarely in the eyes.

'I've been watching you very carefully during this term, Townend,' he said. There was a long pause during which my mind told me that someone must have reported seeing me peddling my old-fashioned bike back from the bungalow through the village during the early hours of the mornings. I sat very still, wondering what he would have to say about such behaviour.

'Yes' he pulled on his pipe and let out a cloud of smoke, 'you've worked hard and appear to be learning quickly. I waited for the blast. Next term, he continued, you are going back to your old Prep School - correct?'

I nodded and said, 'Yes, sir, that has been arranged'.

'The following term you will return here. You will be taking over Shute House as House Master.' I gasped in amazement and was naive enough to blurt out, -

'I couldn't do that, sir.'

He clenched his pipe between his teeth and glared at me - 'I'm not asking you Townend, I'm telling you. He lent back in his chair and smiled. Currently we pay you £300 per annum - correct?'

'Yes, sir.'

'You'll be pleased to know this will be increased to £350.'

'Thank you, sir.' He put a match to his pipe; the interview was over. I got up and made for the door. As I turned the polished brass handle he stood up. -

'As a House Master you'll have to live in,' he said quietly.

'Naturally,' I replied.

'We charge you £50 for living in'. As I closed the door my mental arithmetic was clicking round. £350 minus £50 equals £300 - he had got himself a House Master for the same price as a Prep School Master!

As arranged, the following term I returned to my old Prep School at Stubbington in Hampshire. This School had a remarkable record for producing Admirals, Generals and Air Force Senior Officers - their photographs covered the walls of the hall way where stood the famous grandfather clock. If boys misbehaved

121

in a minor way, they were sent to stand in front of that clock for a set time - quarter of an hour for a minor offence, half an hour for a worse one or an hour or more if really a nuisance. Should the Headmaster pass that way, which he did with regularity, he would, of course, stop and enquire of the culprit why he was standing there wasting time. If he had spoken to the boy previously in front of the clock, chances were that the boy would be invited to follow the Head to his study. The door would be closed and after a suitable chat about wasting time, the boy would receive the stick and be sent back to his classroom to explain, in front of his class, his interview with the Head. I have always felt that this form of punishment should be more widely used. It had the publicity of the stocks, the utter boredom of standing watching the seconds tick away - how slowly those hands moved - and it gave one time to consider the futility of being bolshie. Worst of all was the fear of the Head's measured tread - recognised from afar and remembered to this day.

'Follow me Townend, this is the second time today - isn't it?'

'Yes, sir.

A photo of my schoolboy hero, Captain Robert Falcon Scott RN, (of Antarctic fame) hung in that hallway. As I once more walked across it I remembered his son, Sir Peter Scott, who had been Senior Officer of the steam gunboats at Newhaven when I was in 602. So much had happened since I had stood there as a boy.

Life at this school was much easier for me and I quickly made friends with a young man just down from Cambridge who was an excellent cricketer. It had been arranged, by the Head at Giggleswick, that I should attend a summer school at Loughborough, which would give me a paper qualification as a games coach. Thus, at the end of term I went off to obtain my qualification. My chum from Stubbington took the cricket and we had a great time together. The course was excellent. All the instructors were top class people in their own sports and I learned a lot. I also realised, for the first time, the huge gap between the best in our educational system and the worst when I met some of the other people - potential games masters. Their hearts were very willing, but their knowledge and abilities were hopelessly inadequate.

All too soon the holidays were over. The time to return to Giggleswick and the new challenge as a House Master had arrived. Shute House was the smallest house in the School. It had always had a reputation for being tough and I was determined it would continue to be very competitive. I set out to encourage a team spirit and also tried to encourage the senior boys to run the house themselves. I felt it was important that they should run things, not me. Only that way would they be able to make mistakes and only by making mistakes would they learn.

Because of my tender years, I too made mistakes. It was the Headmaster who kicked my backside. About eleven o'clock one evening shortly after the start of term, I was busy correcting a pile of essays for one of the Prep School forms when the Head knocked on my door and entered.

'Carry on, Townend', he motioned me back into my seat 'Just thought I'd share a pipe with you.' He sat down beside the glowing coal fire and picked up one of the books I had just corrected. He glanced at the boy's name on the front of the exercise book. 'Ah yes, young Smith', he mused half to himself, 'brother doing well too.' Then, turning to me, 'Have you met the parents yet?

'No, sir,' I replied.

'Well', he got up from his chair and looked down at me, 'they are poor people and it is a struggle for them to send their boys to us. They assume we will do a first class job for them.' He paused. 'How many 'm's in immediately?' My mind raced.

'Two, sir,' I replied.

'Correct,' he continued as he placed the book on my desk. 'I pay you for quality work not sloppy correcting.' The page was covered with my pencil-marks where I had corrected punctuation and circled words spelt wrongly but, true enough, I had failed to circle the word in question.

'Good night,' he said. Having made his point he left me to continue. Very seldom did I manage to get to bed before half one or two o'clock all the time I was at Giggleswick. My bedroom overlooked the Head's study and I can honestly state that more often than not he would still be working at his desk when I turned in. He led from the front and set an amazing example. He was also blessed with that special sixth sense which all good commanders have - knowing how to catch their subordinates and thus motivate them to higher standards.

During the next holidays I was surprised to receive a large parcel of books. A curt note inside from the Head stated that the following term I would be teaching Latin. Since he thought my own Latin might be a little rusty, he felt it might be helpful if I studied the primer and grammar in the parcel. I had not done any Latin since leaving my Prep School. Another challenge. The Head would sometimes visit young teachers, like myself, and sit at the back of the class. He would never open his mouth and the boys' behaviour, of course, was beyond reproach. He never did visit me during any of the classes I enjoyed teaching but one afternoon he suddenly appeared as I was about to take a very dull History lesson, which I had not prepared properly. Predictably, I dried up with at least fifteen minutes still to go. All I could do was to say rather lamely, 'Open your books at page 35....'. Eventually the bell rang - saved by the bell indeed. He waited until we were alone.

'You had not prepared that lesson Townend.' He just looked at me.

'No, sir, I'm afraid not.'

'I doubt I'll catch you out again like that, will I?'

'No, sir, I replied. Sure enough, somehow I managed to find the time to make sure he never did.

As well as coaching games every afternoon I became an army officer each Thursday for JTC duties. Indeed this odd additional duty once caused some merriment when we were all fallen in for our annual inspection by a very red-faced Brigadier. When he came to me he poked his swagger stick into my chest and demanded to know why I was wearing the 'Atlantic Star'? In my best Whale Island voice I shouted, 'Senior Service Officer, sir!' The ripple of laughter that shook the ranks of cadets I thought would make him explode. The Head moved him on smartly and the parade was quickly dismissed to the delight of all.

If parents wanted extra tuition for their children, this was given in my study in the evenings. I received no extra pay for this. Corrections would just have to take a back seat. I was on duty from seven thirty each morning to see breakfast through, until my senior boy went to bed around ten thirty each evening.

Society knew we were pretty poorly paid but respected us. There can be few jobs where the element of job satisfaction is greater. You can't buy it, but by God you can feel and enjoy it. The folk I met knew I was poor but respected me for the work I was doing. Obviously such a meagre income was a constraint but it never caused me to suffer or be unable to make friends.

That Christmas I returned to Ireland where my parents had bought a lovely Georgian house on the hill outside Monkstown, opposite the golf course. This was as a direct result of my introducing them to the accountant who had helped sail *Colleen* over to England with Father Mitchell Kelly, Newfy the Boss and me. This accountant played rugby for the Dolphin Club in Cork who at that time contributed three to the Irish national team. My brother Jeremy, an excellent scrum half, and I were invited down to the ground for a trial and were thrilled when asked to play. As brothers we made a very good pairing - I played at stand off. I was invited, along with a few other Dolphin players, to play for a side in Tipperary for an annual match against a Dublin club. As we drove over there was snow on the Galtee Hills. The game was fast and furious - no quarter asked or given. One of the Tipp players, a huge forward, had played against Mike Marshall before the war and remembered him. He was visibly upset when I told him about the tragedy and put his arm around my shoulder and gave me a hug.

The dinner afterwards was an all male affair. Because of the speech making and songs, I began to worry about the wives and girl friends who must have been waiting elsewhere. When I enquired of my table-mate about this, he just roared with laughter and refilled my pint of stout. 'Don't you worry your head about them,' he grinned, 'Sure and they'll be there waiting for us, no problem.'

It must have been close to one o'clock in the morning before we arrived at the dance. Sure enough the girls, pretty as pictures, patient and demure, welcomed us with not a rebuke in sight. An hour later an enormous cold buffet was served. My tummy was still trying to work off the excellent dinner we had had but my colleagues tucked in as if they had not fed for a month. I was impressed. I don't think I have ever been to a more friendly party anywhere. We danced and sang and drank and laughed. Around five thirty they served a full breakfast and afterwards we made our way to our car. I remember walking up our drive with the postman. He gave me an old-fashioned look when I told him I had been playing rugby - I expect my dress suit still had a lingering scent and I hadn't had time to remove any tell-tale lipstick marks from my collar.

124

Eventually the Government decided I was not suitable university material and the Head, probably quite rightly, decided I would not make a good long-term schoolmaster, so my school days were finally over. I learned a great deal from that Headmaster for which I have always been grateful. He was a great man and I was fortunate to have been taken on by him. I like to think that I did make some useful contributions to the coaching of athletics and games at Giggleswick - I would be more than surprised if any of my pupils remembered me for my academic abilities.

I kicked the trusty old Norton 500 which Mike and I had bought in Southampton during the war. Her throaty roar echoed off the now empty school buildings as I left the lovely Pennine scenery for Wales to join the *Innisfallen* once again and sail back to Cork City.

CHAPTER TWENTY-SIX - SUICIDE, ST MALO AND A TASTE OF VETERINARY.

My brother Jeremy was now riding over the sticks for a very well-known Irish trainer. We decided to go to Mallow Races to watch him perform. Between races I went to the beer tent to buy a round of drinks for the family. As I was ordering, a man standing beside me recognised the RNVR tie I was wearing. In those days people did recognise ties. It transpired that he too had been in the Navy and introduced himself as Commander Everett. I excused myself while I delivered the drinks to the family and returned to the tent to continue our conversation. He told me that both he and his brother had just bought a C Class Fairmile each from Admiralty. His was berthed alongside in Cork harbour and he was looking for someone to help him sail it to France. Would I go?

I finished my pint, explained briefly to my folk that I was off to France and the Commander drove me home. I threw a few clothes into a bag and we left to join his new yacht.

Clem Everett was a remarkable man. He and his younger brother, Bill, had both seen service in the Navy in the First World War but the Geddes Axe cuts afterwards had left them out of a job. He told me that their Father had given them both a small amount of money to leave home. Thus it was that they found themselves in South Africa. The businesses they started outside Durban proved so successful that they had retired back to UK before the second war began. They both rejoined the Navy immediately. Bill had gone to Coastal Forces where he first commanded a MAS/B and had the honour of collecting Lord Gort from the beaches of Dunkirk. He later became senior Officer of an MGB Flotilla before taking command of a destroyer. Clem had command of an armed merchant cruiser - a very hairy occupation.

His new toy, named after the wife he had recently married, was lying alongside, immaculate in her new colours. I was fascinated as I wandered around this now very spacious yacht. In place of the three petrol engines he had fitted three diesel tank engines; these he reckoned would produce a cruising speed of around 12 knots. The following morning we sailed. I was on the wheel, his groom acting as deck hand, an old Navy stoker looking after the engines and his newly-wed wife as passenger and cook. That evening found us secured alongside in Penzance.

Having been on the wheel for the whole passage, I turned in around ten o'clock and immediately dropped into a deep sleep. In my dreams I heard seagulls crying. Suddenly I shot bolt upright. Seagulls do not cry at *night*, my mind shouted. In the pitch-dark cabin I grabbed my trousers and fought my way on deck. Those had been human cries for help. Had one of our men fallen overboard? Clem arrived on deck at the same time and I ran forward to check our crew were safe. They were and had been awakened too. I returned to join Clem. He told one of the men to inform the police ashore as we clambered on to the jetty, grabbed a circular life belt and ran around the harbour wall, our eyes searching the black water for movement.

126

Suddenly an arm thrust upwards and we heard a cry for help. I threw the life belt, which landed within grabbing distance of the swirl left by the sinking arm. But now there was total silence, no ripples - nothing moved.

We made our way back to the yacht and soon a police sergeant and a young copper arrived. Having taken statements, the three of us, the sergeant, the copper and I, boarded our dinghy. We had made up a grappling iron with a line long enough to reach the harbour bottom and I now started the long job of square-searching this area, the sergeant and young copper taking it in turns to hold the line while I rowed slowly back and forth.

Around four o'clock in the morning the copper suddenly straightened. 'I've caught something, Serge,' he said. I held the dinghy steady as the young man slowly hauled his line in hand over hand.

'Take it nice and slow son,' said the sergeant. The words were scarcely out of his mouth when an arm nearly poked the young man in his face.

'Christ,' he spluttered, wiping water from his frightened eyes and I knew at once that our trawling would need to start all over again as we watched, in the half light, the arm and its body slide slowly back into the depths.

It took another hour to recover the body and by that time it was daylight. The news spread like wild fire and in no time we were being pestered by tourists and locals alike. It was impossible.

Clem decided to sail at once for France but the police informed him that he would not be allowed to leave the country. It was agreed eventually that we could sail to Dartmouth on condition that we made ourselves available for the inquest.

On the day of the inquest we set out by train. On arrival at the station Clem dispatched me to collect a daily paper and a porter. Having glanced at the racing pages he gave the porter his bets to place - betting was one of his hobbies.

The inquest established that the unfortunate man had run into trouble with the various women in his life. He had decided to resolve the problems by jumping into the harbour to end it all. However, he had obviously had second thoughts, which is why his cries had woken us, but in his case they had come too late. We gave our evidence, collected the very few shillings we were entitled to for our trouble and left the court. Clem dispatched me to buy an evening paper with the racing results. He scanned the paper.

'Find me a taxi,' he smiled. 'I really can't face that train back to Dartmouth.' He insisted a couple of his horses had come good, so we taxied back from Penzance to Dartmouth.

Free now to proceed, we made our way to St Malo. The weather was beautiful and we had a great time. The only trouble, so far as I was concerned, was Clem's personal daily programme. He would rise at 0430 and 'work'. This meant that by 0630 he had completed his 'work' and would be looking for company. He was seldom one for cooked breakfasts, preferring a large 'hair of the dog'. Being on holiday in France, this usually resulted in cracking a bottle of Champers. To begin with I found it different to sit in the sunshine sipping Champagne as the surrounding boats came to life. However, I soon discovered that if I was to stand any chance of seeing the rest of the day through, I was much wiser to keep him company in person rather than in 'spirits'.

By eleven o'clock Clem would be in great form and a party would be in progress. Guests came and went. I became part butler, part Skipper and chief bottle-opener. The afternoons became an extension of the morning session leading into the evening party. His ability to absorb alcohol was truly impressive, but he would then detail me to take his young wife to the Casino ashore. Since I had agreed to this trip to try and make some money, this sort of duty was not much help.

On our return to Ireland, the famous Dublin Horse Show was due to begin. Clem asked me if I would help him take the boat up to Dublin. I had never been to the Dublin Horse Show and there could be no better way to see it than to be moored in the Liffey. Clem was joint Master of his local pack of hounds and a good judge of a horse. He bought a heavyweight hunter the first day, which I assumed was for his own use - how wrong I was. Before the Show ended he had sold it on at a very reasonable profit. We went to one of the fashionable Hunt Balls held in one of the lovely old Dublin Hotels. It was a stupendous party and I have often wondered what the local folk must have thought about us young people, in full evening dress and ball gowns, watching the morning gallops on the Curragh. I believe that that was the first time my brother Jeremy and Clem's daughter, Tina, a young London deb., had danced together. They were guests on board and later married.

When we had returned the yacht to Cork I told Clem that I would have to start looking for a job. His reply, typically, was, 'Time enough.' That night, as Jeremy and I slept in our cabin, he emptied two fox cubs on to the floor before closing the door. We were awoken by a very odd noise. I could not believe my eyes as I found myself looking into the frightened face of a snarling half-grown fox. It was his farewell gift.

Back at the family home, they wanted a tractor trailer built. This helped me pass the time, but when their solicitor saw it during a visit, he asked if I would mend his horsebox. Naturally, they said, I would be happy to do so if he would tow it into the yard. It duly arrived. After inspection it was clear it was so rotten that it would need to be totally rebuilt, from the bottom up - hardly a mend job. This task occupied my time totally and I hoped would result in my earning some badly needed cash. In the event, when I produced all the bills for materials used, a matter of some £60 from memory (a lot of money then), the solicitor thanked me profusely for a wonderful job, reached for his cheque book and wrote a cheque for £60 exactly. Not even any luck money!

However, during my work on this task in our farmyard I had met and got to know our vet, an amazing man called Sean Hyde. He offered me a job as a potential student that I jumped at.

Thus it was that I reported to Conways Yard in Cork City. There I was intro-

128

duced to 'Cookie' the practice administrator. He had been with Sean Hyde for years and ran the show. Every client knew Cookie and Cookie knew every client. No one went anywhere or did anything without Cookie's say so. Sean, of course, was a law unto himself. Each day my first instructions came from Cookie.

Sean Hyde was the sort of character you only read about in books. During the troubles in the First World War he had been picked up as a spy by the British. An inexperienced young army officer was ordered to shoot him, which he did, leaving him for dead in the street. The bullet hit the underside of his cheek-bone and came out through his neck, leaving him bleeding profusely. He was noticed by a passing girl with a donkey cart who took him to hospital. By the end of the war he found himself in trouble from his own people and fled to England. It was in England that he qualified as a vet, returning to set up one of the finest practices in the whole of Ireland. He was a superb horseman. He and his brother used to pair-jump at the Dublin Horse Show and his brother won the Grand National. Tipperary Tim?

He hunted his own pack of hounds aptly named the Sean Peels. They were a Sunday pack and since they did not own country of their own, they hunted what they claimed was the no man's land between the established hunts. They were a wonderful roguish, cheerful mob - their followers coming from all sections of the community. They seldom killed a fox but they rode like hell and enjoyed themselves thoroughly. Sean, as Master, hunted as he rode. Humour was seldom far from his mind and he would delight in bringing down any haughty hunt visitor.

If any man ever had the 'gift of the Blarney' it must surely have been Sean Hyde. He could charm the hardest heart, win over blustering Colonels and sink without trace any other Irishman who dared to oppose him. His beaming smile, twinkling eyes and soft tones would overcome frustrated clients as surely as night follows day. He was utterly fearless of man or beast. I have watched (in abject terror) as he has walked straight up to a wild-eyed horse, nostrils flared and ears flat back, only to see him stroke its taut neck and talk it into submission. Horses loved him and he loved them. Trouble was he could not understand fear in lesser mortals like me. 'What's to be afeared of?' he would say. 'Sure and isn't he the fine big animal.' The fact that the same animal, ears flattened, had swung round and bitten me before trying to kick me out of his box would be totally ignored.

My first job each morning was to open up the kennels in Conways Yard, then to take the various inmates for a swift walk around the streets of the City. On occasions I would bump into a Dolphin Club colleague much to his amusement and my embarrassment - usually when it was not too clear who was taking who for a walk. I recall the local Circus brought the most enormous wolf-hound for treatment for mange. This fearful monster was the size of a small pony and needed a chain like a yacht's cable to lead it. Having exercised, fed and watered and cleaned out the kennels, I would report to Cookie. In those days many of the medicines and drenches used were produced in house at the back. I started a notebook and copied down the various concoctions as instructed by Cookie. Then I would continue to mix and packet until the Doctor (Vets in Ireland are always called Doctor) arrived.

Most days he would take me with him on his rounds as his valet. I found these trips wonderful. He would regale me with stories during the drive and it was an honour to watch a master at work when we arrived at our destination.

A typical episode was the day when we travelled to the far west. On the way down in the car he was telling me what he expected to find. A cow was overdue to calve and the farmer had phoned Cookie to say there were complications. On our arrival at the tiny farmstead, miles from anywhere, I opened the car boot, removed the two white coats, a bucket, soap, a bottle of disinfectant and a towel, put on my white coat and went to the farmhouse for some water. Sean and the farmer were chatting in undertones. On my return I placed the bucket on the ground and held Sean's white coat for him to put it on. Disregarding the proffered coat he turned and looked me in the eyes. Addressing the farmer he said in a friendly voice,

'Right, Paddy, I'll take you up on that offer of a drink,' and walked off to the house.

Left holding the white coat like a surrender flag, I was flabbergasted. I ducked down, entered the tiny byre and came face to arse with the pregnant cow. She bent her neck round and gave me a long silent stare. I went back outside and collected the bucket, soap and towel, removed my white coat, rolled my shirt sleeve as high as it would go and soaped my right arm. My mind was trying desperately to remember what the Doctor had told me in the car. I grasped the cow's tail in my left hand and praying I was entering the right orifice (I had never been inside a cow before) I pushed with all my might. The pressure on my arm was incredible - it had to be experienced to believe it. Now, as my hand felt around inside, I recalled something about the sack being connected by something he had called 'cotyledons'. Yes, sure enough, there were some of these things and I gradually worked my hand around till it seemed all had been freed. I had been so busy concentrating that it was not until I removed my arm that I suddenly realised the calf was lying very still. The cow again gave me her long stare - I felt she thought I had taken advantage of her condition and was embarrassed. As I started to wash my arm and hands I heard the two worthies returning. They had just reached the entrance to the byre when the old cow arched her back and deposited one dead calf at my feet. I felt dreadful.

The Doctor, quite unabashed, turned to the farmer. 'How many times do I have to tell you Paddy? You always leave it too late. Isn't it better to have a small bill and a live calf rather than leave it too late and have a larger bill and a dead calf?'

I replaced the gear in the car and got in beside Sean. Once on the road, I turned to him. 'That, I said, was one hell of a stroke to pull. You frightened me to death.' He was grinning his widest grin.

'Sure and hadn't I told you all about it on the way down? Right down to those little cotyledon things and how to sort them out'

'But,' I insisted, 'suppose I hadn't been paying attention?'

'John, boyo, if I didn't think you were up to it, I wouldn't have given you the chance to work alongside of Wishy and me.' I was forced to grin back at him. He was right, of course, and when I told Wishy afterwards he told me how lucky I was. The first job Sean had given him, to prove his character, had been to castrate a standing stallion in front of the whole of Conways Yard. Sean happened to be an expert at this operation but it is certainly a hell of a job to give an unqualified student. But that was Sean's way of getting his men to prove themselves to themselves. He had the confidence in them; he needed them to have the same confidence in themselves. He was a great teacher.

Sean Hyde

I thoroughly enjoyed my time at Conways Yard. They were a wonderful team - each one an expert in his own right and collectively superb. I found it fascinating to watch sick animals being cured - a cow down and looking set to die, a quick dose of calcium and in minutes she is on her feet again - magic! Horses, torn apart by barbed wire or tin sheeting, sewn up and no infection. Cattle, even greyhounds, with broken bones are wrapped up in plaster; weeks later they are able to walk again without the plaster - magic again.

Enjoyable though this all was, without a University grant I was not going to benefit from this training. Thus, when I was introduced to a retired Air Force Officer at a party, who was looking to start up a shark-fishing enterprise, I decided then and there that I would travel with him to Achill Island and have a go.

CHAPTER TWENTY-SEVEN - ACHILL ISLAND, SHARK FISHING

The Air Commode (as we christened him) wanted someone to go to Achill with him to meet a chap up there who had an idea about starting a new business - would I go?

Achill Island is the largest island off the West Coast of Ireland. It is joined to the mainland by a swing bridge at Achill Sound. Fifty years ago it was a lovely wild place. The Air Commode had bought a bungalow on the lower slopes of Slievemore overlooking the harbour of Keel. He turned out to be totally useless at looking after himself so, to avoid dying of starvation and cold, I became his cook, housekeeper and butler rolled into one.

The man we had come to meet was a most delightful chap called Charlie Osborn. He and I immediately became firm friends as he explained his ideas to me. He was married with two small sons. They lived in one of the traditional three-roomed stone cottages lining the road running through Keel. At the harbour Charlie had a Nissen hut full of gear. An old salvaged wooden lifeboat needing new ribs lay on her side on a turf bank above the high water mark. His interest in engineering and his personal poverty meant that almost all his engines and his car were of a pre-war variety. He was a wizard with old engines and loved them. He was also an ideas man and was always dreaming up some new gadget. The Air Commode decided he wished to invest some money in the proposed shark business. However, it was clear to both Charlie and me that for him to be involved in any practical way would be courting disaster. He would have to be very much a sleeping partner.

One good thing emerged from my first trip with the Air Commode. He sold me a tin box on wheels, which I was able to turn into a super little home. It took me a month to put in windows, construct a ship-like bunk with drawers and hanging space under. A tiny desk and bookcase for office work, a folding table and a built-in seat gave a dining area for four. At the other end I built in a washing and kitchen area. A polished copper deep pub basin let into a polished aluminium work-surface reflected the flames from a primus stove. A polished aluminium hood took the steam away outside. Between the kitchen and the door I had installed a hand-beaten shower area. This was used for bathing from a bucket and for hanging dripping clothes to dry. The floor was polished corticine and after my weekly clean up the whole thing shone like a new pin. I was proud of my tiny home

A gravity-fed paraffin oil fire gave welcome warmth in winter as well as a second means of slow cooking. Dear old Nannie, back with the family after the war, made pretty curtains and my bedspread. Once settled on its rocky foundations between Charlie's hut and the old railway wall, I attached a mobile Elsan toilet at its end. Here I nestled just yards from the harbour and the open Atlantic - I can think of few better sites from which to launch a new basking shark industry.

That first season we had very little success but it was sufficient to enable me to see what had to be done and to work with the other men. I finished up by being

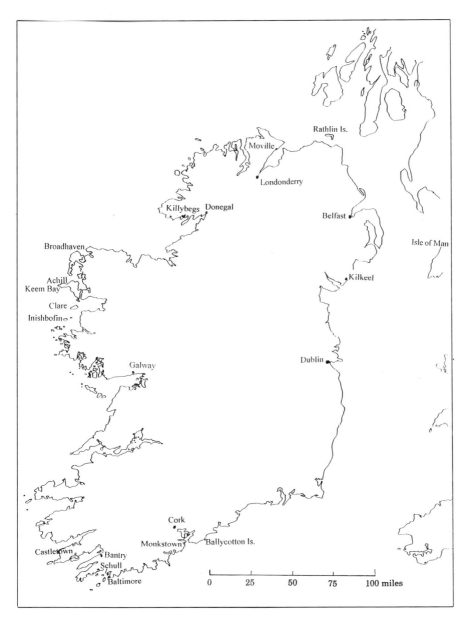

Map of Ireland

133

employed by the opposition and became firm friends with their head man - Jim O'Gorman.

Jim had been brought up on a canal boat. His father always wore a huge leather belt with which, Jim said, he kept the young O'Gormans in place. His formal education was obtained as and when he could attend the various schools on the boat's travels around the Irish canals. Despite these constraints he had acquired an amazing variety of skills. He was a diver, an engineer a fisherman and above all a sailor with an irrepressible optimism. He was strong as an ox and utterly fearless, yet as gentle as a kitten and kind to a fault. None the less he could not tolerate idleness and expected folk to earn their corn.

During the late summer, a small half-decker called the *Girl Pat* was put under my control by Jim. After the shark season was over we took her to drift for herring off Keem Bay. I shall always remember those twilight nights. Lying to our nets under the stars, we talked the hours away between hauls. That year the herring never arrived, so we stored our nets and had to transfer our efforts to the Sound (Achill Sound) where the ancient trawler, *Salva Regina* moored.

During the shark season her hold was fitted out with boilers for rendering down the shark livers. At the end of the season, these had to be removed to enable her to be trawled. The work involved required ingenuity and the stink of the rotting mess in her concrete bilges and the oily slime remaining had to be experienced - it defies description. This was now our next task. Jim would collect me in his jeep each morning and return me to my caravan each evening. My small shower space really came into its own now as I boiled buckets of water on the primus to remove the filth.

At last we had her ready for trawling and Jim signed on another man. He was slight and small, but married to a local girl who could outwork most men. They were expecting their first child and when the day arrived we were all waiting in the bar of the local pub to 'wet the baby's head'. Eventually he was seen to leave his cottage and approach the pub at a run. Breathless and almost speechless he called for a 'large one'. We all waited in silence as he drained his drink. What have you got, asked the landlord? The small man was still in shock. After another 'large one' the story slowly emerged.

He had sent for the midwife but she had been delayed and he was already in a state when she arrived. Anyway, shortly after she had arrived, he heard a crying and the midwife had opened the door and told him to hold a small bundle while she disappeared back inside the bedroom. He was just getting used to the bundle when the door opened again. Again the midwife handed him a small bundle and disappeared back into the bedroom. Our Hero, by now weighed down with both arms full, was almost out of his mind. It was then that the door opened once more. The midwife, smiling broadly, was cradling another little bundle. Realising our Hero's terror - he was about to drop both his bundles on the floor - she placed her own bundle in a cot and relieved him of his two. He had waited no longer.

'Christ,' he said with feeling, 'she's full of 'em!' A great roar went up from the assembled company and his glass was refilled. It was some days later before he recovered his composure.

During the winter Charlie went to England. He worked as a carpenter and did outside broadcasts for the BBC foreign service. At the same time he was getting together a team to return to Achill in the spring to make a film called 'Shark Island'. I fished with Jim while the weather lasted. One evening when bad weather had driven us back to harbour, we returned to Keel to find chaos. The high tide, forced even higher by a full south-westerly gale, had wreaked havoc in the tiny harbour of Keel.

As we approached, the driving rain and wind had made it difficult to converse in the jeep. Now the scene in our headlights was unbelievable. A boat had been lifted on to the stone jetty. The carefully stacked 40-gallon drums of shark oil awaiting collection were, even as we watched, being hurled into the harbour and washed out to sea. Destruction was everywhere. I could not get round to see what had happened to my poor tin hut.

The noise of the wind and the huge waves crashing against the harbour wall formed a deep and constant thunder. Great cascades of dark water, flung high into the air, attacked us like bullets as we got out of the jeep. The force of the wind made it difficult to stand. As the tide began to fall I made my way to my caravan. To my great relief it was still sitting on its rocks. The water level had lapped its base - another few inches and it would have been floating out to sea with the rest of the flotsam.

Early the next morning I called to see my friend Dr King. He had already offered me space in his driveway - now was the time to accept his kind offer. That afternoon Jim towed me up to Ned's bungalow with the jeep and that night I was able to sleep knowing I would be safe for the remainder of the winter.

Ned King, the local doctor, had recently arrived with his pretty Dublin débutante wife. He was a Mayo man but she must have found the change from civilised living in Dublin to Achill a very hard step to take. He decided that he needed me to help him out with various jobs around his place, so I ceased fishing and became land-based for the rest of the winter. It was a change and a joy to be able to help such a happy couple. Ned was incorrigible and I loved him. He was like a small boy and would get so enthusiastic about things that he was a tonic to be with. His bungalow had a bath but no hot water, so I got him to buy a new steel milk churn with a tap at the bottom. I built a stand for it and mounted it so that we could use my primus to heat it. His wife told me she never forgot that first hot bath.

Sometimes I would travel with Ned as he did his rounds. In those days he would never charge the poorer people, only the better off. However, because the poorer folk were superstitious and believed it was bad luck not to give the doctor something, we would return at lunch time with a bag of spuds in the boot and clucking chickens flapping around our ears. Sometimes a bottle of poteen would be hidden under the back seat.

Paying patients used every sort of paper money. We would receive dollars from their children in the USA and pounds from Scotland and England, even, occasionally, golden sovereigns, cheques being favoured by those with bank accounts. I soon realised that Ned was much more interested in treating his patients than he was in sorting out his accounts. I decided to discuss this shortcoming with his wife. A plan of campaign was agreed. Ned had a dispensary attached to his bungalow and it was suggested that his wife and I spend some time sorting this out. Ned thought this an excellent idea and, as we emptied the various drawers, a great pile of notes and cheques was collected by his wife. In future she persuaded him to empty his pockets as a matter of routine after his rounds so that she could bring some order to this very necessary part of his job. The sorting of the medicines and bottles he found useful but was quite puzzled that his wife should bother about such uninteresting things as money and cheques. While later on he realised his wife's contribution, at that time he was young, delightfully idealistic, and charmed all who met him.

He told me about what he called his seasons. In winter there was the measles, colds and whooping cough. Patrick's Day would bring many emigrants home for a party and that would be the mending and stitching up season (result of punch-ups). Summer he always reckoned to have free for fishing apart from the odd birth, but since the men-folk working abroad returned home mainly at the same time each year - nine months later would be the baby season. What more could one want? He would glance at his young wife and grin like a schoolboy. Great days.

On Christmas day Ned had invited the local Guarda Sergeant and his wife for a meal. They were a delightful couple and we both had a very high regard for the young Sergeant. However, we decided it would be fun to get him drunk on poteen. First we sought and found a very fancy old bottle, then using the ingredients in his dispensary we produced a delicate blue liquid with a faintly peppermint flavour and an almost scent-like smell. The poteen suitably camouflaged, the plot was laid. The dinner party was a huge success. When the coffee was served and our cigars lit, Ned introduced the old liquor, which, he said, he had managed to obtain from his Uncle. The guests admired the old bottle and glasses were filled. All decided it really was something quite special. By the time Ned had finished with the Sergeant, he had to be driven home by his wife. She was covered in confusion, as she had never seen him drunk before. It was, of course, much later in the year before a rumour was rife that the Sergeant was a secret drinker of poteen. Later still before he told us that he would get even. Naturally we just grinned but he very nearly did.

One evening Ned and I were in the local pub at an hour when it should have been closed. Suddenly the lady of the house came running to tell us the Sergeant was leaning his bike outside. We both ran down the back passage into the kitchen where the publican was sitting with his feet up, reading his paper. In a flash Ned had grabbed his foot and removed his slipper and sock. As the lady of the house answered the knock on the back door and let the Sergeant in, Ned twisted the old man's ankle. The astonished landlord dropped his paper and squinted at Ned. Ned exerted another twist.' Does that hurt?' The puzzled landlord screamed in pain.

'You're OK', said Ned, as he replaced the man's sock and slipper, 'nothing is broken. If it's still sore tomorrow, pop up to the surgery and I'll give you some pills. He put the man's foot down and turned to the Sergeant.

'Good night to you, Sergeant. Come along, John, we've work to do.' We beat a hasty retreat back to his bungalow. His wife could not understand why we were so jubilant.

My break at the doctor's had come to an end. It was time to move my tin box back to the harbour. I was now approached by the directors of the Dubarry Shoe people who had, I think, five factories in Ireland. They had been looking into the shark fishing and wanted to set up a factory in the harbour. Would I set it up for them and run it? I explained that I worked with Charlie Osborn who was currently in England and that I would have to discuss things with him.

Charlie's reply was to go ahead. He was bringing a film crew over to make this second feature film and would involve my men as extras. I therefore told the Director I would be happy to discuss things with him. I told him how many men I would want, what their terms of employment would be (better basic wage and higher bonus than being offered by the opposition, plus free rubber boots). He agreed these terms, said he would have an old truck sent up for transport to enable me to fetch and carry my men. In the meantime a start was made on building the factory, which he had already had designed. Unfortunately we did not see the design until after it was built. This caused hours of work afterwards to cut out drainage gullies that should have been cast in.

Folk like me, who stayed over the winter on the Island, had the job of knitting the shark nets. These long lengths now needed mounting and stretching ready for the beginning of the season. The anchor points on the rocks at Achill Head also needed checking and renewing, as necessary, with new iron spikes. Such work, which had to be carried out from a curragh or small dinghy, needed fair weather. As spring approached, the little harbour became a hive of industry; a new excitement and expectation filled the air - you could feel the anticipation.

In those days, once the sun shone, hundreds of basking sharks made their placid way up the west coast of Ireland to feed - and possibly to mate? No one knows for certain, even today, but I thought so. When I first started I wrote to the Natural History Museum in London, seeking information about these majestic fish. To my astonishment, although they are the largest fish around our coast, very little is known about them. Because they are plankton-feeders and not taken by anglers or other fishermen, few have ever been caught and studied. I determined to try and learn more myself, but it is only now - 50 years on - that serious scientific study by my friend in the Isle of Man, Ken Watterson, is making any progress. Unless steps are taken soon to control their slaughter, they may disappear.

Historically, in the west of Ireland, these fish were caught by locals with

**A curragh manhandling a shark in a net anchored to the cliffs
The dorsal fin of another shark cuts the water beyond**

harpoons, like whales. When one considers the frailty of the local curraghs, such hunting must have been very dangerous. However, since a good shark (35 - 45 feet long) could produce some eighteen hundredweight of oil from its liver, only a few sharks would be needed to provide lighting through the long winter nights. Being Ireland, of course, many superstitions and stories grew from these 'hunts'. The huge fish would attack small curraghs by tipping them over. The oil itself was attributed with almost magical healing powers.

Once the paraffin lamp had infiltrated into the west of Ireland, the need to hunt these monsters disappeared, but the myths and magic lingered on. When Charlie first tried to get men to help him he met with total disbelief. Only a madman would go after such dangerous prey. It took the whole of the first season and most of the second to convince the locals that the old stories were not true. Once they were laid out on the jetty for all to see and it was explained that they fed on plankton, had virtually no teeth and were harmless to human beings, it was possible to explain why such a fish might swim towards a curragh.

From under water a curragh could look, to a male shark, like a slim nubile female shark with no claspers. So a randy male could be forgiven for wanting to take a closer look at the said boat. The occupants of the curragh, seeing a shark dorsal fin steering straight for them, could be forgiven for getting the wrong idea. If there was a bit of a sea running and they panicked, their curragh could capsize. Since not all could swim, some might be drowned. Obviously any survivor would swear that the shark had tipped the curragh and eaten the crew - except him.

The locals well understood the annual salmon run, fishing off Keel with fixed bag nets and in Keem with sein nets. The sharks tended to follow the same route as the salmon and did great damage if they became entangled in either the bag nets or indeed in the sein nets in Keem.

One day a shark would be sighted, its dorsal fin cutting a clean line on the surface of the smooth spring sea. Great excitement would spread amongst the fishermen - winter was over at last and soon great convoys of sharks would be swimming slowly north. Activity amongst both the salmon and shark men intensified. There were not enough hours in the day to do all the jobs needing to be done. I would rise at dawn, light my primus stove and leave the frying pan on a slow heat with rashers and eggs gently frying. A few steps took me to the edge of the harbour. Assuming the tide was in, I would plunge and swim to the other side. Climbing out, the hot sunshine would dry my naked body by the time I had run back to my tin home. The smell from the pan I had left frying, wafting out of the open door, was the perfect way to start a new day.

Predictably we had all sorts of teething problems with the new factory. However, I was fortunate in being able to employ a lovely man to take responsibility for the boilers. Hans Ott was an ex-prisoner of war who had married an Achill girl. He was working for a retired Colonel (himself a Japanese prisoner of war) but was released to me for the shark season. He proved an excellent choice while I was there and was possibly even more valuable after I had left.

The season was well into its stride when, one evening, as I worked in the harbour with my small team, we noticed a small group of strangers making their way down the turf road. As they got close, I recognised Charlie's red beard.

'It's the film crew', I said, and soon Charlie was introducing everyone. It was tremendous to have him back and there was so much to discuss, so many yarns to swap; could not wait to get back to his cabin. That night we caught up on the missing months. It was great for his wife Brenda to have him back, and the two boys, who worshipped him, were over the moon. Although both he and she were very sophisticated people, he was essentially a simple chap, happiest when in his modest cabin surrounded by few material things, but immersed in his two boys and the film.

Charlie Osborn

Next day I had a long talk to the leading man, Hugh Falkus. His attitude to life was explained by his wartime record. He was a fighter pilot, shot down wearing his pyjamas, and made a prisoner of war. Constant escapes had landed him in a high security prison. His good looks and great charm had attracted the girl he brought with him, his newly-married wife - this was to be their honeymoon. Hugh's enthusiasm for this project was shared by the entire film unit.

140

In no time everyone was hard at it. Charlie asked me to instruct Hugh in the use of the harpoon from our ten-foot dinghy. He was a natural, and the eventual shots, filmed after I had left, are some of the best ever recorded.

The usual method developed for catching these fish in Achill was to allow them to swim into and get entangled by the nets, which were set out from rock stations attached to the base of Achill Head cliffs. The disadvantages of this method were that the sharks took a long time to drown and wound themselves into a cocoon of net, which took hours to disentangle and mend. It also took up a fishing station while this was going on. Charlie's solution was to produce an explosive harpoon. We would station ourselves close to our nets and, as soon as a shark hit one, I would pull the dinghy so as to be directly over the rising shark. As it surfaced, with only a couple of strands of net around its nose, Charlie would harpoon it. The explosion was sufficient to knock it out while we passed a two-inch line through its mouth and gills like a mackerel and towed it to the mother ship. The net was then straightened and fishing continued.

The best time for the entire operation was somewhere around five minutes. No net damage, no loss of fishing time and easily the kindest way to kill these harmless great fish. Naturally such a set-up was far too dangerous for any insurance company to entertain it, so Charlie and I alone were involved

In an effort to try and learn more about these fish I cut through the thick cartilage of the head between the eyes to find the brain. A photograph of an old Irish penny alongside this brain shows it to be about the same size - tiny for such a huge fish. This suggested to me that their reactions are controlled more locally and that the efforts to kill them with shot-guns or lances were probably more dramatic in their blood-spilling than effective in their purpose. I admit to feeling more at risk than the sharks when the boyos got enthusiastic with their guns.

As the day wore on, more and more sharks would become festooned along the sides of the towing ship ready to be taken back to the factory at Keel. The film crew were impressed. Back at the harbour, men with sharpened scythe-blades would expertly joint each shark as it was hauled up the slipway. Our means of hauling them up this slipway was a solid-wheeled 1918 mobile crane, which was driven down from Dublin Docks. It did the job but needed watching, because it would sit up and beg on its back wheels if the shark being hauled was too heavy. The shark flesh was cut into half-hundredweight chunks and loaded on to five-ton lorries at the harbour. These lorries, when full, had to be transferred to ten-ton lorries waiting on the main tarmac road.

Once the ten-tonners were loaded, they set off for the fish-meal plant on the other side of Ireland. The turf road to the harbour would not support anything heavier than the five-tonners. This work was hard, smelly and cut your hands to pieces until they became calloused. The livers, once removed, were loaded into the factory at one end of a simple production line. Here the livers were chopped into smaller and smaller pieces ready to be loaded into the boilers. Once they had been rendered down, the oil would be piped into storage tanks, the sludge emptied, and the boilers readied for the next load of raw liver. We worked from first light till dark. I had chosen my small team carefully - they never let me down.

By this time there would be tourists visiting the harbour. They had to be warned not to allow their children to rub against the sharks. Their skins are covered by millions of razor-sharp spines, which will produce a painful graze on a bare leg, and the slime that covers their bodies is acid and will make any graze very sore indeed. Naturally our men had great fun teasing tourists. They would wait until a pretty girl approached and started to ask questions as they opened a shark. To her horror a lady's shoe would be held aloft from the newly-opened stomach, to be followed by a frenzied search for the rest of the female form. The questioner's rapid departure was greeted by howls of good-natured laughter. Not to be out done, the factory men, working in full view of the public, would play similar tricks. Working with raw liver, their hands and arms were covered in oil and blood. When a suitable audience was gathered and asking questions, one of the men would start chewing. Wiping his mouth with the back of his hand he would ask if any one would like to try a piece, and hold out a tender morsel to the nearest buck male or fair lady. Inevitably the crowd would melt away amidst laughter from my men.

I was proud of our team; they worked tremendously hard and earned every penny of their wages and extra bonus. I was constantly bombarded by requests to join from the opposition's men. Fortunately my friendship with Jim O'Gorman saved any rows on that score. Without it the scene could have been very different.

By this time the war in Korea was well under way. I volunteered my services as a Reserve Officer when it broke out. One day, out of the blue, I received orders from their Lordships to rejoin the Navy. That very day the Director was due to visit us. Having shown him around the operation and received his thanks, we went back to my tin box. I showed him the letter from Admiralty. He asked me if I would request a delay of a couple of months to enable me to see the season finished. I had just agreed to write such a letter when Hans knocked on the door.

He had just heard that Charlie and some of the film crew were missing. Apparently Hugh Falkus had managed to swim ashore. That was all he had heard. I knew they had gone to Keem Bay for some continuity shots. Immediately I excused myself and dashed to the harbour, jumped into the nearest boat and sailed for Keem. When we arrived - it seemed to take ages - we could see flotsam close to the Daisey Rocks and feared the worst. We guessed they must have been taking continuity shots with the rocks as a backdrop for use in the film. We searched and picked up some bodies but there was no sign of the young cameraman or Charlie. They have never been found. Apparently, as we learned from Hugh later, a huge rogue wave suddenly burst over Charlie's boat sinking it. Everyone bobbed to the surface and Charlie fixed everyone with a float of some kind. Since Hugh was reckoned to be the strongest swimmer he was told to swim ashore and raise the alarm. This he had done, but by the time we had received the news and reached the accident spot, the

142

cold water had taken its toll. I was distraught. What was I to say to Brenda and the small boys? The sad trudge back to Keel Harbour haunts me still. As I write I can feel again that awful sickness, tears welling.

The Director was waiting for me. I told him that because of the tragedy I would stick to the programme outlined in the letter from Admiralty. He could see I was in no mood to discuss things and left. First I had lost Mike Marshall, now Charlie Osborn, just when it seemed our fortunes were about to mend. Life was indeed tough, but it has to go on and the next morning I called on Brenda. She was incredibly brave. Hugh was still recovering from exposure and trying to come to terms with the loss of his wife, his film friends, and Charlie Osborn. He decided to return to England to sort out funerals and make arrangements with the next of kin. Obviously the film was put on hold. I arranged for Hans Ott to take over our team and briefed all the men accordingly.

When the day came for me to leave I felt I was leaving part of me on this wild island. I had been accepted by the local folk, who could not have been kinder. I had worked with men who could work. I had become friends with people from every walk of life in the island, folk I would never forget.

To look south from the slopes of Slievemore as the sun sets over the Atlantic to the west, on an evening when the sea is a mill pond of reflective blue, leading the eye to Clare Island and beyond to Bofin and Shark. Surely this must be as fine a view as there is in the whole wide world?

As I sat on the harbour wall that last evening and watched just such a sunset, a popular tune sprang to my lips and I started to sing under my breath,

'Oh some day I'll come back again to Ireland,
Be it only at the closing of my days...'

How easy, I thought, as I half closed my eyes, to believe in the myth of Atlantis.

CHAPTER TWENTY-EIGHT - A RESERVE RECALLED
COLLISION AT SEA.

The 25th of June, 1950, saw North Korean troops advancing into South Korea - the Security Council called for a cease fire. By the 6th of September British troops were in action there.

Although immersed in Achill Island, I followed the news with interest and wrote to their Lordships in Admiralty volunteering my services. It appeared that their policy was to recall folk like myself, with war experience, to help run the Home Fleet, thus enabling younger men to serve in the battle area and gain war experience. Being still single, I thought the strategy eminently sensible.

I reported to Portsmouth Friday 8th June and within a matter of hours I was on my way to HMS *Dryad* for a quick week's refresher course on the various 'radars' carried aboard the destroyer I was to join. The course showed me how far technology had moved on since my last contact with such things; it also made me realise that most of the officers of my own age and experience were now at least Lieutenant Commanders if not Commanders. This was a new Navy. I had a lot to learn.

My appointment was to HMS *Grenville*. She was in dry-dock and as I made my way up the rickety dockyard gangway I thought how awful all ships look, stuck in a dry dock. Removed from their natural element, they take on a hangdog appearance. Dockyard workers and sailors swarmed like ants over poor *Grenville's* inert body while she lay there, defenceless - an abused and naked lady, impatient to become once more her sleek and beautiful self.

The Quartermaster saluted and led me to the Captain's cabin. Nervously I knocked on the door.

'Come in,' a voice shouted above the machine-gun bursts of chipping hammers. A tall, slim Lieutenant Commander, my own age, held out his hand in welcome. He apologised for the din and our first interview was held in the intervals between outbursts of noise. It seemed that this was to be his first command. In fact it turned out that all the officers were doing their various jobs for the first time. In my case, I was to be responsible for the Ship's Office and act as Captain's Secretary - tasks totally new to me. It also became clear that as my Captain's last appointment had been as aide to the Governor of Malta, his requirements of his Secretary would undoubtedly be of a very high standard. Since I had never used a typewriter in my life and had no knowledge of Naval report or letter writing, I felt that my life was going to be pretty interesting, as indeed it was.

I very soon discovered that every piece of paper which enters or leaves a small vessel like a destroyer, at some stage passes through the Ship's Office. It is the co-ordinating area for all the ship's activities and is required to hold the multitude of forms and papers needed to record everything on board, including the people. I have seldom felt more at a loss. The step from running a Coastal Force craft or small inshore minesweeper under wartime conditions to running a destroyer in peacetime was enormous.

When I told my Captain about my total ignorance, as I took the mail in on that first morning for his perusal and signature, he looked at me patiently and smiled.

'Oh I expect you'll soon get used to things,' he said. Then, glancing down at my fingers and hands, still scarred by the shark-skins and calloused from hard labour and immersion in salt water, he said, 'It may take a while for your fingers to find their way around your typewriter.'

However, a lot of midnight oil was to be burned before I could finish my daily tasks like the rest of the officers. It is easy, in retrospect, to wonder why I never asked a qualified Paymaster from ashore to show me how to set up my Ship's Office. I suppose that a natural reluctance to admit one's own shortcomings was one reason and the other was simply that when one joins a ship commissioning, there is so much to be done that there is scant opportunity to leave one's place of work.

HMS *Grenville* had been fitted with a new and secret ASDIC (anti-submarine detection) dome. Their Lordships were impatient to see her out of dockyard hands and completing sea trials for this new piece of vital equipment. After the inevitable last-minute delays, the day arrived. At last the lady took on a different look as she felt the water surging round her bilges and she seemed to sigh with relief as the flood flowing into her dry dock gently lifted her, enabling her to glide alongside the jetty and join her sister vessels. Later that day I had to visit some offices ashore and, on my return, I thought how beautiful she looked as she lay, elegant as a swan, alongside the jetty. I felt very proud of my new ship.

With the minimum of delay our Captain had his ship to sea. There were still various teething troubles to be resolved and the officers and crew needed time to become accustomed to their new roles and the new equipment.

We sailed for Milford Haven at 1800 on Sunday 16th September to act as target ship for the Fleet air arm. Daily we exercised. At 1130 on Thursday 20th we were sent to search for a ditched aircraft but we could find no crew. Life continued until we were sailed back to Portsmouth, arriving at 0930 on Saturday 22nd. This proved to be our 'work up' period, scant time indeed for a new ship's company, and our Captain reported this lack of experience to the Captain of HMS *Triumph*, an aircraft carrier, to whom he had reported to collect his new orders.

On his return, our Captain informed us that we would be escorting HMS *Triumph* as 'safety vessel' while she flew her aircraft at the entrance to the English Channel. Both ships would be calling in at the Channel Islands and it was planned to land both soccer and rugby teams to compete against the Islands. I played for our ship's soccer side. The Islands team had access to a lovely ground and super facilities but after the game the teams departed without any sort of get-together.

The following day I was invited to play rugby for a joint Navy team representing both ships. The whole situation could not have been more different. Before lunch, cars arrived on the jetty and collected as many as possible of the Navy team. Driven by our opponents we were given a conducted tour of the Island and after lunch taken on to the 'field of battle'. Here facilities were of the primitive variety and the playing area showed evidence of the animals (now removed) that had grazed the ground until that afternoon. Our audience was a collection of brightly-dressed and most attractive girl friends, wives, children and club members

Despite the kindness shown by our hosts prior to the match, there was no quarter asked or given during the game. Indeed my own memory of that match is blank because at some stage I received a kick on the head. All I remember is of sitting in the changing room afterwards and suddenly recognising the chap beside me. Apparently I had played on after the short stoppage and no one thought anything was wrong with me. Now it is obvious that I was suffering from concussion. True to form we attended a great party aboard HMS *Triumph,* and although I had a splitting headache, after a few large gin and tonics, I forgot all about everything except our guests. The difference in outlook between the rugby-playing fraternity and their soccer counterparts has always seemed odd to me. I have seen this example repeated many times all over the world.

Monday 1st October found us back at sea - our task was to shadow *Triumph* so that, should any of her aircraft get into trouble, we were available to go to their rescue. By the end of flying that day, both ships were well inside the English Channel. *Triumph* decided to return to the Atlantic ready to fly off her aircraft shortly after dawn and thus chose a course to return us both to such a position. However, as we turned and sailed back, she ordered us to take up station first on one beam, then on the other, to enable both ships to carry out 'darken ship' exercises.

I was Officer of the Watch for the first watch (2000 - 2400). During these various manoeuvres our Captain sat in his chair and handled the ship. I took his instructions and passed his messages down the voice-pipe to the man on the helm. Eventually, the Captain of *Triumph* was satisfied that his ship was darkened and ordered us to take station 4 cables astern. Around 2145, I was told to take over the watch and my Captain went below to get his supper. The course which *Triumph* had chosen took us in the opposite direction to the shipping entering the Channel and a mass of small lights, which we thought were probably fishing boats, turned out to be an exercise involving landing-craft. Soon after the Captain had left the bridge I had occasion to call him on the command inter-com because there was a ship passing us within three miles. I did not think it odd that he did not reply as the ship was passing safely and I thought he would be eating.

Later, in amongst all the other lights in view, I noticed a red light. Suddenly the loudspeaker on the bridge, manned by the signalman, crackled into action. I heard him answer. I had called the Captain to inform him about the red light but had no response. Now the signalman was shouting a message from *Triumph.*

'Execute to follow, sir, four turn,' he said. Again I tried to contact my Captain. The second Officer of the Watch, who had been writing up the hourly log, suggested he ring the buzzer and use the voice-pipe; this I told him to do. Again the radio loudspeaker crackled. By now the red light had altered to show first the white steaming light and then the green starboard light - the bearing was as near as possible steady. This meant that we would collide. Since the new signal was for us to turn to port immediately, I put on port helm and continued to call the Captain.

He suddenly burst on to the bridge. Immediately he ordered the engines to full ahead and the wheel to hard to starboard. By now we could see the tanker clearly, bearing down on us. Collision was inevitable. It was like sitting in a cinema and watching, horror-struck, as the scene unfolded before us. We all knew what was about to happen but were totally unable to do anything to help. It happened in slow motion. The noise and the shock were muted - almost like a glancing blow. *Grenville* was pushed over to port but gradually seemed to regain her proper position. I found myself repeating the Captain's orders down the voice-pipe in a complete daze.

The enormity of my own incompetence frightened me and I felt I had let down those who had placed their trust in me. I was shattered. The Engineer officer and the First Lieutenant made their reports. A medical party arrived from *Triumph* with their doctor. The landing-craft exercise was cancelled and these craft started a square search of the area for survivors. Having established the position, a signal was sent to C-in-C at Plymouth and slowly *Grenville* limped into that port the next morning, a huge canvas covering her battered starboard quarter.

Very fortunately the Italian tanker's bows had struck us in line with X turret's barbett; this probably saved us from being cut in half. The fire in the tanker's bows was put out, thanks to smart work by our own sailors. It was quite extraordinary how well everyone responded to the crisis. We had a crowd of young 'boys' on board straight from their shore training establishment. When the senior 'boy' awoke to find the tanker's bows burning just beside his swinging hammock and water flooding into the mess-deck aft, he collected the rest, fell them in on the quarter-deck, and reported them as all present and correct to the first Officer, just as if this was the most normal of things to happen.

There was no way that I could have slept during the rest of that night. As the reports came in of the death of four of my colleagues I felt distraught. Obviously there was no one else to blame - just me. As I recalled the way the situation had crept up on me, I wondered again and again at what stage I should have realised what was happening and taken some positive action. It had been my inaction that had resulted in these people's deaths. Not only had I failed to ensure that my Captain was on his bridge in time to avoid this catastrophe, but I had not even read the situation correctly as it slowly developed. People ashore often cannot understand how ships, which are travelling so relatively slowly, can collide. Surely, the sea is so large! They forget that the channel sea routes are like motorways. Everyone is using the same lanes and in this instance *Triumph's* Captain had decided that a turn to port was preferable to a turn to starboard because of the proximity of Start Point. His second signal, which was lost in the general confusion, was for us to 'act independently'.

As I sat at my desk in the Ship's Office typing out reports later that morning,

147

my mind went back to my wartime days. The Navy had seen all these things many times before. Life went on. Over the years it had developed a routine to cover such episodes and this now swung into place. First there was an interview with a man from Lloyds; then arrangements were made for an official enquiry to be held aboard the Battleship *Vanguard*. All those people involved in any way were then interviewed by a Board of very senior officers. The proceedings were carried out in a friendly but frighteningly formal atmosphere. I recall being amazed when the Captain of HMS *Triumph* stated his opinion to the Board that the tanker would pass between his ship and *Grenville*. My Captain looked at me in disbelief at this comment. On 5th October I was interviewed by the Treasury Solicitor and in due time, as a result of the Board's findings, a series of Courts Martial were set up.

In the meantime, the ship's company were sent away on a week's leave. There was a pile of paper work and reports to type, so I was happy to volunteer to stay aboard as Duty Officer. A couple of days after they had all left, a signal arrived from Admiralty. This ordered the Captain to transfer with his crew to commission HMS *Launceston Castle* with all dispatch. The Bosun was the senior rating left aboard. Having read him the signal, we took *Grenville's* motorboat to search for HMS *Launceston Castle*. We found her lying at a buoy, 'cocooned' in Reserve. Returning to *Grenville* we set about producing plans to get the crew transferred. On the 10th we took over an advance party, the first crew arrived at 1130 and by 1400 we had them all fed and settled to ship's routine. A stand-in Captain and First Lieutenant arrived that evening. I passed over details of the routine we had set up and returned to *Grenville*.

We had been set the task of a rush commissioning. Their Lordships had decided to use this opportunity to establish how long it would take for a scratch crew to take a cocooned ship out of moth balls and get to sea as an operational working ship. At 1500 on the 11th, HMS *Launceston Castle* was towed by tug to No 4 basin south wall in Plymouth. Work was now in full swing. On Monday 15th I moved my gear across from *Grenville*. By the 18th, when our Captain returned, we were ammunitioning ship and moved to No. 1 basin Flag Staff steps. Despite having to attend the Coroner's court and other activities resulting from our accident, *Launceston Castle* sailed for Portland on Thursday 25th - exactly 14 days from the time she was towed from her buoy by that tug - and returned to Plymouth after various trials on 26th. On Saturday 27th I was granted a long weekend - my first break since the collision - which I spent visiting my sister, a nurse at Newton Abbott Hospital.

It was while we were working away at commissioning that my Captain asked whether I had found an officer to defend me at my forthcoming Court Martial. Since I had no excuses to offer for my failure, I said that I could see no point in asking anyone to defend me. Added to which, as a Reserve officer, I knew precious few regular officers anyway. It then transpired that a certain officer had asked if he might be allowed to defend me. I agreed to talk to him privately in my cabin but was pretty adamant that my mind was made up. I had nothing to say in my defence and would accept full responsibility for my failure to take the necessary avoiding action, which would have prevented the death of my colleagues.

The officer who turned up was a large man. He was a Lieutenant Commander slightly older than myself. He too had served in Coastal Forces during the war. Soon we were chatting away and he told me how he had progressed from MTBs to destroyers. His delightfully informal, confident manner won me over. Here, I felt, I had found not only a wise officer but also a friend. Before he left he invited me to join him and his wife for tea and dinner the following day.

After dinner his wife left us to our coffee. He told me how he had acted for the prosecution at the Nurnberg trials. Now he wished to complete his experience by carrying out my defence. He agreed to make no excuses, and was so persuasive that I agreed to allow him to defend me. In retrospect it was a good decision. Not only did he advise me wisely, but both he and his wife could not have been more supportive at a time when I desperately needed someone to talk sense to me.

My fellow officers had never been other than kindly, but it took a family like his to relax me. For this support I have always been very grateful. The fact that he turned out to be a brilliant defence council I only really appreciated much later on. Unfortunately our paths never crossed again. However, many years later I came upon a photograph in our local Essex paper of a smiling Captain Anderson performing some local duties. I was delighted to see he had made Captain's rank.

CHAPTER TWENTY-NINE - COURT MARTIAL.

On the 24th October a signal had arrived stating that the Courts Martial necessary as a result of the collision between SS Alcoa and HMS *Grenville* would take place in Plymouth on 14-17th November inclusive. On the 10th November a second signal arrived postponing the coming Courts Martial until 10-13th December. In the meantime *Launceston Castle* was hard at work but the strain of having such a trial hanging over us postponed was great.

The afternoon before the fateful day, I was summoned to attend on the Secretary to the C-in-C at Plymouth. I wondered what other awful things were about to happen.

'Come in,' he said cheerfully. 'Sorry to have to drag you all the way up here but you need to sign the charges.' I breathed a sigh of relief.

'Is that all? I was worried sick wondering what else I'd done.' He grinned.

'No problem old boy, but the regulations require that you read these charges and sign them in front of me - OK?'

I read the paper he had put down in front of me:

1. In that he did on the 1st October 1951 negligently, or by default, hazard his ship.

2. Did negligently perform duty imposed on him as Officer of the Watch of said ship, in that he failed to take adequate steps to ensure the presence of his Commanding Officer on the bridge when two vessels approached said ship, on a converging course on the starboard bow at about 2300.

I read the two charges and reached for the pen he was offering. There was no doubt that whatever steps I had taken to alert my Captain to the impending danger, had failed miserably. The loss of four lives, as a result of my failure to take action, would be with me for the rest of my days - even now, all these years later, there is still a cruel hurt deep inside me. I signed the papers and thanked him. Having collected the ship's postman's bicycle, I peddled slowly back to my ship.

Sleep that night was impossible. Having tossed and turned, I gave up the unequal struggle and had a bath. Breakfast, a cup of coffee and a cigarette, was a silent affair and dressed in my best uniform I made my way back to my cabin. Why is it that at times like this the clock seems to slow right down? It took for ever for the minutes to tick into hours but eventually the time came for me to attend as ordered. I grabbed the sword I had borrowed for the occasion and left the ship.

On my arrival, I was ushered into a small room opening off the Courtroom. My Defending Officer had already arrived. He welcomed me and proffered a cigarette with a steady hand. My own, I am ashamed to admit, shook as I reached out for the light he was offering. I felt absolutely awful - the fear of the unknown.

'You managed to borrow a sword OK.' My Defending Officer was smiling at me, trying to break the tension. I grinned back and nodded. Very calmly and quietly he then explained the Court routine. Suddenly we were summoned.

Together we formed up and I was marched into the Courtroom. At the head of the room was a long table on which my borrowed sword was laid. Behind the table sat my inquisitors looking calm and indifferent. The seats in the room were occupied by my brother Officers, the general public and the press. It was as if I was watching a film. It seemed impossible that this was really happening to me and that I was playing 'star role'. My mind was brought back to reality with a bump. I was being questioned. The answers came out in a small voice I hardly recognised as my own. Then my Defending Officer addressed the Court.

'Clear the Court!'. The order rang out and I was marched back to the safety of our small room. My Defending Officer grinned at me. That has got rid of one of those Commanders on the board, he said. It appeared he had discovered a reason, during his research, why that particular Commander was not a suitable man to sit in judgment on my trial. He had been compromised.

'What happens now?' I asked.

'They will call in one of the 'standby' Commanders,' he replied.

'How many of these standbys do they have in reserve?'

'Usually several. Why?'

'Is it normal for the same Commander to appear at the Board of Inquiry and at the Court Martial?.

'Of course not. Do you recognise one of the Commanders sitting at the top table?' I said that I thought so, but could not be certain.

'Great', he said. A few moments later the door opened and we were once more formed up and marched back into the Courtroom. The same routine was enacted and once again my Defending Officer addressed the Court.

'Clear the Court!' Again the order rang out and once more I found myself back in our small room. My Defending Officer took out his cigarette case and laughed openly. For the first time I felt a little more relaxed.

'Go on like this,' he joked, 'and they will run out of standby Commanders.' We just had time to finish our cigarettes before the door opened again. This time, as we entered the Courtroom, there was a feeling of expectation, a buzz of whispered conversation and a rustling of papers from the press area. Before addressing me the President of the Court banged his gavel and called for silence. The nervousness which had built up inside me, a coiled spring of tension, was suddenly released as I saw the humour of the situation. Before the proceedings had even opened, my Defending Officer had removed two Commanders from the Senior Officers presiding. How many more would he discredit? How many more were available in the wings?

God forbid that I should ever find myself in a similar situation but, if I had to be tried again, I believe that the traditional Court Martial (developed over so many years) is the most objective court to try one, and the way that the sentences are arrived at is the most just. The Officers listening to the evidence are all equipped to judge that evidence independently and arrive at a verdict according to the charge.

They consider the experience, or lack of experience, of the accused before passing sentence. In my own case I was cleared of the first, and most serious charge, of hazarding my ship; I was reprimanded for failing to take adequate steps to ensure the presence of my Commanding Officer on the bridge.

For the last time we were marched back to that small room. I turned to my Defending Officer and shook his hand. With tears in my eyes I thanked him sincerely for all his advice and help. He had proved not only a first class Defending Officer but a very real friend. I collected the borrowed sword and made my way outside into a sunny afternoon. As I walked down the stone steps I suddenly glimpsed, out of the corner of my eye, a man holding a camera. Bloody Press, I thought, and raised my right arm to shield my face. The next day, on the front page of a national daily, there I was, my right arm not quite covering my bearded face. As soon as I saw that photograph I went to my cabin and collected some scissors and my razor. Clean-shaven once more, I would be less likely to be hounded.

All the other people involved in that collision were tried. The routine is the same but since the participants are called in reverse order of seniority, being the most junior, I was first. I had not realised just how much strain I had been under until the whole matter was completed. From a purely personal viewpoint, it was a great relief to hear my Captain state publicly that he had then and continued to have complete faith in my ability, indeed he had appointed me Navigator of his new command. He, too, had needed support and I had done my best to help him in this area. After it was all over and he had been quite rightly cleared of both his charges, he sent for me and thanked me for my efforts.

We sailed for Portsmouth after the Captain of *Triumph*'s trial, arriving at 0815, despite fog, ready to welcome Captain D aboard at 1030 on the 14th.

Having cleared my work I was able to set off for Christmas leave in Ireland on the evening of the 15th.

Admiralty, S.W.1.

N.L. 199/52   8th March, 1952.

The Commander-in-Chief, Plymouth.

I am to refer to your submissions 21/AS.151, 22/AS.151 and 23/AS.151 of 3rd January, 1952, with which you forwarded the proceedings of the trials by Court Martial of Captain U.H.R. James, C.B.E., R.N., Lieutenant Commander J.M. Cowling, R.N., and Temporary Lieutenant J.S. Townend, R.N.V.R., respectively, and to inform you that Their Lordships have not interfered with the findings or sentences.

2. The conduct of these trials was exceptionally good and reflects credit on all concerned. In particular, the speech of Lieutenant Commander C.C. Anderson, R.N., for the defence at the end of the trial of Lieutenant Townend was excellent. Any member of the Bar, whether junior or Queen's Counsel, would be pleased to have put his client's case so forcefully and so well. Lieutenant Commander Anderson is to be informed accordingly.

BY COMMAND OF THEIR LORDSHIPS,

(Sgnd) J.G. Lang.

II

No.P.131
COMMODORE,
ROYAL NAVAL BARRACKS,
DEVONPORT

Forwarded with pleasure.

(Sgnd) M.J. Mansergh

Plymouth.   VICE ADMIRAL
10th March, 1952   COMMANDER-IN-CHIEF.

'....Lieut. Commander Anderson to be informed accordingly.'

CHAPTER THIRTY - EXERCISE 'CASTANETS' - CONVOY COMMODORE.

HMS *Launceston Castle* was built by the Blyth Dry Dock Company, she was completed in June 1944. By November of that year she was part of the 30th Escort Group. On the 11th of November, in company with three other Castle Class frigates, she sank U-1200 in the North Atlantic south of Cape Clear. Her final task with this group was to escort some thirteen U-boats from Bergen to Scapa Flow. After a short stint doing Air/Sea rescue duties from Freetown she was placed in reserve at Devonport in 1946.Now, due to an accident, she was to have a new lease of life. Having commissioned her in the minimum of time, morale aboard was high. Ship's companies need sea time and positive work where they can see the results of their efforts. Working mainly from Londonderry and Milford Haven, we were soon busy acting as a target ship for the Fleet Air Arm. This meant spending time at sea during the week and at weekends our sports sides more than held their own in matches ashore. Very quickly the ship became a tight knit and proud small family. While I had personally learned a lot from my time in the Ship's Office and as Captain's Secretary, I was much happier as Navigator and Sports Officer.

'Castanets' was the first of the large-scale post-war naval exercises. We were sailed to Milford Haven to act as the Commodore's ship in charge of an escorted convoy approaching the Channel from the Atlantic. So soon after the real Battle of the Atlantic, the scene was set for a very interesting and demanding exercise.

On our arrival at Milford Haven, a very senior four-stripe RN Captain came on board. The mass of medal ribbons on his chest, including First World War ones, indicated that he had been a very gallant officer in his day. Now we were honoured to carry him as Commodore of this convoy. The briefing was organised for the following day. Our small boat delivered the Commodore, my Captain and myself. As we climbed the ladder I delayed my own approach while my superiors were piped aboard. Then, armed with my roll of charts, I joined them. The convoy conference was presented by young officers, all with war experience. It was business-like, practical and very professional. The objectives were clearly defined. Communications, codes and recognition signals were all confirmed, charts detailed and the general plans explained. The various sorts of attack to which the convoy was vulnerable were discussed, as were general strategy and tactics, by the Senior Officer of the escorting destroyers. I was impressed by the expertise of each speaker and scribbled notes frantically. I had never before been the Navigator to such a Senior Officer and was concerned in case he should ask me for information afterwards, which I was unable to supply.

Having covered all aspects of the briefing and taken questions the Senior Officer turned to the Commodore and asked him if he would like to say a few words. That grand old man stood, one hand in his reefer pocket, and looked slowly round the silent room. He had been listening intently during the briefing and now it was his turn. Quite old enough to have fathered everyone else there, he appeared to be searching for the right words to use. Then, in a quiet voice he spoke.

'The convoy' he said, 'must get through.' There was not a sound as he again looked around the attentive lines of faces. There was another long pause as he again searched for words to express his thoughts. Suddenly his free fist rose and banged the table. 'The *convoy,*' he accented the word, '*must get through.*!'

Blank astonishment was on almost every young face. The Senior Officer who had invited him to say a few words stood up. 'Thank you, sir, for those words of wisdom. I know we all agree with your own assessment and I'm certain under your leadership we shall be successful in attaining that aim.' Turning to the assembled officers, he said, 'Thank you all for attending, if anyone has any problems or needs further information please catch me before I leave for my ship.

I collected my papers together and followed my Captain. He was escorting the Commodore back to our motor boat. Once back aboard I went to the chart-house to prepare for the exercise ahead. Suddenly I realised someone was behind me and turned to find my Captain standing there.

'I am afraid', he said in an undertone, 'we are going to have problems with that dear old man. I believe he has 'flipped'. I stared hard at my Captain. The Commodore was such a super old boy that I found such a comment hard to accept.

'Do you really think so, sir?' I queried and paused. 'Well, the next few days will decide won't they.' I turned and continued my work on the chart.

To accommodate the Commodore our Captain had moved out of his day cabin and turned these quarters (and his steward) over to the old man. At around eleven o'clock on our first night at sea, I was working in the chart house when the Captain's steward came in.

'Excuse me, sir.' I looked up; he was obviously agitated.

'What's the problem?' I asked.

'The Commodore has gone, sir.' I placed the dividers back in their rack.

'What do you mean, the Commodore has gone?'

'Well, sir... ', he hesitated.

'Get on with it', I snapped. He then told me how he had popped in to see if the Commodore would like anything before he himself turned in, but the old man was not in the cabin. He had searched the wardroom and made enquiries from the other officers but no one had seen him since dinner.

'I thought I'd better let you know, sir.'

'Thank you', I replied, as I climbed the ladder to the bridge. I was in the middle of explaining the position to the Captain when a sailor arrived with a mug of steaming cocoa from the galley.

'There is an old chap in outsize pyjamas and no teeth holding forth outside the galley,' he said with a grin. The Captain looked at me and I recalled his earlier comment.

'Take over Pilot,' he said, 'I'm going below to return our hero to his bunk. Tell the Officer of the Watch I want a sailor to be permanently on watch outside my cabin door from now on. His duties are to keep an eye on the old man in a friendly and diplomatic way so that he does not feel he is under surveillance - is that clear?'

'Yes, sir', I replied.

As the night wore on and various convoy manoeuvres were needed, we acted as if nothing had happened. However, at some stage it was obvious we would be obliged to own up. Our Captain was considerably junior to many of the escorting Captains, and there could be serious repercussions once it was discovered that decisions assumed to have been made by the Commodore, had in fact been made by our Captain. Having gently persuaded the old man back to his cabin, my Captain joined me in the chart-house. It was decided that he would talk direct to the Senior Officer of the escorting force and explain his predicament. As the night was well advanced, this 'chat' was delayed till after breakfast the following morning. Content that the old man could not escape again, we both turned in.

The first part of the exercise involved attacks by submarines and it felt very odd to be sitting in the middle of a convoy organising their weaving and zig-zagging instead of being outside as one of the hunting pack. As the days passed and we continued our role as organiser of our small convoy, despite air attacks, we found ourselves slowly edging our way up the Channel. My mind flew back to the massive array of shipping during those weeks and months after the invasion of Europe. Then, as darkness and the Straits of Dover approached, just as in the war, we were attacked by E-boats. It was so reminiscent of the nights I had spent convoying coastal convoys in the B class ML. Once again I could feel the excitement of it all as the intervening years fell away. Despite these attacks we steamed on, and in due time reached our Scottish destination. The Old Man was delighted; he had achieved his aim - his convoy had *got through*.

That final evening we all dressed for dinner. A special meal had been produced to wish the Commodore 'God speed'. I believe he was in fact one of the first (if not the first) lower-deck man to rise to the rank of Captain RN. In those days that really was a terrific achievement. He had charmed us all with his total honesty and his experiences, obviously happy to be back in the environment that had been his life. It was a tragedy for such a man to suddenly find his mind let him down. The fact that he did not know was only overshadowed by the fact that their Lordships did not know either. The dinner was a huge success. We all drank rather more than we should, perhaps, but the speeches were unprepared and genuine. As the old man got to his feet a great round of applause greeted him. He eyed us all quietly and then, as tears rolled down his weather-beaten face, he just murmured,

'Thank you all for being such good messmates,' and sat down.

As the applause died down, our Captain rose to his feet. 'I think,' he said to the old man, 'you and I will leave these youngsters to their own evil ways. A nightcap in my cabin is more in our line, sir.' And together, arm in arm, they left the wardroom.

CHAPTER THIRTY-ONE - LAST YEARS IN THE NAVY

As the Battle of the Atlantic had shown, effective methods of finding and attacking submarines were essential for safeguarding our shipping lanes. *Launceston Castle* was employed to help train air crews in hunting skills, using the latest technology, and occasionally being involved in joint exercises.

We sailed for Londonderry from Portsmouth on Friday 30th January 1953. The south-westerly gale blowing up the English Channel retarded our progress somewhat. I remember suggesting to our Captain when he visited the chart-house that once Ireland offered some protection and we were sailing up the Irish Channel life would become easier. Almost as soon as he left, a new weather forecast arrived stating that the winds would swing round to the north-west and increase! Very shortly afterwards we received a signal from Plymouth that the Ferry *Princess Victoria*, en route from Scotland to Ireland, was in distress and we were instructed to increase to full speed to help.

The Irish Sea, when a south-westerly gale swings round to the north, becomes a most uncomfortable place. Bitterly cold winds funnel their way south with increasing ferocity and poor old *Launceston Castle* was now ordered to slam her way at ful power into this mayhem. It became almost impossible to see on the open bridge, which was almost constantly being covered by green seas and blinding sleet. In the chart-house I had to place buckets under the bridge voice-pipes to avoid everything being swamped. As Navigator and Signals Officer I remained in the chart-house all night and continued through the following day as we, too, searched.

By the time we arrived and joined the searching ships already there, the weather was easing. A very cold but bright day revealed only bodies and flotsam. It was a silent *Launceston Castle* that entered Derry, without any casualties, but with damage to our ship.

As a target ship we spent most of every week at sea. We were still sailing around the coast serving the various RAF Fleet Air-arm requirements from Ireland in the west to Scotland in the east. In May we returned to Portsmouth to 'dock'. On my return from leave it was time to prepare for our duties during the coming Coronation Review.

On the 9th of June the Fleet began to assemble in the Solent. We were open to the public on the morning of the 11th and took our first guests on a trip around the Fleet that afternoon. The Queen arrived aboard HMS *Surprise* on Sunday 14th and on Monday we left our berth to anchor with our guests aboard - the only ship to leave Portsmouth. After the Queen had inspected the Fleet, we were allowed to land some of our guests and collect some more to watch the fireworks display. I had Stella Marshall and her children as well as my brother Pat aboard. Having watched the Review in 1937 from the shore as a schoolboy, it was wonderful to be taking part now. On the 16th the ships dispersed and the Solent seemed terribly empty.

On the 4th July we were informed that we would be exchanging crews with HMS *Hedingham Castle*. To this day I do not know the reason, but that is what had to happen. It was swift, like all good partings, but painful. On the 7th they sailed away with our crew, and on the 8th we sailed away with our new crew for Invergordon.

By August we were back in Londonderry, then sailed for Oban to act as Guard Ship for the Highland Games in September. Being asked to supply some athletes to take part, I hurriedly detailed off any likely lads as volunteers and we duly turned up. What none of us had realised was that, even then, Highland Games were attended by Olympic athletes. We could hardly lift the 'stones' used for the weight-put, and I could walk under the high-jump bar where one competitor was doing some practice jumps! But we entertained the locals aboard and 'Guns' and his lads put on a super fireworks display, so honour was satisfied.

December saw us back in Plymouth for the Christmas leave period. On my return from leave 'Guns' and I made contact with the local panto cast, and by the time the rest had returned we had a great party lined up, both at the theatre and back on board.

In February the Captain and I visited Launceston to make final arrangements with the Council for a ship's company visit -soccer match, dance, the lot - which turned out to be a great success.

March saw us visiting Antwerp for a few days before returning to our normal duties. There was a most unusual accident when a fridge suddenly exploded, burning and freezing our poor engineers and causing havoc. Fortunately no one died, but it was serious.

On 20th May 1954 I was demobbed for the second time. From now on I would be doing just two weeks a year as a reserve .I see from my diary that on the 9th of June I was signed on by Tom Swan as his skipper for a weekly wage of £10. A new and very different sort of life was beckoning - youth is resilient.

CHAPTER THIRTY-TWO - A DATE WITH *MAEVE*.

Tom Swan had first approached me late in 1951. He had seen my efforts in Achill Island and asked me to join his fishing boats. In September 1953 he and his family visited Londonderry and I entertained them aboard *Launceston Castle* and was able to get his son a visit to one of the submarines, which he thought was wonderful. So after demob I returned to my folk's home in Monkstown and, having enjoyed a family reunion dinner, left my naval gear, collected the few clothes I would need as a fishing skipper, and set off for Donegal to meet Tom Swan, the owner of the *Maeve*.

Tom's family had originated in Scotland and had done very well over the years. They lived in a large manse-type dwelling at Ballyshannon and he owned salmon-fishing rights, eel-netting rights, a small knitting factory employing a lot of local women and three inshore fishing boats. MFV *Maeve* was the newest and largest. He was a pillar of the local church, where his wife played the organ, and his children were being brought up in a strict Presbyterian household. He showed me round his small factory and then told me all about the boat which was to become my new home. By the time he had finished I was eager to see her for myself, and the next morning we set off for Kilkeel, the other side of Ireland, in his car.

As we drove he told me about the overhaul the boat had just completed and I asked about the crew members who were apparently already working aboard. He went into detail about only one of the crew - he called him 'Old Willy'. It seemed that Old Willy had been employed by Tom for many years in a variety of positions. He had the ability to turn his hand to many tasks and it was, I gathered, this ability (rather than any qualifications) that had encouraged Tom to appoint him as engineer to *Maeve*.

The closer we got to Kilkeel the darker the sky became and very soon we were driving with our lights on into a steady drizzle. A cold biting wind drove in from the Irish Sea as the car stopped on the empty jetty. I thanked Tom for driving me over and told him not to delay; I would get my gear onboard and 'phone him once I knew when we would be ready to sail.

Shouldering my kit bag and grabbing my suitcase I made my way to the ladder leading down to *Maeve*'s deck. The tide was out and evil-smelling black mud complemented the unhappy picture before me. She looked filthy, forlorn and forgotten. I swallowed hard. After the great build-up Tom had given me I could not believe that this was the same vessel. A strong icy gust and a smattering of cold droplets across my face encouraged me to throw my gear on board. Opening the door at the back of the wheel-house, I lowered my things down the steep ladder into the flat below. It was pitch black and it took a few moments for my eyes to pick out a light switch. The galley, which is where I was, was filthy and stank. A small sliding door opening from the galley led into the skipper's cabin and I entered what was to be my home. It was tiny but quite adequate. A bunk along the ship's side had

158

drawers under it and a wardrobe for hanging garments. There was a small desk for paper work, a chair and bookcase.

I immediately unpacked, made up the bunk with a coloured spread and pillow, set out some books in the bookcase and stowed the other gear. Already it looked lived in. I glanced at my watch. There was still no sign of any crew so I went into the galley

Maeve

The first priority was obviously to get a fire going. I opened the solid-fuel stove fire-box. It was full of clinker and very out. Having found lighting material and fuel I cleared the fire-box, laid a new fire and in no time at all the range was hot enough to boil a kettle. In the meantime I had opened the oven to be faced with a green glow; an evil smelling dish of rotting fish made me retch as I threw the whole lot into the incoming tide. As I turned to go below I noticed a small knot of men, bent against the wind and rain, making their way down the jetty from the town.

What is the best way to meet a new crew? I assumed they were wondering about me too. Tom would have undoubtedly told them that I was a retired Naval Officer - such a description to fishermen would have been damning enough, but to Donegal men (citizens of the Irish Republic) the fact that I was an Englishman as well must have left them with very serious doubts indeed. It did not surprise me that they would prefer to put off such a meeting as long as possible and the local pub was as good a place as any considering the awful state of the boat. I pretended not to have seen them and went below to continue my labours. The kettle was now singing on the range, which was roaring away, and the heat was beginning to permeate the after cabin to the extent that all the scuttles were steamed up.

I waited in my cabin until the last man had climbed down the ladder and I heard them all in the after-cabin. Then, very nervously, I entered and introduced myself. Steaming mugs of very strong tea eased the stunted conversation and by the time a fried evening meal had been consumed, we had managed to break down the initial barriers. I made no secret of the fact that I knew nothing at all about sein-net fishing. They were interested in my experiences in Achill Island and, as I lay in my bunk that first night, I wondered just how long it would take to get poor *Maeve* into a reasonable state.

A watery sun shone from a windy sky as I walked the deck for the first time with the Mate. He explained the machinery before I went below to have a conducted tour of the engine room with Willy. There were still some jobs outstanding and I went to the boatyard to chase these up. Meantime one of the crew had been sent ashore for provisions. The work continued slowly.

In a very short time we fell into a routine. As I was keen to return to Killybegs as soon as possible I 'phoned Tom and told him that we would be sailing the following morning - whether the few outstanding jobs were completed or not.

The day dawned bright and it was a joy to slip the last warp and feel the throb of Willy's engine as we made our way up the Irish Sea. A short swell tumbled her about and I found how she handled. The design was odd to say the least, as they had placed her seven-ton engine, a four-cylinder Blackstone, where one would have expected the hold to be. This meant having a very extended series of shafts to drive the propeller. We had not been at sea many hours when Willy came into the wheel-house wiping his hands on an oily rag.

'She's at it again', he said as he gazed out of the window. I looked at him.

'She's at what?' I asked, wondering what on earth he was talking about. He continued laconically that he had started the auxiliary bilge pump as well as the one driven off the main engine. I nodded and proffered him a cigarette; obviously he expected me to know what the trouble was. My Mate appeared and I asked him to take the wheel while I went below with Willy the better to understand his concern. Willy led me below and showed me the first bearing grease-cup, which he had had to remove because it was getting too hot. We then went aft and, as he lifted a bilge board, a sudden swell sent water spilling over the after-cabin deck. I straightened up and asked where the water was coming from.

'Bloody stern post,' he replied.

'But wasn't this what the refit was supposed to have cured?' I queried.

'Until they shift that bloody engine aft', Willy spat out the words, 'she'll continue to leak like a bloody sieve.' He replaced the bilge board and we made our way back to the wheel-house. I thanked my Mate and took over the wheel. Willy then told me of the trouble they had had since she was built. It appeared that I had not only taken over a very dirty vessel but also one with a built-in problem; certainly the sooner I got her back to Killybegs the better.

At the north-east corner of Ireland is a tiny island shaped like a boomerang called Rathlin Island. If the tides are right, a vessel can save hours on a passage by cutting inside this Island, rather than going round it. As we made our way towards it I found the tides were right and decided to cut inside. During my time as Navigator in HMS *Launceston Castle* operating out of Londonderry, we had several times done the same thing. However, what I had not reckoned on was the difference between travelling in a ship with a gyro compass, radar and the ability to fix one's position even in bad visibility, and travelling in a small inshore boat where you alone have to steer, fix the position and keep a look-out all at the same time. That night, as the weather deteriorated and visibility went from bad to worse, I learned a valuable lesson that I never forgot. Truthfully I made a very bad judgment and we were all extremely lucky that we were not destroyed by my stupidity. Seldom have I been more concerned than I was that night as we fought our way through increasingly rough water with flying spray making it almost impossible to see the lights. No skipper has ever been more thankful than I was to reach the open water to the west and I swore that never again would I chance my arm. There are so many things which one takes for granted in a naval or merchant ship which are just not available in a little vessel like *Maeve* and it took such an error to drive this home to me.

Although we had only sailed the day before, we needed to call into Moville to collect stores and water. Again I was amazed. I now realised that it was up to me to see such things were done. (I am not recording these things as any complaint against my crew; I am recording them to illustrate just how naive I was.) I was having to learn a completely new way of life and I needed to learn jolly quickly. In those days the inshore boats sailed each morning and landed each evening, so it was never necessary to have food or water for more than that time. We collected our stores and water and sailed on for Killybegs.

CHAPTER THIRTY-THREE. - BACK TO THE DRAWING BOARD

Killybegs is a beautiful natural harbour at the head of Donegal Bay. In those days it had a jetty, where the few inshore fishing boats berthed, and a sea fisheries warehouse and office at the harbour end where, each evening, the landings would be auctioned or loaded for the Dublin market the following morning. Apart from the tiny boat yard on the shore opposite, that was the extent of the facilities. There was no ice-plant, which meant boats landing their catches daily - real fresh fish.

The boats ranged in age from *Maeve* and James McCloud's new boat, back to the *Mulroy Bay* which had been fished by the same family of brothers for years, the only boat, so far as I know, which has ever caught *two* sturgeon in Donegal Bay. This small group of fishermen were a tight-knit community, hardy and very hard working.

There was great excitement when we arrived. Tom met us and introduced me to old Charlie McGowan who was to show me the ropes. A most delightful, quiet and genuine man whose son, young Charlie McGowan, was skippering one of Tom's smaller boats. As soon as possible Tom whisked me away in his car to his home in Ballyshannon. By the time we arrived I had already explained the cause of the problem. I agreed with Willy. Until the engine was moved further aft and the shafting reduced in length, the poor lady would continue to spring the joints at her stern post and water would continue to fill her bilges. To Tom, who had just had his boat slipped and the sprung joints all refitted at some considerable cost, this must have seemed like heresy. He said he would have to think about it and the next morning I was dropped back at the harbour by his handyman.

The only person on board was Willy. He was lying in his bunk and was obviously recovering from a fairly extreme hangover. I stoked the range, boiled a kettle and presented him with a mug of tea and a cigarette. He turned on to his elbow, drew on his cigarette and looked at me long and hard.

'You don't have a crew any more, Skipper.'

'No, Willy', I replied. 'I expect they are with their families after our passage.'

'No, *no*, Skipper,' he continued, 'you don't understand. They've left. They say they're not sailing *anywhere* in this old girl while she leaks like this.' With that he swung his thin legs out of his bunk and started to drag on his shoes. 'Come with me', he said over his shoulder as he led me to the engine room. There he lifted a bilge board to reveal water just below the level of the deck-boards. I was astonished.

'How long has this taken?' I queried.

'I've had the auxiliary pumping since I returned on board around five o'clock,' he replied. 'It's beginning to fall now, but even at rest she is still making water.'

I thanked him for his efforts and returned to the after-cabin. We drank our tea and I went into my cabin to think. I heard Willy climb up on deck and watched as he made his way to the nearest pub.

What on earth was I to do now? I had no crew, a boat that was unseaworthy, and only by getting her to a boatyard could she be made seaworthy. I decided to 'phone Tom and explain once more the predicament. I did not have the ability on the phone to show, as Willy had done with his gnarled old hands, the effect of the shafting turning the stern tube in the stern post and thus working all the planking joints loose but Tom could see the simple logic. He promised he would start to seek a yard to accept us as soon as possible. Armed with this promise I returned on board. The tide was low. *Maeve* lay there silent, apart from her faithful Lister auxiliary chuffing away and a constant stream of bilge water spilling into the harbour. I stoked the range and cooked myself an egg and bacon, washed up and sat in my tiny cabin, smoking and thinking. I started to smile inside. A short time ago I was the Navigator of a Royal Navy Corvette, paid, fed, watered and able to rely on a whole host of other trained men to take a well-found ship from place to place to do Her Majesty's bidding. Now I was the Skipper of a leaking hulk with no crew, no money and, unless I saw to it, no food or water either. Life, I thought, could only get better from now on.

I made my way ashore and phoned Tom Swan.

'Yes,' he said enthusiastically,' I've found a yard which is just starting up at the mouth of Cork Harbour. It's called Session's Yard and they can take you at once. How soon can you sail?

I explained what Willy had said about the crew. There was a silence from the other end. Then he said he would see if he could find anyone to keep me company for the passage and rang off. I walked slowly back down the jetty, but when I reached *Maeve* I found a smiling Irishman there to welcome me. He introduced himself as Paddy Sharkey.

We went below and I made two steaming mugs of tea. He listened intently as I poured out my heart to him. 'It would not be a good idea to sail alone, John,' he said. I knew he was right, but I was so angry that I was determined to leave next morning.

Suddenly I realised how rude I had been. 'I'm sorry,' I said, 'I'm so tied up in my own worries I never even asked why you had come to see me'.

He grinned broadly. 'Sure and hadn't I come to find out when to fit the new radio? Pity it hasn't arrived 'cause you're going to need at least a receiver for the trip you're taking if only for weather forecasts'. He stopped and thought. 'Tell you what, I've an old receiver at home.' He got up and, thanking me for the tea, said he would be back later to fix something up. With that he climbed the ladder and departed up the jetty.

I made my way to the engine room. The sooner I got to grips with my machinery, I thought, the better. I had just shut down the main engine and was checking the compressed air bottles to ensure they were ready for the following day's start, when a very Oxford accent shouted from the jetty. 'Below there, Skipper!'

Grabbing a piece of rag and wiping my oily hands as I went, I climbed on deck. A very erect, grey-haired man was climbing on board. He held out his hand and introduced himself. A black patch covered one eye. 'Hear you require a chap to keep you company for a passage to Cork,' he said. 'I was astonished and led him below to the cabin. It transpired that he and his wife ran a small guest house inland and he was bored. He had flown with the Royal Flying Corps during the First World War, continued between the wars introducing aerial surveying and reckoned he could cope with the engine. He was one of those men you take to instantly and I was delighted to have such a companion. What he had told his long-suffering wife when he left home I hate to think. Anyway he now persuaded me to accompany him back to his house. On our arrival he introduced me to his wife and left to collect a tooth-brush, razor and a few clothes. In no time he returned and took charge.

'Right chaps, no time to waste - just off to Cork with John here.' He addressed his comments to the large Labrador dog as much as to his wife. 'You and the dog sit in the back. Skipper, you get in front'

In a trice we were on our way back to Killybegs. On the jetty he kissed his wife, patted the dog and turned to board *Maeve* without further ado. 'We'll phone when we arrive,' he shouted over his shoulder. I waved and we went below. I had just completed showing my new engineer round his domain when I heard Paddy shouting from above.

Back on deck, I was astonished to see Paddy with a woman carrying what appeared to be miles of fine wire. He introduced his wife Peggy and as I handed her on board, he lowered a tool-box and followed with a radio receiver. I followed him into the wheel-house with his tools. 'I hope you are good at shinning up masts,' he grinned, handing me one end of the fine wire. 'I want that secured like this' (he showed me what he had in mind) 'up there to that point,' and he indicated a position close to the masthead. I set off and managed to do as he had bid, sliding down again exhausted. 'OK so far,' he said. 'Now the other end fixed there.' He pointed aloft again to the after-mast above the wheel-house. I set off once more and under his eagle eye passed the wire back to him. There was then much screwing and adjusting of the old set until suddenly I heard music.

'It works!' I said amazed.

'Of course it does you bloody ignorant Englishman,' he replied. I passed him a cigarette and smiled. A small figure with very thick-lensed glasses was making his way on board. 'Good man,' shouted Paddy from the open wheel-house window. 'I knew you wouldn't let me down.' I looked at Paddy for an explanation. 'I told you,' he said, 'I did not think it a good idea to sail alone so I arranged for this fellow to keep you company. Come on,' he said, 'it's time we went below for a mug of tea.'

As we made our way below a wonderful smell of stew wafted upwards from the galley. Paddy's wife, Peggy, had been brewing up a meal fit for a king. I did not know what to say. For strangers to put themselves out in such a way for an idiot Englishman was incredible. Even worse, they refused point blank to join us and all I had to offer them was a cup of tea.

'Come on, boys,' said Peggy, 'the table's laid and the stew's getting cold. Sit you down and feed. Skipper tells me you are in for an early start tomorrow.' I tried to thank them both for all their kindness and help.

'Will you sit down and shut up,' said Paddy. 'Come on, wife, we have things to do.' As they left, he shouted back, 'I'll let you know when the new set arrives and will come down to Cork and fit it. Safe journey!' They were gone.

I looked round the cabin table and grinned at my two newly-found friends. They grinned back and we all tucked into Peggy's stew. I have never been more grateful for a meal in all my life and, had it not been for her kindness, I am sure we would have all finished up in the local pub that night and would never have sailed. It also gave us the opportunity to get to know each other a bit. The new engineer was an incredible character; they don't build them like that any more. His attitude to life belied his years. The newest arrival we immediately christened the 'Dormouse' because of his hunched up appearance and his glasses. He too was a character. Some years before, whilst diamond prospecting in South Africa, had made a very substantial find, but the very day he recorded his stake, the laws were altered, making him a pauper instead of a millionaire. He had every right to drown his sorrows, which he had been doing ever since. Paddy had hijacked him from the boatyard for this trip and I was doubtful about the stories he told us that night in our smoke-filled cabin, but years later I read a book which substantiated all he had said.

Before turning in I explained just how I intended to handle *Maeve* so we could be away before the local boats left in the morning. I did not want them to see a crew of landlubbers making a mess of things. My alarm clock went off and I was so keen to leave that I was dressed and in the main cabin within seconds. Shouting abuse in the time-honoured way, I retreated to the galley, stoked the range and had the kettle boiled and the tea made before the first bleary-eyed crew member showed his face. As we sipped our tea, I again went through the way we would warp ourselves clear of the other moored boats. Then I would start the engine. It was absolutely imperative that no warp be allowed to fall into the water anywhere near the propeller because as soon as I started the engine the propeller would start to turn ever so slowly. Having got things started on deck I went below to ready the engine; a voice from above told me they were all ready and I turned the compressed air valve to turn the engine over. She fired at once, but just as I was about to close the valve the engine stopped abruptly. I knew instinctively that we had picked up a warp round the propeller. I rushed up the ladder. Sure enough, there was the Dormouse gazing in disbelief at the stern rope leading straight to the propeller. This was no time for niceties.

'Follow me,' I screamed as I ran forward. *Maeve* was being taken into the middle of the harbour by the breeze and tide. I cleared away the anchor - yelled for them both to stand clear and let go. A splash and the noise of the cable running out I was sure would awaken the whole town. As soon as she had swung to her anchor I turned to the shaken crew. 'Fetch that ladder.' I pointed to the ladder in question.

'Lash that inboard and throw the ladder over the side there.' They both ran off to do as bid. I removed my sea boots and by the time they had the ladder over the side I was stripped to my underpants with just a knife on a lanyard round my waist. I plunged over the side and swam to the stern. Taking a deep breath I dived to the propeller. Sure enough there were a couple of turns of the stern rope wound around it. I had just sufficient breath to make a start before surfacing for more air. The water was ice-cold. After a few more dives I had managed to clear one of the turns but was breathless and frozen. I swam back to the ladder and climbed on board. Still furious, I turned to the Dormouse. 'You put the bloody rope round the screw, your turn now to take it off!'

To his eternal credit he never argued. Stripping to his underpants he went over the side. As I pulled on the stern rope he dived and suddenly we were free. As our engineer helped him back on board I made sure that all the warps were properly stowed. The poor Dormouse, teeth chattering his apologies was congratulated for his efforts and I took the new engineer below to show him how to start the engine. We had just weighed the anchor and were steaming out of harbour as the first of the local boats started up her engines. I hoped they had not seen our display

Donegal Bay is huge. By late that afternoon we were approaching the western end of it when I received a gale warning on Paddy's receiver. South-easterly gales were forecast. The constant pounding and movement had increased the inflow of water from the stern post and it would obviously be fool hardy to attempt a passage down the west coast of Ireland with the possibility of the gales swinging round to the south-west or west. With both pumps going full blast we were keeping the water at bay, thus I sought shelter in the first possible anchorage.

The gale raged all night but by the following afternoon it had eased, so we put the dinghy over the side and rowed ashore to find a telephone. I knew the people at home would be worried having had no news of our progress, and any calls made to the local Coast Guards could have caused concern. On our return we decided to sail at once and by ten thirty that night I picked up Johnny Corrigan's moorings off Inish Galloon just south of Keel in Achill Island. At once we were visited by my old shark-fishing friend, Jim O'Gorman, and we had a great reunion. The following afternoon the wind had gone round to the west north-west and we sailed on. I see from my notebook that we needed to stop once to clear the 'limber holes,' but the rest of the passage went without incident. At eleven o'clock on the night of the 12th of July we were moored alongside at Monkstown pier; it had taken us three days and nights but she had made it. We were all tired, filthy but very content.

At six thirty the next morning I roused the crew. 'Come on chaps,' I said, 'I know where we can get hot baths and the best breakfast in the whole of Ireland.'

The home my folks had bought was only a mile from this jetty. Still dressed in our sea-going clothes and (though we did not realise it) stinking of diesel, we made our way to the back door. I could hear the dogs barking and knew that our old family Nanny would be right then boiling water for the early morning tea. I knocked on the door. A few moments later Nanny opened it. Her eyes were a sight never to be forgotten. She just looked at me, filthy and unshaven, and then at my two companions. 'You'd better leave your boots in the yard,' she said, 'then come in and sit down.'

By the time we were seated I could hear voices shouting from upstairs. Suddenly the entire household was in the kitchen all talking at once. Introductions were swift and my two colleagues were led away to bathrooms. An hour later we were all enjoying the comfort of clean clothes, very full tummies and the absence of constant motion; no explorers had ever been made more welcome. I 'phoned Tom Swan whose relief one could hear in his voice.

Like all good things, this particular meeting had to end. The three of us walked slowly back to the poor old *Maeve*. As I unlocked the door at the back of the wheel-house, the smell of diesel smote us. I turned to the old engineer. 'Contrast,' I said, 'has always seemed to me to be the beauty of living.'

He smiled back. 'I agree, but I've often thought that I could well do without some of the unpleasant things first.' I was never to see that fine gentleman again, but the Dormouse I was to meet again, many moons later, in Killybegs. In retrospect I could not have chosen a more cheerful or willing crew for such a passage. It was amazing, too, that, although neither had ever done anything like that in their lives before, despite severe weather and filthy conditions, neither was sick. I have always been very lucky with my friends and I hope they both knew just how grateful I was for their assistance.

Old Willy's logic could not be faulted. Until the engine was moved further aft in poor *Maeve*'s ample bosom, she would continue the indignity of being branded as unseaworthy, due to the constant inflow of water from her abused stern end. An Englishman called Sessions, whose brother ran a boatyard in England, was just setting up a new yard in Monkstown. We were to be his first clients. After an initial inspection all haste was made to finish the slipway and haul *Maeve* out of the water, and then new drawings were produced to enable the engine to be moved as far aft as the existing bulkheads would allow. I left my small cabin and retreated to the luxury of my folks' home.

The weeks passed and the work progressed. It was time for Tom Swan to pay a visit. Meantime Paddy Sharkey phoned to say that the radio had arrived and he came down and installed it. My folk looked after him and, as soon as the crew turned up, I moved back aboard. Now, however, *Maeve* was a different vessel. During the refit we had painted her throughout. The new engine room was spotless white gloss, the various pipes were all colour coded for ease of recognition and the copper work shone like burnished gold. She really did look a picture. At last I was proud to show people around and the crew were delighted with the changes. We had stripped down and overhauled all the machinery so now we *knew* everything worked. On our transom we had a new net and newly-spliced ropes filled the 'waist' on each side.

167

The day set aside for engine trials dawned bright and beautiful. As we moved slowly away from the jetty I called the Coast Guard on the new radio and it was wonderful to feel the lady lift her skirts to the Atlantic swell as we turned west to put her through her paces. After a couple of hours the engineers said they were satisfied. It was such a beautiful day the passengers all said, why didn't we shoot the gear to show them how it all worked and we could check the 'coilers' too. I must admit I would have preferred to head home but the volume of opinion was such that it would have been churlish to have done so.

This was the first time I had 'shot' the gear and only by the grace of God did I manage to find the dan boy holding our rope. At one stage, as we hauled, my Mate said we were fast, but gradually the ropes were recovered and neatly coiled down either side in the waist. Eventually the gulls, which had been following us, started to dive on our cod end as it surfaced. No one was more relieved than I was to see that net back aboard although it was badly damaged. The problem now facing me was what to do with the fish we had caught? First thing, of course, was to land the various passengers, including Tom Swan. Then with a motley gang trying their hand at gutting fish for the first time, I sailed up the river to Cork.

One of the crew went ashore to find a buyer for the fish. In his absence the rest of us were all gutting as fast as we could to the delight of the local seagulls. Suddenly a very angry harbour official roared his disapproval from the jetty above. Who the hell did we think we were and what the hell did we think we were doing?

'Do yer want some fish?' Willy grinned back at him. Before he could blow his top totally, Willy climbed the greasy ladder built into the wall carrying a wire basket full of still flapping fish. The irate official, measuring the gift in his mind in the potential number of pints it would purchase, looked at Willy.

'It's against the law to gut alongside here,' he announced.

'And what, pray, do you suggest, sir?' asked Willy. 'Tell you what,' Willy continued, 'there is more where that came from, fine fresh fish. We're awaiting a buyer right now. You've done your duty and as soon as the buyer turns up we will be away out of it.' The official smiled at last. We parcelled up his fish for him and eventually a little man turned up and said he'd relieve us of our burden. We had only just completed things when a steamer rounded the bend and we had to slip to make room for her. In those days before ice was available, you either got rid of your catch or by the following afternoon you had a nasty smell on deck .

That night, before turning in, I sat down at the little desk in my cabin and drew pictures. The way a fly-seiner worked was to drop a dan buoy, with one end of its rope attached to it, and then steam away paying out a mile of rope. This was attached to the net, which was then 'shot' and the remaining mile of rope allowed the boat to return to collect the first rope from its dan buoy. Having then both ends of rope aboard, they were led through the coiler and as the boat steamed very slowly forward the coilers would retrieve the ropes. Finally the net would arrive back on board full of fish. So much for the simple mechanics of the system. But how do you steer a small vessel, bouncing all over the place, in a nice smooth circle while you shoot two miles of rope and finish up back at the place you started from? Obviously the simplest way would be to steer a series of straight courses that would in total bring you back to your starting point.

We had spliced ten reels of new rope together and each splice had been painted. If I shot five coils (I could count the coloured splices) then altered course and shot another three coils before altering course again and shooting two coils, I would be at my net, shoot that, and by reversing the procedure should theoretically end up steaming back to the dan buoy. I drew out the theoretical courses to be steered and made a gadget which would translate these courses whatever heading I needed. I now felt confident that I could shoot my gear and return to my dan. Contented, I turned in.

The theory of this method of fishing is that the ropes, as they stutter along the seabed, disturb the fish and frighten them into the centre of the huge rope circle. The boat steams slowly forward and, as the ropes are coiled in, the net slowly follows, scooping up the fish in its path. It is a very efficient way to catch fish if the ground is clean, but inevitably rocks, wrecks and other obstacles, even very soft mud or sand can cause problems. Since I had no one to discuss these things with at that time, I had to use my own initiative to resolve the problems as they arose. In retrospect I would have been better advised to go back to Killybegs to learn rather than do it the hard way as I did.

We were about early next morning. The damaged net was landed on the jetty and spread. I was astonished that a net so tattered and torn could hold any fish. Although I had once spent the winter months in Achill Island knitting shark nets, I had never been taught how to mend a net. The destruction now facing me really frightened the life out of me. Where did one start? Fortunately for me, one of my crew, Jackie McGowan, *did* know how to mend nets. My job now was to learn from him as quickly as possible. When it became apparent that Jackie was the only one who could mend, discussion began about how the shares were to be allocated, another question that, till then, had never even occurred to me. Any fisher folk reading this narrative will be astonished at my naiveté. For the benefit of my readers it could be helpful to explain how the share system works.

In those days in an inshore vessel, the catch would be divided into two initial shares. One half went to the boat. The other half would be broken down into shares. The Skipper would be allocated two shares, the Mate and Engineer one and a half shares each. The deck hands who could mend and splice and knew their job would each receive one share. Any other crew, unqualified, would get half a share. Thus in monetary terms, if a catch was worth say £100, the boat's share would be £50. The remaining £50 would be split into shares according to the number and constitution of the crew

This age-old well-tried method, as can be seen, is designed to recompense those in authority for their added responsibilities and knowledge. It is also designed to encourage the learners to learn their trade. Few things are more annoying for a crew, after a bad day's fishing in the depths of winter, than to return to harbour and have to spend half the night, under a spotlight, in wet and freezing conditions, mending a net for the following day, in the knowledge that some of their members are tucked away in warm beds because they cannot mend even simple holes in nets. I felt it was a very sound system and certainly it encouraged other members of my crew to learn how to splice and mend.

The crew of the *Maeve*

CHAPTER THIRTY-FOUR - *MAEVE* REBORN.

Any bloody fool can be uncomfortable. Somebody, maybe my father, had told me this simple truth many years before and I have always believed that wherever one is it's worth the effort to make oneself as comfortable as is possible. This refit had given us the opportunity to turn poor *Maeve* from a dirty, stinking, unseaworthy hulk into a spotless, comfortable home. The crew were proud to show her off and I was proud to show them off. They had stuck with me during the dark days and I was determined to do the very best I could for them in return.

The news from around the coast (now we had a radio, we could talk to other boats further afield) was of a poor fishing everywhere. Typical south-westerly gales and November weather prevailed. It was decided that we would start off by trying our luck locally. Thus at six o'clock on the 17th November we sailed from Monkstown. The day dawned grey and overcast with a light south-easterly wind. By eight thirty we had shot our gear. This was it, I thought, as the crew went below for their breakfast. Slowly I steered *Maeve* into the Atlantic swell. What, I wondered, would our first haul produce? At ten o'clock we found out. The net was in tatters.

A three point fix in my notebook still warns me to stay well clear of that patch of sea where some 'fast' exists which did not show on my echo-sounder trace. Back in harbour we spread the net and set to mending.

Six o'clock the following day we were off again. This time I ran over the ground with my echo-sounder running; it all seemed clean and my Mate confirmed with an 'armed' lead-line that the bottom was sandy. We shot our gear. Fifteen minutes later we had become fast on our starboard warp. It was solid. We fixed a dan buoy to our port warp and hauled ourselves back on the starboard one; after much manoeuvring we cleared this, recovered our net and then the port warp. Time to start all over again.

This time, as they were shooting the net over the stern, a piece of the cod end caught on one of the rollers and the net was ripped. Once more the gear needed to be hauled, the net mended and then shot once more.

It was almost midday as we started once more to tow our gear. Again we were fast. We retrieved our gear and started off again. Almost at once both warps were fast. Now my Mate said he felt we were in a patch of very soft sand so we steamed further to the east. By this time a steady drizzle had set in to accompany the cold wind; we decided to have one more shot before the visibility and light left us. As we shot our gear I prayed for a break. Imagine my heartache and dismay when on turning on to the final course to return to our dan, there was no sign of it anywhere. I have never felt so awful. What sort of a clot of a Skipper did my crew think they had got? There was nothing for it but to retrieve our gear once again. It was a very silent and dispirited crew that tied up that night. Such was the life of the inshore man in those days. It called for enormous patience and determination. I am still amazed, as I read my old log book, at the trials and tribulations we took in our stride day after day, and still tumbled out of our bunks next morning, bright and early, to continue the battle. It is noticeable in life that when one is down and everything which can go wrong appears to do so, those able to keep going are the ones to survive. We went through some really dreadful days when whatever we did went wrong. The harder we tried, the worse things appeared to get. I do not believe any Skipper ever had a more patient bunch of men with him.

In retrospect, some of our problems were self-inflicted because we were all learning to some extent, but our run of misfortune took its time to change. The effect, however, was to produce a very tight-knit bunch of men who believed in themselves and showed their mettle over the years ahead.

One of the advantages of having a radio, as I have said, was that now we could talk to other boats and listen to them discussing their catches. In those days, if one walked up a street in a fishing area, one would have heard the 'Boats Frequency' from every house. Every woman going about her work would be tuned to the 'Boats' and that way one knew we could always get news ashore quickly and reliably. This fact had all sorts of interesting possibilities. There was the famous occasion when an Income Tax Inspector appeared on the jetty seeking a particular Skipper. One of the boats alongside noticed this man and sent word out on an open line. That night, the Skipper in question failed to return to harbour. The same thing happened the next day and the day after. The poor Inspector was bemused. The rumour was that the boat had sailed for Bantry. In desperation the Inspector departed back to Dublin and that night the Skipper returned to Killybegs. Each night he had passed his catch to another boat to land for him, and they in turn had provisioned the boat the following day. They could have kept it up for weeks had they needed to do so. On the more serious level though, it enabled medical attention to be available as soon as a boat landed with an injured man. Without such prior warning, the delay could be a matter of life and death.

Each Skipper had his own 'whistle', which he would use to warn other boats he was about to pass a message. So, as soon as he had hauled his gear, and could see what was in his fish ponds on deck, he would operate his 'whistle' and give a brief synopsis of what he could see. Something along the lines of, 'Five or six boxes, mainly haddock with a few small plaice.' Then silence. Everyone afloat and ashore knew his whistle so no names were needed. Because the Spanish 'pair trawlers' also kept a listening watch on this frequency it was vital to keep the messages brief and never to mention hake. On one occasion, at least, when an over-excited Skipper made such an error, he was literally swept up, gear and all, by these larger and more powerful boats. The only hope of escape was if the Irish Sea Fishery patrol happened to be about, but with only three boats to cover their entire coastline, that chance was remote in the extreme. I like to think that I may sometimes have been able to help because one of the Irish Navy's vessels was called *Maeve*; so on the occasions when I used my vessel's name, perhaps I made a few Spanish Skippers think twice before coming too close.

We decided to try our luck further to the east and we set off for Dungarven. Tied up that night in Helvick, we walked up the hill to the pub at the top. As we entered we could hear a murmur of English conversation emanating from the bar. I led my men in and ordered pints for them. A silence followed as we were eyed by the assembled company, then conversation started again, this time in Gaelic. The intention was obvious. I looked at the bar-tender as he uncorked the bottles of stout.

'Are you Irish speakers?' he asked without looking at me.

Before I could say a word my Mate, eyes blazing, said in a loud but low tone that he most certainly *was* an Irish speaker. The bar-tender passed the filled glasses over the counter, took his money, and gradually the conversation resumed, in English. We decided we did not like the atmosphere and returned on board. The following day we fished alongside the local boats. We found them, like their colleagues the night before, less than friendly and turned our bows west again. This was the only episode during my years working in Ireland that I ever encountered any hostility.

The remainder of that December we fished from Castlehaven, Baltimore and Schull - names to conjure with, lovely places and full of lovely people. We could not have been treated more kindly and it came as something of a surprise to me to learn that my Donegal men were treated as much as strangers as I was. The men from the West would travel to America, Scotland and England but, as I was to find out later, they would not travel to Donegal.

The morning of the 18th December saw us fishing out of Baltimore. It was a dismal, drizzly dawn with a rising south-westerly wind and a heavy Atlantic swell rolling in. We had started our first tow. The sea was steep and the wind was rising. Almost at once the starboard warp tightened; immediately I slowed and shouted below for the crew to come on deck. Having buoyed the offending warp we very slowly hauled our way back on the remaining warp towards our net.

Willy was seated on the starboard gunwale, balancing his swaying body in time to the pitch and roll. As the coiler did its work he would rise and take the coiled rope aft. The wind and sea was making it very difficult, at such slow speed, to keep *Maeve* steering and I was fighting the wheel with spray stinging its way across the boat. Suddenly, as Willy rose to collect another coil of ropes, the roll made him slip and, just for a second, his right leg moved inside a coil of rope. I saw it all as in slow motion and screamed at my Mate, pointing to Willy who was even then being dragged over the starboard bow.

As *Maeve* heaved upwards and then dropped ten feet, Willy was tossed overboard. I was frantically trying to bring *Maeve* head to wind and could only shout at the men forward to get a line around him. As soon as I could, I lashed the wheel and ran forward to inspect the situation. As *Maeve* rose to the swell Willy was clear of the water, holding on for grim life to the warp, his right leg held tightly by the coil into which he had stepped. They had managed to get a heaving line round his body before he had been hauled further away from us, but unless we could

173

free his leg we could not get him back. *Maeve* dipped into the trough of another swell and Willy disappeared from view below the angry swirling waters. Shouting above the din of the weather, I told my Mate that I intended to drive *Maeve* forward slowly. He would need to indicate where Willy was as I couldn't see from the wheel-house. As long as they were very quick, we might just be able to collect him between swells and whip the coil off his leg then haul him back aboard. I ran back to the wheel-house, my heart thumping as never before.

Easing the throttle forward and grabbing the wheel I managed to get *Maeve* to react. The small knot of men in the bows, balancing as best they could, were lying right over the side. I could see an extra high sea approaching and yelled to them to stand by. Then it was on us. A great surge of spray and green water landed in my face through the open wheel-house window. As I wiped my eyes clear I could see a mass of bodies sprawled in the bows -they'd done it, they'd got him back! I eased the throttle back and lashed the wheel once more. Rushing forward I grasped old Willy by the hands. 'You stupid old bastard', I cried. 'What on earth did you do that for? You frightened the life out of all of us. Get below and dry out.' Turning to my Mate I said, 'I think we've had enough excitement for one day. We'll dan this warp too, then return to harbour and get Willy to a doctor.'

As we turned for home I glanced back; somewhere in amongst that stormy water was all our gear, ropes, net, everything. I only hoped that the knots we had used to hold the warps to the dan buoys held and that the buoys themselves would ride out the storm. Priority now was to get a doctor to see old Willy. He had taken a terrible bashing apart from being near drowned every time he was dunked under water. His only comment during the whole awful episode was made as he surfaced on one occasion. 'Don't delay too long, lads, my arms are giving out.' He was, as the Irish would say, a tough one and no dispute

To everyone's astonishment the doctor gave Willy a clean bill of health. Bruising apart, he had no broken bones. We all went ashore to the local pub and held a well-earned celebration, joined by the local fishermen. It really was a miracle that he was still with us. The locals were as happy as we were. Willy had become well-known to them as a most generous, delightful man who would drink with anyone, and they showed their delight by their hospitality and friendliness.

The storm, like all storms, eventually blew itself out and, although it was a Sunday, the locals came out with us as we went in search of our gear. Sure enough, to my delight, as we made our way to the 'fix' I had marked on the chart, I suddenly caught sight of the tiny dan buoy, its tattered flag still fluttering bravely. By that evening we had everything back on board and were able to take a trip ashore for a final celebration with clear consciences.

Now Christmas was upon us, so we returned to Monkstown. My crew went back to their families in Killybegs and I spent the festive season with my folks. On the evening of the 6th January we sailed for Schull. I wondered, as we ploughed our way westwards once more, what the new year would hold in store. The fishing around the coasts was still very patchy and we had decided that we would work our way around the western tip to Bantry, but we needed an extra man as we had lost old Willy to hospital. Having spread the word ashore through the local agent that a man was wanted, we were met one evening by two local men. The elder was a trained fisherman, the younger one a learner - I engaged them both.

What a pity that we did not have tape-recorders in those days. The older man was one of a dying breed, a storyteller, and a magnificent one at that. How I wish I could have recorded the stories he told us in that smoke-filled cabin during those long, winter evenings. With the wind howling outside and the boat straining at her mooring ropes, he would entertain us with his stories. His ability was such that on one occasion, I remember, we had the greatest difficulty in getting his young friend to turn into his bunk, being quite convinced it held a ghost. His stories held all the charm of the ancients but he told them as if they had happened the day before yesterday.

'You know old Paddy Joe,' he would say to his young friend. The young man would nod.

'I know him well,' he would reply.

'But did I ever tell you about his uncle?' Then would start a fascinating tale, made all the more interesting since we all knew the characters involved and of course the places were all local too. While I was Skipper I refused to have alcohol on board, so these evenings were conducted in total abstinence and yet were as fraught with tension as any cinema I have ever visited. He truly had the gift of the Blarney in the very best sense - I often wonder what happened to him. Perhaps he is still telling his stories; if not here then, I am sure, with huge success in the great beyond.

One of the things I learned from him was a respect for local superstitions. He explained, for instance, it was very bad luck to go fishing if you met a red-haired girl on your way to the harbour. It seemed, too, that pigs and hares could also put paid to fishing that day. Many moons later, I was to remember this man when, having waited for two hours one morning for a crew member, I at last sailed without him. When we returned that evening, there he was, bold as brass taking our lines and chatting to his mates. I was about to blow my top when he explained quite casually that he had to turn back because he had seen a hare that morning. Forewarned is forearmed. I looked at him long and hard and drew on my cigarette.

'Of course,' I answered, 'but we still waited for you for two hours.' It may be coincidence but that was the last time any of my crew was ever late.

We were happy in those western places. Does the Frenchman still have those lobster ponds where he collects lobsters from all over Ireland and then, when the price is right, flies them alive to London or Paris? I remember the sight outside my caravan in Keel, in Achill Island, of the strange curragh with eight large feet sticking out from under its upturned body. These had been lobster fishermen from the west whose catch went to swell the Frenchman's ponds. What has happened to that tiny smoke-house on the jetty where the local merchant smoked us our own haddock for breakfast, and the Skippers and boats that fished out of Berehaven and Bantry - such helpful and friendly folk.?

But now the news from Killybegs was of an upturn in the fishing while the local Bantry fishing was poor, so this was the time to return to our home base at last. When we told the two new crew members about our plans we were already steaming north. To my amazement I was immediately approached in the wheel-house by the elder man.

'You can't take us to Donegal,' he said. 'You must turn round and land us back where you collected us.' I looked at him in surprise; they had become such a part of our team it had never occurred to me that they might not wish to continue with us. I tried to persuade him to change his mind, but I was forced to turn the boat round and do as he requested. We really were very sorry to see them go, but they were quite adamant that Donegal was not for them. A small group had collected on the jetty at Schull as we dropped them off and waved goodbye - genuine and decent folk.

Now we headed north again. It was seven months since I had left Killybegs with my two cronies to sail a leaking hulk to Cork. We were returning in a spotless, seaworthy boat with a proud crew. Under these circumstances a night passage can be very relaxing. Below, my crew slept their well-earned rest. Alone on the wheel I had time to enjoy the night; the long even swell, with only a touch of wind, required just the tiniest movement of the helm. The regular rhythmic engine noise, like the base of some great symphony, was a fitting accompaniment to the swish of the water. Astern, our wash, a silver ribbon of bubbles, ahead the loom of the light beckoning us home.

The following morning my Mate relieved me. I had a quick breakfast and a cat-nap. I was sorely tempted to call and visit my old shark-fishing friends in Achill which we passed that evening, but the wind had backed round to the north-west and it was prudent to press onwards. By midnight we were altering course into Donegal Bay, our last leg home. By three o'clock, visibility had closed right down. I knew Jackie McGowan knew his bay well but thick fog can play very funny tricks. It was another five hours of peering into murk and fog before he suddenly recognised Rathlin O'Birne and another few hours before we were safely berthed once more alongside in our home port.

CHAPTER THIRTY-FIVE - KILLYBEGS

After the initial home-coming welcomes were over, I called on James McCloud, the acknowledged expert on sein net fishing. I explained that, while I had taught myself how to shoot the gear and handle that side of things, I knew nothing about how to set up our nets. One of the Skippers at Berehaven had explained to me the importance of having them set correctly. James could not have been more helpful.

'You land your nets and get them stretched, he said, 'and I'll explain to you what is needed.'

As soon as the crew returned the following morning we landed every net. James, true to his word, came over and inspected them. He explained why they would not fish properly and what needed to be done to put them right. It also gave us the opportunity to put right some of the 'mends' that had been done at sea in a hurry. By the time we had finished, our gear was in proper shape and we were raring to prove our ability alongside the other boats.

Although angling is one of the most popular of our national sports, the closest most people get to a whiting, haddock or plaice is when they undo the paper surrounding it and add salt and vinegar. Where do fishermen go to catch these fish? How do they know where to shoot their gear?

Donegal Bay contains around seven hundred square miles of sea. On any given day, where, in this vast area, should a fisherman look for fish? James McCloud had been fishing this Bay since before the war. Like all great fisherman he had kept records over the years and had as good an idea as any man alive where to go, given the season and the prevailing weather. I asked him now if he would mind if I followed his lead. Being a good-natured and honest man, he instantly agreed.

Tom Swan had arranged for old Charlie McGowan to accompany us, and I was delighted to learn from Tom, after the first day's outing, that he had reported back favourably on the way our team worked. Over the past months we had become as proficient as any other boat at the mechanics of shooting and handling our gear. Now, fishing alongside James's boat, we started to catch fish, never, I must admit, in the same quantity as he did, but certainly up to the level that other boats managed. We were learning fast. All the Killybegs boats worked well together as a direct result of the example James had set over the years - Killybegs has much to thank him for.

The local hotel at the head of the pier supplied most of our needs. The widow who owned it said I was welcome to use one of her bathrooms, once a week to clean up. Thus, every Saturday evening, I would make my way there to reappear an hour later a rather more wholesome-smelling man. The Skippers and their crews met there every Saturday evening and I was invited to join them. These get-togethers were fabulous. We would discuss every subject under the sun and really put the world to rights. When it was time to close the pub, the widow would move our small party upstairs to a private room, then, placing the keys to the bar on the table, would wish us good night. So long as anyone wanted to continue, the party went on. It was a great way for everyone to get to know each other.

It was during one of these evenings that I became involved in one of the most interesting 'nights out' I've ever had. Big Georgie Buchan approached me on behalf of his wife to ask if I could drive a car. I replied that I could.

Fine, said Georgie, in that case would I do him a favour and drive his car out into the mountains because he, his wife and some friends needed to attend a wake and by the time they had finished no one would be able to drive home again. Naturally I agreed. We finished our pints and piled into Georgie's car. The road out of Killybegs led us to an isolated cabin in the hills that took quite a time to reach. On our arrival I was all set to stay in the car but Georgie and his wife were adamant that I accompany them. I explained that I had never been to a wake and did not know how to behave.

'Just follow me and do as I do,' said Georgie. 'Everything will be fine.' Two young men were relieving themselves into some bushes as we approached. There was the noise of music from an open window. Georgie pushed his wife ahead of him, removed his cap and ducked under the lintel. I followed. I heard what Georgie said and repeated the same words to the person who welcomed us in. We were led into a small bedroom to the right of the door and given a chair each. Instantly we were handed a half pint glass each of neat whisky. I glanced nervously over at Big Georgie; he was beaming and gave me a huge wink. Raising his glass he proposed a toast to the house and to all in it. We drank with him. Somebody had produced some old photographs and these were passed from hand to hand. Naturally they meant nothing to me so I just made non-committal noises of admiration and passed them on. The laughter and music from the other end of the small house made it difficult to hear what was being said, but I gathered that Georgie and his wife had known the personage who was sitting up in bed.

To start with I had assumed that the bed held an ageing widow to whom we had come to pay our respects. It came as a shock to realise that this was no widow but the dead man. Dressed in his best night attire, propped up by spotless pillows, he sat there at peace with the world, while all around him was a hum of conversation. A voice in my ear enquired if I had known the old man? Feeling myself redden I replied that I was driving the Buchans.

'Sure and you must be the new English Skipper,' said the voice, at the same time refilling my tumbler to the brim. I again glanced at Georgie, but he was in deep conversation and my eyes were drawn back to the corpse in that bed. Suddenly I had the awful feeling that the old man was going to open those eyes, fix me with a glassy stare and enquire in a stentorian bellow 'Who are you, and what the hell are *you* doing in my bedroom?'

By now the whisky was taking its effect and I had a great urge to giggle at the prospect. Fortunately, before I lost control, a new couple arrived and we were politely shepherded into the other room where the party was in full swing. I glanced at my watch. There was no doubt that this particular party was going to watch the sun rise - I decided I had better take refuge in the car before any more whisky was poured into me.

Around five o'clock I went back inside and found Georgie's wife. She, in turn, eventually found Big Georgie and the other passengers. Full of good humour and with the cries of the party-goers still ringing in our ears, we bumped our way back to Killybegs. The snores from the back seat indicated that everyone had had a superb wake and I felt privileged to have been invited to attend. I cannot think of a nicer way to be seen off by all one's friends and shall always be grateful to Big Georgie and his diminutive wife for taking me along with them.

As the days lengthened, we were able to increase the hours we worked. By March a fifteen-hour day would be the norm. The Skipper would be on his feet at the wheel for most of this time unless the catches were big enough for him to have to lash the wheel and help with the gutting on deck. Food was taken as and when possible, so the evening meal on return to port was savoured to the full.

James had trained a young man called Tommy Watson over the years and had sold him his old boat. Tommy was a natural and I became very friendly with him. We decided to look for new grounds further to the west and together went exploring. This involved leaving Killybegs very early in the morning, steaming for five to six hours into the Atlantic and fishing all day, riding out the hours of darkness and continuing the next day before landing that night. April, May and June saw us fishing all the daylight hours available, and as July passed into August the return of the whiting and haddock swelled our catches. We were at last keeping pace with the majority of the other local boats, never the master, but our hard work and long hours did gain us respect. It was during this time that my father visited me and spent a day with us. He enjoyed himself hugely but it took me all my time to retrieve him from the hospitality of the other Skippers who made him so welcome.

Tourists came to Killybegs during the summer season and, if asked, we would happily take them to sea for the day on the understanding that they would be ready to leave at our sailing time. We never charged them and fed them along with ourselves. Usually, they would ask before they left what they owed me and were delighted when I told them, nothing. It was nice to have had their company and I hoped they had enjoyed their day. Without exception they would leave a note with the pub to buy the crew a drink. It cost us nothing to carry them and gave them an insight into the way we earned our living.

Saturdays were usually spent in settling the crew's wages and other administrative jobs while maintenance of all sorts was being completed. It was on one of these days that a young English lad, on holiday with his aunt, asked my crew if they could find him a job as he was bored and liked boats. They duly fixed him up with a paint-brush and paint and he was as happy as Larry.

On Sunday morning, as I returned from church, there he was back again. 'Hello,' I said, 'you still bored?' He grinned and nodded. I beckoned him aboard and asked what he would like to do.

'Can I do some more painting, sir?' he asked very politely. So I fixed him up, then went below to change into working clothes. There were jobs I needed to do in the engine room before we sailed on the morrow.

Sunday in Killybegs was a non-fishing day. When I went back to the main cabin at lunchtime, there was the young lad tucking into a great fry-up. The crew had taken him to their hearts and he was grinning from ear to ear. He stopped his eating when I arrived and looking up at me asked if he could come fishing with us? 'Of course you can,' I said, 'but you'll have to get permission from your auntie. Do you think you can get out of bed in time to be ready to sail at three thirty tomorrow morning?' He nodded. Collecting a mug of tea I returned to my jobs in the engine room and thought no more about the conversation.

By five o'clock that evening I had finished the job. Covered in oil and sweating from my efforts I went back to the cabin to grab another mug of tea prior to cleaning my semi-naked body. To my embarrassment there, seated in the corner of the cabin, was a most beautiful young lady. She was dressed in a pretty summer frock, which showed off her figure to perfection. She was truly lovely and as her blue eyes met mine I could see she was enjoying my embarrassment. I was lost for words. A voice was saying, 'This is our Skipper.' Then the young lad, pointing rather rudely, added, 'And this is my aunt.' It's true that I had assumed 'Auntie' would have been a rather older woman.

'I'm sorry if I don't measure up to your idea of an aunt,' her soft voice was mocking me. She had read my mind and I just grinned. Very much aware of my semi-nakedness and filthy condition, I apologised.

'I don't think I have ever met a prettier aunt,' I rejoined. 'Now please excuse me while I get cleaned up.'

'Before you go' that same soft voice made me turn, 'would it be possible for you to take both of us fishing with you tomorrow? We'll be on time, Skipper, I promise.' Her demure smile and sideways glance would have melted an iceberg. I was aware of my crew's eyes and the young lad's too, fixed on me.

'Of course', I said with a smile, 'we'll be delighted to take you, but we shall be sailing at four, and we do not wait for anyone. Look forward to seeing you both then. I turned and left.

Next morning, as we shortened the lines, I could see the young lad with his beautiful escort walking briskly down the jetty. They were helped on board and shown to the wheel-house. At least now I was properly dressed and clean. Within minutes of them boarding we had slipped our ropes and were steaming out of harbour. Astern the peacefully sleeping village, ahead the swinging beam of the lighthouse beckoned us seawards. To the east the first streaks of dawn were appearing but we turned westward towards the fast-receding night sky. Every dawn at sea is different and I just hoped that this one would produce some spectacular colours for my lovely guest to enjoy. In the event we were not disappointed. It was a beautiful sunrise, but the wind was enough to produce quite a choppy sea and I wondered just how long my demure young lady's slim tummy would be able to cope with the unfamiliar motion.

As soon as it was safe to do so, I put the young lad on the wheel. He was so keen to learn, it took him no time to get the hang of things and while he had something to occupy his mind I was not worried about him getting seasick. Auntie, meanwhile, was asking intelligent questions, but when she was presented with an egg and bacon sandwich and a mug of tea she whispered to me that she thought she might like to lie down for while. Leaving my Mate in charge and the young lad on the wheel, I escorted Auntie below to my cabin. Having removed her shoes I helped her on to my bunk and gently placed a cover over her shapely young form. I remember thinking rather wickedly that it was she who needed a chaperone rather than her nephew. Looking down at her I said, 'You just lie there and relax. If you want anything - shout. Otherwise we'll leave you in peace. When you feel like it just come back to the wheel-house' Back in the wheel-house my Mate gave me an evil grin.

'Got her bedded down, Skipper, have you?' I suddenly realised that I would now have my leg pulled by every sailor in Killybegs.

'I don't suppose I can bribe you lot to keep this to yourselves?' I queried. He grinned back at me.

'You haven't enough money to buy the pints that *that* would cost Skipper,' he said, as he went on deck to prepare the gear for our first 'shot' of the day. The wind eased back and the sea calmed. By lunchtime I once more had my pretty companion beside me in the wheel-house. The young lad was now learning how to hold and gut fish and was hanging on every word the crew told him. All too soon that sunny day came to an end. For once everything had worked to perfection.

As we carved our way back through a golden silken sea, I plucked up courage and asked if I might see her again. She looked up at me and smiled. The evening sunlight silhouetted her youthful figure through her summer blouse and I was sorely tempted to take her in my arms then and there.

'Why don't you take me for a walk tomorrow night when you return to harbour?' she answered in that soft beautiful voice. My heart missed a beat as I swung the wheel over to take us up the last stretch to the harbour. The crew were readying the ropes and fenders, assisted by the young lad. Now I must achieve a professional berthing with no bumps. As we glided into our berth and I stopped the engine she held out her slim hand. 'Thank you for a lovely day and for looking after both of us so well.' Adding with a smile, 'Your bunk was much more comfortable than I ever thought possible.'

At that moment my Mate put his head round the door. He handed her to the deck before seeing both of them safely on to the jetty. I lit a cigarette, inhaled deeply and waved back, as they walked away into the approaching dusk.

The following evening she was at the harbour to meet us when we returned. We went for a walk as she had suggested. I learned that her holiday was almost finished;

my disappointment was so obvious that she laughed at me. Sitting looking out to sea, we chatted as if we had known each other for years. Suddenly she looked at me and said very seriously, 'Do you know, you have the most beautiful shoulders and back?' I swung round. Looking straight into her beautiful eyes I replied,

'And you, my darling, have the most beautiful front.' Before the impact of my words had time to enter her mind I had her in my arms. As our lips met a great surge of pent up emotion engulfed us both. I could hear her heart beating through her flimsy blouse. Memory does not recall how long we lay there. Suffice to say that she had to return to being an Auntie and I had to return to being an English gentleman. Often since, I have wondered what became of my delightful and pretty Auntie. I hope she met a good man with a beautiful back. As for the young lad, I hope he went to sea. Perhaps today he is Captain of a famous liner or an Admiral. He was so keen, I hope life has been kind to him too.

The father of another family we took to sea turned out to be an amateur photographer. In fact, since I did not own a camera in those days, I am indebted to him for the few photographs I have of *Maeve* and my crew, which he very kindly sent us after their day out. We only had one couple who turned out to be troublesome but, as is the way of the sea, their own seasickness sorted them out.

In September, Tom Swan approached me with the proposal that I should accompany him to Canada on a business trip. I had never been to Canada and such an opportunity was not to be missed. He told me that he was thinking of shifting all his interests over to Canada and wanted to go and see for himself what the Canadian government would do to help him. My job would be to 'carry his bag' and act as personal private secretary. While I was away, *Maeve* would be fished by young Charlie McGowan who had worked on board. He knew and got on well with my crew.

It felt odd to be wearing a collar and tie once more. We made our way up the gangway and a steward showed us to our cabin. I had never been in a liner in peacetime and I was amazed at the comfort surrounding us and the extent and quality of the menus. Tom turned out to be a rather silent companion. I explored the ship and wondered how to spend my time. It was, I found, boring not being able to be part of the ship's company. All my days at sea, I had had duties and responsibilities, but as a passenger I had nothing to do all day except laze around and, even for a short passage across the Atlantic, I was bored to tears.

The trip up the St Lawrence was fascinating, with visits to Quebec and Montreal before making for Ottawa. Here we were entertained by some of the top people from the Department of Immigration. Because Tom was thinking of transferring his business interests, which would produce new jobs, and they were keen to hear about his ideas. However, it soon became apparent to me that they were not over-impressed by his presentation of these ideas. I held my own council, but it was noticeable that their enthusiasm waned rather than gained as the days passed. Nevertheless, a fairly hectic programme had been arranged and off we went.

182

Canada in the autumn was as beautiful as the postcards suggested. The Maritimes, where the various Fishing Companies were sited, were no exception. The volume of fish being handled by these plants was impressive and I was most interested in their methods. One plant, I remember, used fresh sea-water, pumped from the ocean surrounding them, to transport the landed fish in open pipes around their plant. Either side of these pipes stood men with knives. As a fish floated past, it would be grabbed, dealt with and the filleted pieces placed back to float onwards. It was here that I first saw a machine for skinning flat-fish fillets and here, too, that I saw for the first time the now familiar 'Fish Fingers' being produced. At that time these things had not crossed the Atlantic and it was fascinating to see ideas in action before they reached our country. As the days passed and we visited more and more plants and factories, I got the impression that Tom Swan was being seen more as a dreamer than as a serious businessman. The people we were introduced to were very professional and knew their businesses inside out and in depth. Poor Tom, I felt, was a bit lost in their company. So it was a relief when we made our way back to Toronto where I was met and entertained by my old Canadian friend, David Fry, who had served aboard *Launceston Castle*. I well remember him showing us the Toronto Stock Exchange - a real madhouse! Our hosts could not have been more kind, but I had this nagging feeling that Tom's ideas would never get off the ground.

All too soon our time was up. We said our goodbyes and set sail for England. That night at dinner Tom asked me what I thought of Canada. I replied that what I had seen I had enjoyed. It was undoubtedly a beautiful country although our own glimpse had been very limited. It was also a country with tremendous potential. He nodded. What did I think of the people? I told him that the Canadians I had met, both during the war and since, I had liked very much. They seemed to have been able to hold on to their British attitude to life rather than just becoming North Americans. He nodded again. How would you feel about emigrating to Canada? Now this was a leading question and not so easily answered. I paused before I spoke. We had finished our meal and I reached for a cigarette.

'Tom,' I said slowly, 'at the moment I am a bachelor but, God willing, I do not intend to die a bachelor. I know it will sound stupid to you, but although I've met beautiful Canadian girls, I want my wife to bear me English children who will understand all that England means to me. If I emigrated to Canada I would undoubtedly marry a Canadian girl and those children would never know about England. I am also too set in my ways to start a new life in a new country. This is a young man's country.' Suddenly I felt stupid and stopped. He was considering what I had said.

'How do you think my work force would settle down over here?'

I pointed to a couple at a neighbouring table who had been on the same boat as us on our way out. He was a doctor. His wife had decided during the short time we had been visiting that she was too homesick and they were even now on their way home again. 'I believe, Tom,' I replied, 'that quite a lot of the folk back in Bally-shannon would find life so different and miss their friends and relations so much that they would not be happy in Canada.' He looked crestfallen. 'But I believe this trip has been worthwhile,' I tried to cheer him up, 'if you have absorbed new ideas for your business. We've seen some most interesting ideas, which I'm sure you can use.' This subject was never raised again.

November saw me back again skippering *Maeve*. The weather was foul and the fishing worse. Tommy Watson was now involved with another boat purse-net fishing for herring. I went out with him to watch this new operation and was fascinated. One could see the terrific opportunities such a method opened up. Unfortunately there was no boat for us to 'pair up' with. Soon Christmas was upon us again. We doubled up the mooring lines and left *Maeve*. My crew rejoined their families for a well-earned break and I joined my father and his sister in Yorkshire.

Eight days later we were hard at work again. As often happens at that time of year, with short daylight hours, gales and the cold, the rewards for the hours put in are meagre.

As the spring approached we were able to travel further afield, and it was during one of these trips that we had trouble with the drive from the main engine. Having stripped down and removed the offending part, my Mate and I went ashore looking for help. The local taxi-driver recommended he drive us to a blacksmith he knew who was 'a great man for these sort of troubles'. When we arrived, the black-smith was shoeing a horse, with another waiting. We must have looked pretty incongruous in our jerseys and long white sea-boots but he paid scant attention and continued with his task. Having finished the first horse he looked at our taxi driver.

'What the hell have you brought these idiots here for?' he shouted. 'I'm a bloody blacksmith not a fish buyer.' Our friendly taxi-man, quite unconcerned by his welcome, handed the blacksmith a cigarette.

'And aren't you the best engineer in the whole of Donegal, so you are.' With that he lit the man's cigarette and stood back. We lifted the offending part up for the blacksmith to see and I explained what we needed doing. After a second he turned to me and said,

'I could do what you want, but it'll take all day 'cause I don't have the right tackle, but I'll tell you where to go to get it done right and quickly.' He motioned to our driver and gave instructions. Thanking him we got back in the car and sped eastwards. As we drove and the miles passed, I asked the driver where this place was that we were seeking. It then transpired we were driving right across Ireland. I looked at my Mate in astonishment, but there was nothing for it, we were committed. By then I had worked in Ireland long enough to appreciate their saying, 'Time enough' This saying is not, as many folk think, just a way of putting things off; it is a philosophical way of accepting the inevitable. My Mate and I now decided that we might just as well enjoy our ride as complain about it. 'Time enough,' said our driver, and we both agreed. Although the rest of the crew would have no idea where we were or what was delaying us, we knew that they would busy themselves with the various tasks that are always there to be tackled aboard a fishing boat - we sat back and enjoyed the lovely scenery.

Our driver was a fund of information and seemed to know all about each small village through which we passed. In one almost every house was unoccupied. This was so obvious that I asked him about it.

'Mostly gone,' he said, 'some to Scotland, some to your country, but mostly to the States.' How crazy, I thought. As human beings we are very good at resolving scientific, mathematical or engineering problems but when it comes to resolving human problems we fail over and over again. Soon after passing through this village we drove past mile after mile of brand new fencing. The contrast was immediate and I asked our driver what it was for. 'Ah sure, and that's to keep the reindeer in,' he said with never a smile. I glanced at my Mate.

'Pull the other one, Paddy, I suppose Father Christmas lives up that road over there.'

'No, Skipper,' he said, 'I'm serious.' Apparently a wealthy American had bought thousands of acres and was in fact introducing reindeer. The contrast between the empty, derelict cabins and the obvious wealth needed to install such fine fencing moved me. Perhaps, I thought, some day the children of those empty cabins will return and once again those small villages will become alive. I started to laugh.

'What's the joke, Skipper?' asked our driver.

'I was just thinking about some of my friends who go poaching the salmon. I wonder how long it will be before they are offering venison as a second course.' I replied in explanation. He laughed out loud.

'Sure and aren't you the queer fellow indeed. Would a country boy do a thing like that now?'

When we arrived at our destination it took but a short time to explain our problem to a very efficient engineering manager, once he overcame his initial shock at the sight of two dirty, diesel-impregnated fishermen still in their long white boots. While he did the job we entertained our driver to some liquid refreshment (no drink and drive rules then) and soon we were on our way back again. Having paid our driver, and with many a cheery farewell, we returned on board. While my mate related the day's happenings to the crew, I repaired the damaged engine ready for an early start the next day.

One day, on our return from an extended trip, I was surprised to find Tom Swan's driver waiting for us. He had been instructed to collect me and drive me to Tom's home. It was all very mysterious. Tom was out when we arrived, but his wife made me welcome and we chatted about her children and such things. On Tom's return we all sat down to high tea. Nothing was said about my sudden invitation until the table had been cleared and Tom and I were alone.

'How would you feel about fishing out of Fleetwood in England?' My surprise must have shown on my face.

185

Photo supplied by Paddy Sharkey

**Paddy Sharkey beside the Killybegs memorial
to 'those who have lost their lives at sea' 1994**

'I'm quite happy to fish your boat anywhere you want,' I replied, 'but only if my crew are happy to come with me.' He looked at me quizzically.

'Perhaps if *you* were to ask them they might agree.' I said I would like to know more about his ideas. He then explained that there were seining boats fishing out of Fleetwood, which were doing very well. He had been in touch with an agent who said he would welcome handling our catches and would put men aboard to guide us to the right grounds for a start. I replied that there would be two problems. First, most of my men were married. I could not predict how their families would feel about having their men folk so far away, and secondly, *Maeve* would need her hold remodelled to be able to carry ice. The boats in Fleetwood stayed away for up to fourteen days at a time. We agreed to sleep on it.

The following morning Tom's driver returned me to Killybegs. At lunchtime, when all the crew were together, I explained the reason for my call to Tom Swan's home. There followed a long silence. Then my Mate spoke.

'Some of us have worked in England' he said. 'I have for one and always got on OK with your lot. If you're prepared to go, Skipper, I'll keep you company.' I thanked him for his confidence in me and for his loyal support. I glanced round the rest of the familiar faces. In turn each man agreed to 'give it a go'. In principle we would all stick together but naturally, the married men wished to obtain the blessing of their wives before they were definite. I thanked them all and went ashore to 'phone Tom Swan. He was delighted and said he was arranging for Session's Yard at Monkstown to receive us as soon as possible to sort out the hold.

The following day the crew returned to say that all the wives were happy. Tom phoned to say we could sail at once. So now all that had to be done was to say our goodbyes. Like all sailors I hate saying goodbye. I had made so many good friends in Killybegs and been treated so kindly that it was hard to keep back the tears as I did the rounds.

At four thirty on the morning of the first of May 1956, *Maeve* slipped quietly away from her home port for the last time. A great sadness gripped my heart as we steamed west. The day dawned and my Mate appeared with a steaming mug of tea. Together we gazed silently ahead - smoking but not speaking.

CHAPTER THIRTY-SIX - THE ENGLISH VENTURE

As *Maeve* rolled and pitched her way towards Eagle Light my mind flew back to my first passage across Donegal Bay. What a long time ago it all seemed. We had decided to anchor off Keel to say farewell to my old shark-fishing friends in Achill Island. This we did, but the weather worsened and the next morning we sailed for the lee of Clare Island and anchored again. By that afternoon the wind had eased and we decided to press on. Just before nine o'clock that evening I intercepted a distress message being passed to the local lifeboat. Having plotted the position on our chart, I informed the local radio station of our own position and said we were altering course to assist in the search.

Now the wind was increasing all the time and when, having searched fruitlessly for a couple of hours, Valentia broadcast a new gale warning, it seemed prudent to sail on. By three o'clock the following morning the wind had backed to the south and was blowing a full gale. I was obliged to ease back our speed as we thumped our way into the white-topped rushing rollers. Even so, *Maeve* took a terrible hammering as we edged our way past those rocky headlands, which reach like fingers out into the Atlantic Ocean. It is at times like this that Skippers really pray for their engines to keep going. As we crashed our way south, spray and great walls of green water hurling across our decks and over the wheel-house, I wondered at the confidence of my men doing their best to sleep below on such a night. Eventually, at four forty-five that morning, Bull Light was abeam and I was able to ease *Maeve* round on to a south-easterly course.

Change at sea can be dramatic. Within a couple of hours we were sailing into dense fog and I was forced to slow right down. My Mate arrived with an egg and bacon sandwich and mug of tea. We both peered into the surrounding murk while the echo-sounder ticked away beside me. 'Where are we Skipper?' he asked as he pulled on his cigarette. I waved a hand in the direction of the shore and he returned to his window, straining his eyes for a glimpse of land. Suddenly he shouted. Sure enough there was the land we sought. Taking a quick bearing I adjusted our course to take us to the Fastnet. The tension disappeared. I switched off the echo-sounder and, as we increased speed again, looked at my Mate.

'It's a pity, we don't have time to call into all our old haunts and look up old friends.'

'It is indeed, Skipper,' he replied. We were just passing Baltimore. 'Do you remember the night we had to run there for shelter and were followed in by an old English trawler?' I grinned back. Would I ever forget? We had sought shelter, followed in by a rusty old English trawler. I had just anchored when she steamed slowly past us and I read her name. *Night Hawk*, it said, out of Milford Haven. I could not believe it. That was the very first ship I had ever sailed in during the war. Then she had been commandeered as a minesweeper. When I told my Mate he agreed to keep me company, so we lowered our dinghy and rowed across.

Photo supplied by Ray Harding

Steam Trawler Night Hawk GY15

All sailors have many things in common but there are very real differences between the type of men who manned our deep-sea trawlers and the men who fished inshore vessels like *Maeve*. At that time I did not realise there were such differences. Having tied our dinghy alongside I asked to be taken to their Captain's cabin and my Mate was taken forward to meet the crew.

The Captain's cabin, as I entered, was still littered with items thrown about by the storm. The Captain, fully clothed, lay on his bunk smoking a cigarette. Rather blearily he enquired who the hell I was and what the hell I wanted. I explained that I too was anchored because of the storm but that I had served in his ship during the war. He got out of his bunk and grabbing a bottle of whisky poured a large drink for himself and pushed the bottle at me. 'Help yourself,' he growled. For an hour or so we talked and then I suggested he might like to see how the other half lived. Perhaps he would like to drop over and see my small vessel. As his whisky intake grew, his temper improved. 'Why the hell not?' he shouted. I made my way back on deck, collected my Mate and we rowed back to *Maeve*. He too had been amazed at the mess aboard the trawler and the fact that no one seemed very interested in doing anything about it - a different world. They carried drink and issued it. I would not have drink aboard. Not that we were teetotallers by any means; once in harbour we would drink with the best of them, but I considered the sea to be quite dangerous enough without the added danger of drunk men around.

189

Half an hour later the Captain and his Mate arrived. Seated in our comfortable snug cabin with steaming mugs of tea, it was their turn to be amazed. 'This ain't no fishing boat,' said the weather-beaten old Captain 'more like some bloody yacht'. We grinned at him. Come and have a look at the engine room, I said. When I switched on the light, his face was an education. The sparkling white gloss paint, the polished copper pipes and the gleaming, green-painted diesel engines were set off by the bright red compressed air cylinders. He just looked in disbelief. 'Does anyone ever get their hands dirty in this bloody palace?' he asked.

'Never read a book by its cover,' I rejoined, holding up my hands for him to see. They were salt-hardened, calloused by hard work and still ingrained with the old sump-oil stains from the last repairs. He had shaken his grizzled old head.

'Never seen nothing like this before, Mate. Come on, man cannot live by tea alone.' And they climbed back on deck. As they rowed away, my Mate turned to me and grinned.

'Don't know which upset them most, Skipper, your Oxford English accent or the contrast between our two homes.' We both laughed as we recalled this episode.

We had all decided that we should call in and see the folk at Castle Townsend who had shown such kindness after the Willy incident. So, just after midday, we anchored and rowed ashore. Time now to let our hair down and we had a great party.

The following day, after the unusual luxury of a 'lie in', we waved our friends farewell and by that evening were berthed once more alongside at Monkstown pier.

This time, though, it was a very different *Maeve* and crew that welcomed Mr Sessions aboard. He shook hands all round and told us there would be a meeting the following day to thrash out the details of our new hold layout.

Boatyards I have always found fascinating, as indeed are the men who work there. They are all professionals and collectively need to cover a tremendous number of skills. Because the end results of their work are going to be tested by the elements, they know that things have got to be right. Few yards exist for long that produce sloppy or sub-standard work. Many of the people involved have themselves been to sea in some capacity or other, very knowledgeable and highly practical men, a joy to work with. Their job now was to design and construct wooden bays in our hold so that we could take aboard tons of ice, which would then be used to keep our catches fresh ready for landing on our return. Each bay needed to be able to be taken to pieces for easy cleaning in harbour and easily rebuilt to contain the different sorts of fish and their layers of ice at sea. The work progressed and we were glad of the chance to catch up on the multitude of jobs that tend to be put off while busy catching fish. At seven in the evening on June 20th, we sailed for England.

As a passenger we had a young Irish doctor. I cannot remember how we met him, but he was keen to come so we took him. Our own duty-free allowances I had locked in my cabin for safe keeping; naturally he had kept his own in his baggage.

190

Our passage to Holyhead was uneventful but, being unsure where to berth, I secured alongside in the inner harbour and went ashore to find the necessary authorities to ask. On my return I was met by my Mate with the news that there were two Customs Officers waiting for me below. As I entered the cabin it was strangely silent. The senior Customs Officer stood up, shook my hand and introduced himself and his colleague. Our passenger, an inane smile on his face, was humming a jig to himself behind a large bottle of John Jameson Irish whisky.

It appeared that the two Officers had been walking along the jetty when they had been halted by a shout from our fine doctor. His accent and the Irish flag interested them and when he invited them to join him for a 'spot of the hard stuff', how could they refuse? I listened intently and enquired what I had done wrong.

They were highly suspicious, especially since our gallant passenger, realising his mistake, had compounded his crime by trying to bribe them. I explained the reason for our trip and that we were bound for Fleetwood. I told them the only duty-free stores we carried were those authorised by their colleagues in Cork and showed them the papers to prove my point. They were singularly unimpressed by my explanation and said they would have to search the boat. I took them through to my own cabin and showed them the stocks safely locked away there. They could see for themselves that there was not a cigarette too many. Eventually a compromise was reached. The stores must be secured in a locker in the galley. Having locked this, they placed a large red seal on it. 'Heaven help you, Skipper, if this seal is broken,' they said. 'What are you going to do with that fellow?' The senior Officer was pointing at our doctor friend.

'You'd best take him ashore with you and shoot him,' I said with some feeling. They laughed at last -they were human after all. The following morning we waved goodbye to our passenger. Suffering from a mammoth hang over, he apologised for the trouble he had caused. We forgave him and sailed on We had only been at sea about an hour when my Mate came into the wheel-house.

'You're in dead trouble, Skipper.' I looked at him. 'That great, big, beautiful seal the Customs chap put on that locker in the galley...'

'Yes,' I said

'It's fallen on the deck and it's broken into a thousand pieces. As soon as she rolled, the locker opened. I've put all the stores back in your cabin. I hope that's OK.' We laughed together.

'I just hope the chaps in Fleetwood haven't been told to come and inspect us.' As soon as we had been allocated a berth, I went ashore and found the agent for whom we would be landing. He was a pleasant middle-aged man. Between answering telephone calls he told me that he had been in touch with Tom Swan and had arranged for a local man of experience to sail with us to introduce us to the fishing grounds. I invited him to come aboard when he was free. Later in the day he called and had a look around. The local expert arrived, showed us where to go to receive our ice and, once all was ready, we sailed on our first trip. He marked on our chart where he would like to try for a start. Since it was some hours' steaming time away, I suggested he turn in. When we arrived at the fishing ground chosen we shook the expert. For the first time I learned he had never been in a seining boat before. He was a trawler man.

My log states that our first haul achieved about ten boxes, but once we had sorted out the trash, there were only about two boxes of fish, mostly small dabs. Not a very encouraging start. The second haul was not much better and the third shot we came fast. Having retrieved our gear and dumped the shoulder of an old trawl, which was all that filled our cod end, I was already beginning to have doubts about the 'expert' who had been wished on us. The weather now took a hand and over the next week we suffered both a gale and fog. The various 'grounds' which our expert had suggested had resulted in our losing one cod end, almost certainly being over - weighted by shells and trash, a series of 'fasts' and a very meagre catch to show for our efforts.

As we steamed into Fleetwood he was beside me in the wheel-house. 'Not a very successful trip, Skipper,' he remarked as he gazed out of the open window.

'Not to worry,' I said, 'we all get poor trips once in a while. Now then, where do we berth?' He pointed to the Jubilee jetty ahead of us. 'If you berth there,' he said, 'we will be all ready to enter the fish dock when they open it on the incoming tide.'

Once secured alongside, he took two of our crew with him to collect the aluminium kits used by the market for landing fish. On their return, our catch was sorted and loaded, under his direction, into these kits and we were in the middle of landing our catch when a strange Irishman tapped me on the shoulder. I was busy operating the winch and apart from talking over my shoulder, paid but scant attention to his questions. By three o'clock in the morning we were finished and I had just turned in when all hell broke out on deck. Hurriedly I threw my clothes back on and, as I stepped into the galley, heavy boots came thumping down the ladder into the after-cabin. By now the entire crew was awake. Some very irate officials were banging the table. In a break in the furore I enquired what exactly their problem was? Immediately they flew into another tantrum. By now I could hear the kettle boiling on the range and withdrew to make a pot of tea. Armed with mugs I returned and suggested they sit down while we sort out what had got to be done. They then told us that we had taken kits that we were not allowed to take - landed fish in an area where we were not allowed to land and, as an Irish boat, who the hell did we think we were? When I tried to explain that we were operating under the instructions of a local expert they just laughed in disbelief.

'Tell you what, Skipper,' they said. 'best thing you and your Mate can do is to get up to that Fish Market as quick as you can and stand beside your fish. Your catch has been blacked by the union, OK?' And they left.

My Mate and I followed them on to the jetty and did as requested. Fish Markets are interesting places and we stood beside our few kits. A man in a white coat approached me. 'Are those fish yours?' he asked. On being told they were he disappeared. We waited and watched as the various landings were auctioned. No one came near us. Then suddenly a couple of men in white coats appeared again. Turning to my Mate one asked what sort of fish were in the kit nearest him.

'Medium plaice,' he replied, having packed them himself.

'How do I know?' asked the buyer 'Tip them out and let me see for myself.' Angry but with no option, my Mate did as he was bid. Then it was my turn as another white-coated buyer told me to do the same thing with the kit beside me. We were made to tip and repack every kit. I thought my Mate would explode at this indignity and certainly I was fuming inside too. When we had completed this task to their satisfaction a further white-coated buyer appeared and placed a label on each kit of prime fish. We looked on in amazement. The labels spelled out our rewards for all our efforts, 'SCRAP' they read. By this time it was midday and we returned to *Maeve* disconsolate and absolutely furious. The local 'expert' had wisely decided to return ashore and there was a message awaiting me to report to the agent as soon as possible. I grabbed a new packet of cigarettes and set off ashore again.

The agent was in a state of high excitement. What on earth had got into me, he asked, to land my fish the way I had? I drew hard on my cigarette before daring to open my mouth. 'I understood,' I said, in as even a voice as I could muster, 'that the local hero you placed on board knew the ropes round here. We now know he doesn't have a clue about the local fishing grounds, but at least I thought he would know about his own home port.' The agent went from red to white and I could see his hands trembling.

'*He* told you to land at Jubilee?' he queried.

'Who else? I replied. The agent shook his head in disbelief.

'Anyway,' he continued, 'we are in all sorts of trouble. I've had a delegation from the Union and they are refusing to handle any fish from any source until I get your signature on this document.' While he was speaking he was pushing a piece of paper towards me. It was now my turn to show surprise.

'I'm not signing any bits of paper for anyone,' I said, 'until I understand exactly what the hell is going on around here.' He looked at me like an imploring puppy.

'You must,' he said, 'or they'll close the whole port.'

The impasse was broken by his telephone ringing. He picked it up and I heard him say, 'I'm talking to him right now. I'll phone you later.' He replaced the instrument and looked at me. 'That was the local Union boss,' he said and waited. I lit another cigarette.

'I don't know where all this trouble started,' I said, 'but perhaps you can explain.' It appeared that the strange Irishman who had visited us as we were landing was, in fact, a Union man and had rushed back to his cronies and organised the whole episode. Having established where the cause lay and been promised that the 'expert' would never set foot aboard *Maeve* again, I signed the piece of paper as requested. In effect it promised that we would only land, in future, inside the fish dock. Had we been so advised before we would have obviously done so anyway. The agent, much relieved, thanked me and promised to find me a more suitable 'expert' before we sailed next. I was drained, hungry and thoroughly fed up.

As I trudged back to *Maeve* I thought about the disaster our first trip had turned out to be. When I explained to my crew who had started all the trouble, they were as furious as I had been. The Irish have very long memories and I would not like to be in that Irishman's place if he ever visits Donegal.

Having had some welcome food and explained the position I felt much better. My Mate and I went ashore that evening and had a pint at a dockside pub. It was busy and crowded and we found a small table where we could talk in relative quiet. I apologised to him for the crass bad manners he had had to put up with at the fish market. He grinned back at me and replied that I too had had the same treatment. We both laughed. Just then a drunk bumped up against our table and spilled my Mate's beer. I looked at my Mate and could see he was getting angry.

'Bloody Irish,' the drunk slurred as I guided him into an open space.

'Come on, Jackie,' I said, finishing my pint. 'Early start tomorrow.' But as I left, Jackie veered off to the Gents. I waited outside. After five minutes I entered. There was my Mate, just standing there.

'Come along,' I said, but before I could get any further Jackie exploded.

'I'll kill him,' he spat the words out in fury. It took a little time to calm him down during which, fortunately, the drunk did not reappear. Still fuming we boarded *Maeve* and slept the sleep of the just.

Our next trip took us to the Clyde, fishing south of that superb rock, Ailsa Craig. Few sailors enjoy spending any Friday the 13th at sea and after our immediate past problems I was not looking forward to that day either. However, we never came fast all day, and in the evening, as we watched the local boats leave for their home port, we decided to move inshore to where they had been fishing all day and have a final shot. I continued inshore until the marks showed me we were inside the limit; we shot our gear as the light was fading and I was towing back out to sea when my Mate entered the wheel-house. He stood silent, gazing out of the half open window. Suddenly he said, without turning round, 'I'd have killed that son of a bitch last night Skipper, if you hadn't interfered.'

'I know, Jackie,' I replied softly. 'and today you'd have been in a gaol not with us here.'

'But he asked for it didn't he?' he continued. I agreed but pointed out that that was exactly how the Irish got their reputation for causing trouble. It wasn't his fault but he would have ended up by being blamed. I turned to have a look at the warps we were towing, they seemed to be coming in nice and level.

'Skipper,' Jackie's voice attracted my attention, 'is that the Fishery Patrol ship?' I strained my eyes. Sure enough steaming towards us was a ship, which looked, through the murky drizzle, very like such a vessel. I glanced at the marks ashore - our gear must still be inside the limits. There was nothing for it but to haul as fast as we could and plead ignorance. We were trapped.

The vessel continued towards us and then circled at a safe distance. Through the worsening light we could see that it was, in fact, a Dutch ocean-going tug. A loud hailer voice boomed across the waters, 'Haf you any feesh?' Very relieved that it was not the Patrol boat I shouted back,

'Just hauling.' As the cod end emptied into the fish ponds, it was clear that there were quite a lot of Dublin Bay prawns and a selection of small fish, ideal for his crew's supper. I suggested to my crew we hand over the lot to the tug. They agreed. The Tug Captain had positioned his ship so that we could touch against his quarter with our bow and my crew handed them our catch in baskets. Having emptied our baskets, they returned them filled with duty-free cartons of cigarettes and the biggest stone jar containing Bols gin I have ever seen. It was enormous and my Mate carried it aft like a baby in his arms. It was laid on my bunk for safety. The Dutchman waved his thanks; we did the same and I studied the chart.

'I think we'll anchor in Loch Ryan for the night,' I said as we swung round on to a new course. The crew were busying themselves clearing up on deck and below the cook was brewing. By the time we had anchored, the crew were ready for their meal and we uncorked that Bols bottle.

'It's not over yet, lads,' I said as I raised my glass to them all, 'but this must be the best Friday the 13th I've ever had at sea.' A general murmur of consent greeted my toast and certainly, anchor watch apart, every man Jack aboard slept like a baby that night.

We had by now got into the new routine and landed our fish in Fleetwood without any further troubles. Our trips took us to Campbelltown and the Isle of Man but then our dynamo burnt out and we had to return to Fleetwood to obtain a replacement. Two days later we sailed, but after a couple of fruitless days of 'fasts' and associated problems a northerly gale blew us back to Fleetwood for shelter. On the 2nd of August we sailed once more and fished away but on the 10th of August disaster struck. Our faithful Lister auxiliary stopped. We berthed alongside in Ramsey in the Isle of Man. My Mate and I stripped the small engine down for the umpteenth time. On each occasion, having found nothing wrong, we would reassemble it, it would start and run for a short time then, quite suddenly, die again. We were totally bemused and I went ashore to find a diesel engineer.

He returned to the boat with me, took a look at the stripped engine and suggested we reassemble it again in front of him. He then poured some chloroform onto a piece of rag and told us to swing the engine over very slowly while he held the rag over the air intake. Removing the impregnated rag, he said, 'OK, boys, give her a whirl.' There was a huge bang and a cloud of soot blew into the spotless engine room. We swung her once more and off she went. Before the engineer could turn round she died again.

'Shall we swing her some more?' we said wearily. He looked at our blistered hands and laughed at us.

195

'With a diesel engine, boys, if she doesn't go, there's always a simple reason and swinging won't find out what it is. Strip her down again.' We did as he had asked and stood back while he examined the engine in detail. Straightening up, he smiled. 'There's your trouble' he said. 'Feel there.' He took my fingers and pressed them inside the cylinder wall. As he pushed my hand very gently round the circumference my fingers could feel a tiny indentation. No wonder my Mate and I had been puzzled. It was hardly visible. 'Whoever put this engine together after its last refit,' he was saying, 'failed to replace one of the surclips holding that gudgeon pin in position. Ever since then the gudgeon pin has been able to wander back and forth. In the course of time it has worn that tiny indentation you can feel and that has now become sufficiently deep to reduce the compression in the cylinder on which all diesel engines rely to work. Sorry, boys, you need a new cylinder.' We thanked him. I radioed ahead to Fleetwood to our agent to advise him of our latest disaster and, since we could not fish without this engine, we once more returned to Fleetwood.

As, all these years later, I read my old log I am amazed at the fortitude of my crew. At every turn we seemed doomed to come face to face with problems, but they never moaned at me and continued to work all the hours that God sent. No sooner had we overcome one problem than another would attack us. Having berthed and landed the small amount of fish in our hold, I left the crew cleaning up and went ashore to chase up the agent.

As usual he was deep in telephone conversation when I arrived. Between calls I asked him when our new part would be available. To my astonishment he said he had not ordered it. I was all set to blow my top when he held up his hand.

'I have been trying to talk to your boss', he said, 'but I have not been able to contact him.' I stared at the agent in disbelief. 'Have you sent him a telegram telling him that you wish to talk to him?' I asked. He looked drained and told me he had been trying to make contact without any joy for some days. I was absolutely stunned.

'Please let me know as soon as you have any further news,' I said and walked slowly back to *Maeve*.

Once everyone was sitting in the after-cabin I passed on what the agent had said to me. When I had finished there was a total silence. Everyone was obviously as stunned as I had been. 'First thing tomorrow I shall revisit the agent and perhaps by then the mystery will have been solved,' I said. There must be some simple solution - perhaps he's been called away on business and the family are away with him.' We turned in but I couldn't sleep. What on earth was I to do now for my crew? They had come with me to England in good faith. What was Tom Swan up to?

The following morning the agent managed to contact another Director. It appeared that Tom and his family had flown to Canada and disappeared. I could not believe he could behave in such a way but, as the old Yorkshire saying has it, 'There's none queerer than folk.'

Back on board, I passed on the latest news. They too were dumbfounded. 'Anyway,' I said. 'we have a roof over our heads and food, so there is no immediate problem. What I want each one of you to do is to let me know whether you wish to be returned to Ireland, or whether you wish to remain in England to work over here. I'm deeply sorry. I got you into this mess and somehow I'll get you out of it. Whatever you decide, I'll make sure that your wishes are fulfilled.' The agent had promised me he would give me an advance to settle my crew.

Gradually they each decided what course they wished to follow. Tickets were purchased and bags packed. Came the day when they all mustered on the jetty awaiting their taxis to take them, each to his own destination. We had been together for a long time and it was like a family parting as we shook hands. My own tears were barely kept in check until I reached the safety of the wheel-house. Then, I confess, I blabbed like a schoolboy.

I went slowly down the ladder to the cabin. The empty bunks stared back at me reproachfully and I turned to the galley. The kettle was still boiling from their final mugs of tea and I filled my mug and took it into my small cabin, lit a cigarette and pondered on the extraordinary events of the past few days.

Tom Swan had been a pillar of his kirk, his wife had played the organ and his children were being privately educated. His family held a special position in their community and he employed a lot of people. What on earth had got into him?

Maeve rolled ever so slightly as a trawler passed. I went on deck and adjusted the mooring lines. Then, starting right forward, I walked slowly aft, tidying as I went till the upper deck was spotless. Below I carried out the same exercise. In the engine-room I started the main engine and pumped the air bottles up and the bilges out. Eventually, having tidied the after-cabin and galley, I decided it was time to go ashore and have a final meeting with the agent. I had phoned my father in Hertfordshire and asked him if he could send me £10 to buy a ticket to Hitchin.

When I arrived the agent handed me the letter from my father and told me that the boat was being impounded until he could get one of the other Directors to come over. I told him everything was ready for someone else to take over, ship-shape and Bristol fashion. He asked when I would be leaving and I told him I had a few odds and ends to pack but would leave him the wheel-house key the following day. In the event, I had about a dozen cardboard boxes tied together with twine, apart from my dunlopillow mattress and suitcase. It amazed me how much stuff I had collected over the past years. That evening I have seldom felt so lonely and alone. The utter silence of poor *Maeve* tugged at my heart-strings. I wondered would I ever see those brave men again. How would they get along in their new jobs? How would their families feel now about my taking them away from Killybegs?

Next morning I woke early, boiled a kettle and shaved. When I went into the wheel-house the sun was shining and I tuned the radio to the BBC news. Life goes on, I thought to myself, no one knows but me that I'm so empty inside. Below again I rustled up a last breakfast. Eat well while you can, I mused, may be a long time

197

before your next meal. I cleared everything away, washed up and dampened the galley fire which was almost out. I took the key to the agent, thanked him for his help and returned to *Maeve*. Having phoned for a taxi, I collected all my gear on deck and waited. The taxi-driver helped me pack the boxes, suitcase and mattress into his cab.

'Is that the lot?' he smiled at me as he spoke. I had turned for a long last look at the lady who had been my home for the past years. As I got into the seat beside him he glanced at me out of the corner of his eye and must have noticed my eyes wet with tears.

'You bloody sailors come to love your bloody boats like other men love bloody women.' He spoke it as a statement rather than as a question.

'Unfortunately,' I replied softly, 'we bloody do.'

Willy, Skipper and Skipper's father in *Maeve* berthed at Monkstown pier

CHAPTER THIRTY-SEVEN -. BEACHED AND BROKE - TIME TO START AGAIN.

My father helped me load my worldly possessions into his small motor car. As we forced the last cardboard box into the back-seat space he smiled.

'You haven't seen the tiny cottage we live in. Jane will have a fit when she sees this load.'

My sister Jane, a nurse, had given up her work to look after Dad after he and Mother had decided to divorce. My brother Patrick, then a successful shipbroker in the City, had found this small cottage to rent for them. It really was tiny, with the upstairs room just big enough for two single beds and downstairs a bathroom with loo and kitchen, plus a tiny eating and sitting room. That night I had to stack the furniture in the sitting room to lay down my mattress and the following morning it was quite a job to find a space to stow the mattress away. Obviously I needed to buy wood to make a folding bunk top for the bath so that I could sleep there, and a storage shelf above the stairs to stow my mattress and bedding during the day. Dad and I went into Hitchin to buy the necessary materials and to call on the manager of the local branch of Barclays Bank. By coincidence, Dad had taught this man many years ago and he could not have been more helpful. I told him my unlikely story and he immediately agreed to open an account for me although I had no collateral and he only had my word that my story was true.

It was at this point that the Royal Navy came to my rescue. As a Reserve Officer I needed to carry out a fortnight's training each year. I telephoned the appointments officer in HMS *Caroline*, in Belfast, and told him about my problems. It was vital for me to be able to visit the Director who lived outside Belfast, I explained; could he arrange for me to carry out my training in one of the ships operating out of Londonderry? As ever he was immediately sympathetic and constructive.

'Leave it with me, John,' he said. A week later I received a warrant to take me to Londonderry and orders to report to HMS *Whitby* for a fortnight's sea training. The Captain welcomed me with a large gin and tonic. After he had heard about my unhappy experiences he insisted I go ashore to make contact with Tom Swan's accountants before we sailed. The last time I had met them was when they had visited me aboard *Maeve* in Killybegs. We had got along fine then and I wondered what sort of reception I would get now as I entered their offices without any appointment or prior warning. I need not have worried; they could not have been more helpful. Obviously they could not answer all my questions, but they did say they would not dispute my claim that I was owed money by the Directors, which was all that I was seeking.

My fortnight's training at sea was, as always, great fun but the weather turned beastly towards the end and we were berthed the wrong side of the Irish Sea. It was essential to end up in Ireland if I was to be able to visit the Director outside Belfast.

Having no money, I would never be able to get back to Ireland from home. I called on the Captain in his cabin and explained my predicament.

'My dear chap,' the friendly Captain exclaimed, 'let's get a signal off to their Lordships,' and he rang for the signalman.

Sure enough, the following day, I was informed that I was required for 'additional watch-keeping duties' for a further week. I thanked the Captain for his help and went back to my duties knowing that in a week's time I would be able to visit that other Director.

It was seven thirty on a dry cold morning as the taxi dropped me off outside the Director's house. I rang the bell and waited. I could hear dogs barking and then a bolt slid back - the door opened and the Director could not conceal her surprise when she saw who her caller was.

'May I come inside?' I asked politely. She beckoned me in and led me through to a sitting room. I had established that, so far as I was concerned, their company owed me £500. Sitting there in her lovely home, with the farm she owned adjoining, she told me seriously that she had no money. I replied that I was not asking for my £500 now but I did need a promissory note to the effect that it would be paid off at the rate of £10 per week, adding that I needed that amount to pay my father for housing and feeding me. Eventually she agreed and wrote out such a note. Thanking her for her hospitality and help I got a taxi back to Belfast, and made my way home.

When you have nothing, a note promising to pay £10 a week is like a miracle. Ten pounds may not seem very much today, but nearly fifty years ago it would buy a lot of stores. I called on my trusting bank manager and told him about my trip. He was happy that I had been able to obtain my 'piece of paper' but explained that if she went back on her word, it probably had little value. When I rejoined my father in the car, I was less buoyant but at least I had made a start. Now for a job.

Fifty years ago, industry in England was still trying to overcome the enormous strain of seven years of war. The release of hundreds of thousands of servicemen and women on to the job market had caused huge problems. However, I was convinced that I could prove myself, given the chance. The question was what sort of a job should I be seeking? Apart from a couple of years teaching immediately after the war, I had spent all my working life at sea. I scanned the job ads daily and soon realised that I had no clear idea what those jobs really involved. What was the difference between a tool-maker, a capstan-operator and a fitter, or between an agricultural engineer and a work-study engineer? The more I replied to the ads, the more it became clear that I needed a 'box' into which I could fit so that other people could recognise me. Obviously I needed to go for some job offering me training so that I could obtain a 'box'. My interviews had taught me that no one wanted sailors ashore.

At length I was taken on by a firm of Management Consultants who were seeking work-study trainees. The Consultants had been employed by an Aluminium Company to introduce a new wage-bonus structure into their die-casting foundry and other factory activities. Inevitably I was much older than the rest of the trainees but, after a pretty shaky start, I managed to hold my own. I decided to study as hard as I could and obtained text books, which I found dry and difficult to absorb. The lectures at a local Technical College were much more interesting. Dad had a part-time job as gardener for the lady of the manor and I would help him in my evenings and at weekends. He was not as strong as he had been, and it annoyed me sometimes to hear the way the lady spoke to him. When I bridled on one occasion, he rebuked me. Afterwards he said, as he gently pulled on his old pipe, 'Thanks for your support, John, but you should never bother with folk like that, they don't understand.' I don't think I have ever met a more patient or understanding man.

My new job was at London Colney and it soon became clear that it would be sensible to try and find lodgings closer to my work. That weekend there was an advert in the paper for a room in Wheathampstead and we set off at once.

White Cottage proved to be opposite the church in the high street of Wheathampstead. I knocked at the front door and a lady about my own age opened the door. Inside she took me into a small sitting room and we talked for a few minutes before she asked me to follow her. The room was small but comfortable and I assured her it would suit me fine. I said I would bring my few belongings over on the Sunday night. At the door, she shook my hand and I waved as I drove off. My sister said she thought my landlady looked very attractive and I told her not to be such a romantic.

The summer weekends I spent playing cricket for the Offley village team and studying. That Christmas, brother Pat arrived from London with all sorts of exotic things to eat and drink. Obviously he was doing very well and my own tiny salary £8.50 per week was an embarrassment. Still, I was earning my living and on the way to becoming a qualified work-study engineer. The bad weather during the winter and the difficulties of public bus transport convinced me that I needed to obtain a car. I mentioned this to my landlady (Lorna). One evening, on my return, she showed me an ad she had saved. We set off immediately and found the old Rover car at a house behind the gasworks in St Albans. It was well pre-war and built like a tank. It went, and I bought it for £13.50. Triumphantly we drove it home and down the little side road that led into the Club car park behind.

The Club had been built and created by Mac who had once owned White Cottage. He had a wonderful cook, Ruth, and the Club thrived. In celebration of my new acquisition we decided to tell Mac and have a drink. He showed great enthusiasm and I was delighted and amused to see my old lady parked beside his clients' modern and very expensive models. Mac had two old Railtons.

Just before lunchtime one Friday, the Foundry Manager called me to follow him outside into the scrapyard. I wondered what my crime had been and was totally taken by surprise by his opening question.

'How would you feel about working for me?' he said. I was so surprised that for a moment I just looked at him in silence.

201

'I'm sorry Jack', I said, 'but I don't understand. I'm very happy working for the Consultants and am on my way to getting myself qualified as a work-study engineer.'

'My assistant Foundry Manager is being transferred to Sales,' he said. 'I have selected you to take his place.' I smiled back at him.

'That is a great compliment, Jack, for which I'm very grateful, but I don't know anything about aluminium casting or metallurgy. I think you've got the wrong bloke.' It was now his turn to smile.

'I hear that you are thinking of leaving the 'bachelor's club' at last - is that true?' I felt my face redden.

'Well yes,' I admitted.

'Right then. Join me and your salary will be increased to £10 per week.' He turned away. 'Think about it over the weekend, discuss it with Lorna and let me know on Monday.' He disappeared back into the smoke and noise of the foundry

The car had given me the ability to take Lorna out and about. She had met my father and sister in their tiny cottage and I had met her father and step-mother in their lovely house near Harpenden. We were invited up there for the doctor's tennis parties and when they went away to Switzerland we played singles on our own. The summer sun shone and I even made runs for the village side ending up with a silver cup for my efforts. Then, early one morning, the phone rang. It was my sister.

'John,' she said, 'can you drive over straight away. Dad has just died.' A great pain tore at my inside as I threw clothes on and ran to the car. In the early light my mind failed to function logically and it was not until I stood looking down at his peaceful face that I accepted the truth of what Jane had said.

Dad was one of a large Yorkshire farming family. He had taught French, Geography and Games at a school in Norfolk just before the First World War. I remember him telling me that he was trying out his motor bicycle on Porlock Hill at a meet of the local hounds the day the First World War broke out. The Master had stood in his stirrups and called for silence.

'Ladies and Gentlemen' he announced, 'I've just heard that we are at war with Germany.' Turning to his whips he cantered off shouting,. 'We'll draw Furze Bottom first!'

Dad, as a Territorial, kicked his bike into action and drove back to Yorkshire to join his regiment. He eventually went to the front as a dispatch rider and interpreter before being accepted for training as a fighter pilot and returning to Blighty. In 1917 he was a Flight Lieutenant at Rochester airfield. It was there that he met my Mother whose family farmed Apton Hall near Pagglesham. Mother, only 17, had had to sit and watch with envy as her elder sisters came and went with their exotic boyfriends. Her favourite brother had lied about his age and left Felsted school to serve at the front. He was commissioned from the ranks and collected a Military Cross. Dad with his Air Force Cross and other medals must have swept her off her feet. Despite their age difference (Dad was over ten years older) they must have made a handsome couple. However, Mother worried about Dad's test pilot job and was less than happy at being left all alone all day in digs. She insisted that he leave the Air Force and return to his previous job of teaching.

Although Dad proved to be a born schoolmaster, he always bitterly regretted leaving the RAF. He was one of only a few men I have ever met who could teach not only the University Scholarship boys, but also the idle ones at the bottom of the school. Excellent cricketers or footballers are not always good coaches - Dad *was*. My main regret, in retrospect, is that there are so many things I never asked him, partly because the war took me away and partly because, until I returned to that tiny cottage in Offley, we seldom had time together to talk. Now it was too late.

Not long after the funeral I asked Lorna to marry me. I also arranged an appointment to call on her father, a doctor, in the old-fashioned way and asked for his blessing as well. I explained that I had nothing except hard work to offer. He gave his blessing and invited me to join him for a morning's rough shooting the following Saturday.

The Doctor was from Aberdeen. He had joined the Navy from college as a Surgeon Probationer during the First World War and on his return was made by his father to work his way through college to qualify. His brother and he (both doctors) made their way south and practised in Essex. Lorna's father then decided to specialise in Public Health and spent the Second World War years in Chatham, which had more than its share of bombing and other problems. He then wangled his way into the Army and served in Europe after the occupation. He was a great chap and I thoroughly enjoyed the hours we spent together. Lorna, his eldest daughter, he had always treated like a boy, so she had shot and fished alongside him, which enabled her to understand the things which we enjoyed doing together.

Our wedding was a very simple affair. Lorna had married a soldier during the war and produced her first daughter, Jane, in 1945. She had been left to bring up Jane alone and in due course she had divorced the soldier. Just twelve people sat down for the wedding lunch and, as soon as they had departed, we returned to White Cottage and spent the afternoon resting in bed. We had arranged a candle-lit dinner in St Albans that evening and drove back in our faithful old Rover - there were no laws then about drinking and driving - so midnight saw us, well refreshed, driving home once more for the marriage night. Jane had been invited to stay with her grandparents and we were alone for the first time. Lorna had a large, old, four poster bed which she had brought down from Scotland - that bed was to sire all four of our children.

Monday morning saw me back at work - Lorna was running her guest house and we had no money for honeymoons or holidays. A few pints at the local with our friends was the limit of what we could afford. In the autumn I returned to do my Reserve Training. The additional money now was very welcome and it never occurred to me to discuss my appointment with my new wife. She had been in the WAAF during the war so was used to Service things. It was not until I returned, full of enthusiasm about the submarine I had served in, that she blew her top. Like many other folk she wrongly thought submarines more dangerous than surface ships. But it did remind me that I was no longer a bachelor and had got to get used to discussing things of this nature with my wife in future.

As I blew a smoke ring into the air, I pondered, 'Ain't life odd.' With all its ups and downs, excitements and sorrows, almost by mistake I had suddenly found myself a wife. I could hardly believe it. Both being closer to forty than thirty, we decided we wanted a family sooner rather than later. Neither of us could have guessed that Lorna would produce two boys and two girls in the next four years. Inevitably we were permanently 'broke', but the chickens laid, the garden kept us in vegetables, we made our own beer and life was tough, but fun. The future would look after itself. We loved, laughed and worked like hell - a new life was starting for both of us and we grabbed it with both hands.